MW00398956

Final Treatment

Final Treatment

THE FILE ON DR. X

Matthew L. Lifflander

W · W · NORTON & COMPANY
New York

Published simultaneously in Canada by George J. McLeod Limited, Toronto. Printed in the United States of America.

First Edition

Library of Congress Cataloging in Publication Data

Lifflander, Matthew L
Final treatment.

1. Forensic toxicology—Cases, clinical reports, statistics. 2. Curare—Toxicology—Cases, clinical reports, statistics. 3. Trials (Poisoning)—New Jersey—Hackensack. 4. Jascalevich, Mario. 5. Surgeons—New Jersey—Biography. I. Title.
RA1228.L53 1979 614'.19 78-26176
ISBN 0-393-08833-2

Typefaces used are Korinna and Times Roman.
Book designed by Jacques Chazaud.
Manufactured by the Haddon Craftsmen, Inc.

1 2 3 4 5 6 7 8 9 0

For Barbara

"When you have eliminated the impossible, whatever remains, however improbable, must be the truth."

—Sherlock Holmes in *The Sign of Four*
(Sir Arthur Conan Doyle)

Contents

PART III

PART IV

PART V

PART VI

List of Illustrations

Illustrations by Al Herr

Acknowledgments

Fred and Paula Morgan convinced me that this story should be told and that I could do it. I am forever grateful and hope that I have given them no cause for regret.

My wife, Barbara, has shared in my effort, editing and reacting to my drafts and tolerating me whenever I became insufferable. Her criticism was severe and invaluable. With pride and understanding, our children, Clay and Justin, accepted a great deal of absence on my part.

Helen Guelpa did some of the research, typed every word, and shared valuable insights.

The encouragement of Eric Swenson and the patience of Starling Lawrence of W. W. Norton & Company, Inc., enriched my experience.

Quality research was provided by Robert Sullivan, Caroline Hill, and Jill Gordon.

I also benefited from the excellent manual for writers by William Zinsser of Yale University.

Finally, I am especially grateful to my law firm partners, Earle K. Moore and Michael T. Sullivan, for their good counsel and representation in our successful effort to protect this manuscript against Dr. Jascalevich's attempt to obtain it prior to publication.

Prologue

At six o'clock in the morning of May, 19, 1976, the police appeared at an expensive suburban New Jersey home and arrested the successful surgeon who lives there. Just the day before, a grand jury had completed two months of deliberations by finding reasonable cause to believe that, some ten years earlier, the doctor had murdered five hospital patients by administering lethal doses of curare, an asphyxiant developed by South American Indians to poison darts.

The dramatic, emotional question of the doctor's guilt or innocence is perhaps less significant than are the reasons why certain people and institutions failed to reveal or resolve the mystery of these deaths ten years earlier. This is a study of failure and institutional inadequacy in the professions of law and medicine.

Final Treatment

PART I

CHAPTER I

"A Little Child Shall Lead Them"

The houses, the streets, the neighborhood, and the people are similar to those of hundreds of suburbs developed after World War II to house middle-class refugees from New York City. It is not a fancy place, but it is solid. The town itself, Bergenfield, New Jersey, is so uniform that neither side of its old railroad track is the wrong side.

Across Prospect Avenue from the high school field, on the lawn of a split-level house, is a discreet sign: "Dr. Allan Lans, Physician."

His waiting room is at the end of a short driveway and was once the garage. The entire ground floor, garage included, had been paneled and converted to a doctor's office when the Lans family moved to a larger house in nearby Teaneck.

On March 19, 1966, Marie Savino and her four-year-old daughter, Nancy, arrived in Dr. Lans's small and crowded waiting room. The doctor took them ahead of his other patients because he had not liked what he heard when Mrs. Savino telephoned. The Savino family had been Dr. Lans's patients for a number of years, but little Nancy was one of his special people—he had delivered her.

Nancy arrived suffering from nausea and a severe "tummy ache." Her eyes were red from crying most of the day. The doctor found that there was tenderness in the lower right section of her abdomen, and, after an extensive office examination, he asked Mrs. Savino to drive her to Riverdell Hospital, only a mile away. There, a blood count revealed an increase in white blood cells, and further examination seemed to confirm Dr. Lans's diagnosis of acute appendicitis. Such a diagnosis can be very difficult and is not sure, as the symptoms of an inflamed appendix resemble those of several other serious disorders. However, an appendix about to burst can be life threatening, and the accepted procedure in such cases is: when in doubt, operate.

The hospital's newest surgeon, thirty-four-year-old Dr. Stanley Harris, was called to handle the case, and at 9 P.M. that same evening, Harris, Lans, the anesthesiologist, and a team of nurses went to work.

The appendix is a wormlike structure, normally as thick as a lead pencil in a fully grown person. When inflamed or infected, it may be enlarged eight to ten times its normal size. Once it is surgically exposed, it is not difficult to determine if appendicitis is the cause of a patient's discomfort. Nancy Savino's appendix was normal.

A series of tiny, lymphatic cysts on the small intestine was the apparent cause of Nancy's pain, and Dr. Harris decided that resectioning the intestine was the appropriate cure. That involved removing a small piece of the organ and reattaching the remaining portions. There were no complications, and the entire surgical procedure took an hour and one half. Both doctors were satisfied when Nancy Savino was moved from the operating room at the far end of Riverdell Hospital's main floor to a cheerful, private room some two hundred feet further down the long corridor. It was 11 P.M. by then, and Mr. Hall, a private-duty nurse, was already on hand to watch over the little girl throughout the night.

During that first postoperative evening, the patient was fed intravenously, as is usual in such cases. At ten minutes after midnight the private-duty nurse made his first entry on the hospital chart. Nancy was sleeping soundly, and such sleep after the anesthesia has worn off is a sign of good progress. The little girl awoke for the first time at 12:49 A.M., and Mr. Hall administered the sedative, phenobarbital, as Dr. Harris had instructed. She awoke briefly at 2:05 A.M. and more medication was provided. In thirty minutes Nancy was asleep and didn't awake again until 5:20 in the morning, when she tearfully told the nurse that she wanted to go home and she wanted her mommy—a healthy postoperative reaction for a four-year-old spending the first night of her life away from home. Again, Nancy went back to sleep, and at 6:45 Mr. Hall made another entry on the hospital record: "Restful night except for brief periods of crying. Slept most of night. Extremely homesick."

At 7:00, his assignment completed, Mr. Hall left.

The floor nurse came to check on her patient only nineteen

minutes later. It was breakfast time. Nurse Irene Nelson began her turn at the chart, "Child sleeping, no untoward symptoms." She came back at 7:40 A.M. and once more recorded that the little girl was sleeping.

Twenty minutes passed before a technician arrived to draw blood. Her entry on the hospital chart at 8:00 completed the nurses' notes: "Was unable to awaken patient. Dr. Jascalevich was called." Dr. Mario Jascalevich headed the four-man surgical department at Riverdell and was already in the hospital making his morning rounds and preparing for surgery.

An intern, Dr. Jorge Ortega, had been close to Nancy's room when he heard the commotion caused by the technician's urgent search for help; Ortega was there applying mouth-to-mouth resuscitation when Dr. Jascalevich entered the room. Jascalevich checked the patient with a stethoscope and, at 8:15 A.M., pronounced her dead.

In his own words, the chief surgeon, an Argentine to whom English is a second language, described what he found when he rushed in from the operating room: ". . . there it was, this creature . . . They gave me the stethoscope . . . it was dead. . . . The girl was dead." Assuming the accuracy of all the notations on the hospital chart, the little "creature" died during the twenty-minute period between the floor nurse's last visit at 7:40 A.M. and the arrival of the blood technician at 8 A.M. She was recovering smoothly from uncomplicated surgery, when suddenly, very suddenly, Nancy Savino, age 4, was dead. There was no reason for her death, no warning that she would die.

That evening an autopsy was performed by the Riverdell pathologist, Dr. Laurence Markley, assisted by Dr. Harris. In accordance with the established procedure in Bergen County, the county medical examiner reviewed the autopsy report.

The autopsy confirms the original diagnosis of lymphatic cysts and the apparent success of the surgery. Anything defective in the surgery should have been readily identified, and whether Dr. Harris's presence at the autopsy simplified or complicated that process is only a matter of conjecture. Unlike most autopsy reports, this one is inconclusive. Every organ appeared to be normal. The autopsy report confirms that four-year-old Nancy Savino came to Riverdell with the symptoms of appendicitis, had intestinal cysts, was operated on, and, in less than half a day after surgery, died.

Under the heading "Immediate Cause of Death," the experts wrote:

> The relationship to sudden death is not understood. A definite diagnosis is thus not made and remains as a sudden, unexpected death, cause undetermined, possibly due to an unexplained physiologic catastrophy.

In laymen's terms they meant, "We don't know."

Dr. Lans explained to the Savinos what had happened as best he could. He remembers it as probably the most unpleasant moment of his career.

Doctors frequently encounter the unexplainable, but Dr. Lans found himself unable to get the Savino child out of his mind throughout the summer of 1966. Dealing with the problems of hundreds of other patients, coping with the administration of Riverdell Hospital, where he was secretary of the board of directors, and even a vacation in the wine country of southern France did not dim that memory. He says that his thoughts kept returning to the case, reviewing it again and again. The fact that she was only a child made it harder to accept, but beyond that, there was something about the case that was out of the ordinary, and which he could not identify.

Seven months passed before the significance of Nancy Savino's death became clear to Dr. Lans.

On October 23, 1966, Eileen Shaw died at Riverdell Hospital.

She was a short, obese woman, and she was nine months pregnant when she entered the front door of Riverdell Hospital on October 19 to have her third baby. She had just turned 36.

Riverdell was familiar to Mrs. Shaw. She had delivered a normal baby there and then two who had died in childbirth, the second after a caesarean section. In 1964, she had given birth to a second healthy child, also delivered by caesarean. She understood that after one more caesarean delivery, common medical practice recommended that she be sterilized by a simple tubal ligation to avoid the dangerous pelvic stress of another caesarean.

On October 21, at 8 o'clock in the morning, her surgeon, Dr. Stanley Harris, performed the routine operation by opening the abdominal cavity with a six-inch longitudinal incision and another cut through the wall of the uterus, from which he delivered a healthy baby. There was no appreciable loss of blood, so no replacement blood was required. In short, no complications. Her postoperative course was normal for twenty-four hours.

At 8:00 the next morning, Dr. Harris's patient was visited by Dr. Jascalevich, who was making his morning rounds. At the time he came to her room, the hospital chart does not indicate that Mrs. Shaw was in any difficulty. Her routine intravenous feeding was running and the doctor changed the bottle, although the written hospital record does not indicate why he did so. He was doing this when the nurse accompanying him left the room momentarily. When she returned, she found that Mrs. Shaw's color had changed, and she was complaining of shortness of breath and a pain in the chest. Her pulse had dropped dramatically—she had become convulsive, and she was turning blue, "cyanotic," in the terms of the medical chart that recorded the events. Help came quickly: the grey curtains were drawn around her bed, an oxygen mask applied, and her color and pulse improved. After an hour of medication and a blood transfusion, her symptoms were relieved.

Later that morning, however, Mrs. Shaw had another convulsion. She became cyanotic again, and the medical team, now working with a sense of desperation, applied mouth-to-mouth resuscitation and then inserted a trachial tube to facilitate her breathing. After considerable time and attention, the convulsion passed and the patient began breathing easily once again. Later in the morning, the hospital chart recorded, she was comatose, and for most of the day the new mother slept soundly. The nurses noted that her hands were returning to a more normal color.

In the late afternoon, after the brief period of stabilization, the patient's color changed from dusky to cyanotic again, and her breathing and pulse became irregular. At times it was difficult to find a heartbeat, and signs of heart strain became obvious. Again she was given medication, but as the afternoon waned Eileen Shaw's cyanosis became worse. Her pulse began dropping again, and despite the close attention and all the energy of the hospital staff, at 3 o'clock in the morning of October 23, her heart stopped. Dr. Harris filled in the form with pulmonary thrombosis as the cause of death.

After the body was embalmed the next day, Riverdell's pathologist, Dr. Markley, performed an autopsy and found a perfectly normal heart. Mrs. Shaw was not the victim of a heart attack.

As in the Nancy Savino case, the autopsy report was inconclusive. Under the section "Cause of Death," Dr. Markley wrote, "See summary." While the pathologist took no firm position on the cause of death, he pointed out in the summary that the body contained evidence of a massive fat embolism and cited a recent medical journal article indicating that sudden and unexpected death can occur as a result of fat embolism from a fatty liver in cases of alcoholism.

The people who had worked to save Mrs. Shaw's life at Riverdell were extremely upset. Although most of them accepted the pathologist's excuse, several discussed the case among themselves. Experts agree that in cases of a fat embolism, the fat should be found clogging the lungs. Eileen Shaw was not an alcoholic, and though she was considerably overweight, her lungs were free of fat. Any careful reader of the report on the autopsy of Mrs. Shaw would conclude that medical science had not explained her death. The details of her case traveled through the hospital corridors and the doctors' lounge.

Mrs. Shaw became the sixth of Dr. Harris's patients to die postoperatively since he joined the Riverdell staff only seven months earlier. None of the deaths had been anticipated, and he considered all of the explanations to be dubious.

It was one hell of a way to begin a career. Harris, a Yale University Medical School graduate, came to Riverdell with six years of surgical training at the Bronx Municipal Hospital Center at Albert Einstein Hospital, one of New York's best.

Although Harris maintained an outward calm, the experience was shattering. His mortality rate was unprecedented, worse than that of a wartime field hospital. Statistically, he was already a failure, a surgeon who had spent half a lifetime preparing for a career that was already in jeopardy. The confidence created by surviving the competition for years of medical and premedical training drove him to find an answer better than those on the death certificates.

Harris could have found a modicum of morbid comfort in the fact that Dr. Robert Briski, one of the other surgeons who joined

Riverdell in 1966, had already lost two patients unexpectedly, and the ascribed causes of those deaths also seemed questionable.

The day after Eileen Shaw's death, Harris was in the doctors' lounge reviewing the autopsy report which the pathologist had left in his message box, when Allan Lans suggested they go over to the Colonial Inn in Englewood for lunch.

Lans, one of the hospital's directors, was concerned about the mortality rate, and he had not recovered from the experience he had shared with Harris in March when the Savino child died.

He had never lost confidence in Harris. Like his fellow hospital directors, Allan Lans was impressed with the credentials that Dr. Harris had brought to Riverdell. Harris was confident to the point of aggressiveness. He was familiar with the most up-to-date methods. From the vantage point of the operating table, Lans could see that Harris was both knowledgeable and quick, and Lans was comfortable when recommending the new man to his own patients. Besides, despite his aggressiveness, the younger man was much easier to work with than the chief of surgery, Dr. Mario Jascalevich, who, Lans felt, treated doctors, nurses, and patients in a manner that bordered on arrogance. Jascalevich had a highly developed sense of self-importance, and he frequently expressed the conviction that his skills were superior to anyone else's. Born in Argentina, his foreign accent made him more difficult for Lans to communicate with. While Dr. Lans had only the highest regard for Jascalevich's surgical speed and skill, it was Harris who was always eager to be accommodating.

At lunch in Englewood, Lans commiserated with the young surgeon while they reviewed the latest autopsy report. Another Harris patient was dead and again the pathologist's explanation was inadequate. Lans, sympathetic by nature, was sensitive to the surgeon's feelings. Harris finally felt able to confide in him.

As they discussed the Shaw case, the circumstances of her death triggered Allan Lans's memory to a chain of events leading back to the previous March. A parade of cadavers passed through his mind. That intangible question in the case of the death of Nancy Savino suddenly became tangible.

Lans and Harris started to discuss the particulars of several other cases which, it turned out, both had mentally categorized as "unsatisfactorily explained." Nancy Savino was the first, and yesterday Eileen Shaw had become number eight. In between, the list showed Margaret Henderson, died 4/23/66; Edith Post, died 5/18/66; Ira Holster, died 7/29/66; Paul Grisel, died 8/4/66; Frank Biggs, died 8/28/66; Emma Arzt, died 9/23/66. Each had undergone surgery at Riverdell. There was no reason to suspect faulty surgery in any case, and none of these eight died as a result of any operative or postoperative complications connected with the surgery. All the deaths were unanticipated. While no one of these cases by itself would give rise to a question, together they constituted a pattern. To Lans and Harris, something was amiss—something terrible. Eight people who should have been alive were dead. They had to find a reason.

Leaving the restaurant without waiting for coffee and dessert, the doctors returned to Riverdell. There, the two began pulling hospital charts out of the rows of pale green file cabinets, until they had gathered the documented histories of all the cases they had been discussing.

A hospital chart actually consists of a small pile of different records: the admission record, the patient's history, operative and discharge summaries; the doctor's orders on pink paper; the light blue record of medication; and the canary yellow progress record upon which doctors and nurses note significant occurrences as they happen.

They selected first the file on Margaret Henderson. The twenty-six-year-old woman had died only one day after an exploratory laparotomy to find the source of her abdominal pain. Nothing was found. Robert Livingston, Mrs. Henderson's family physician, was another surgeon who had just joined the Riverdell staff. He had assisted Dr. Harris, and they had operated on her despite the advice of Dr. Jascalevich, when he was called for an initial consultation. Her postoperative course was uneventful. At 8 A.M. on April 23, 1966, the first morning after surgery, apparently in response to her complaints of difficulty in swallowing and pain in the chest, Dr. Jascalevich himself started an I.V. feeding of glucose and water. Forty-five minutes later she was dead.

An autopsy was performed on April 24 by Dr. Raphael D. Gilady, the long-time chief medical examiner of Bergen County, assisted by Dr. Vincent Gillson, the Riverdell Hospital pathologist. Their report attributed the death to "acute hepatic Necrosis—

probably toxic," but they provided no apparent basis for reaching that conclusion, and their official form said practically nothing at all about what was actually done at the autopsy. As a routine procedure indicated by the pathologist's concluding words "probably toxic," the vital organs were sent to Edel Laboratories in Newark, New Jersey, for a toxicological report. That report, dated July 7, 1966, stated that nothing the laboratory tested for was detected in any of the organs analyzed, a finding which certainly refuted the original conclusion set forth in the autopsy report. But laboratories can only discover those things that they look for specifically.

The two troubled physicians placed the Henderson file on top of the Savino and Shaw records and began to review the charts of Edith Post, a sixty-two-year-old lady who had had undergone surgery by Dr. Robert Briski. They chose the case because, just as in the cases of Mrs. Henderson and Mrs. Shaw, her death on May 17, 1966 was only one day postoperative, and she had also appeared to be recovering uneventfully when, following a visit by Dr. Jascalevich in consultation, she developed shortness of breath and severe chest pain. Within an hour's time she expired without further warning or explanation, and the autopsy report was another case of vague and inconclusive language ascribing a heart attack as the "possible" cause of death.

Striking similarities were also found in the files on Frank Biggs, age 59, and Emma Arzt, age 70, who had much in common with each other and with some of the other victims of Riverdell's surgical department. The postoperative death of each in 1966 was preceded by cyanosis, chest pain, and shortness of breath, while I.V.'s were running.

Certain circumstances were common to each case. At some time during the hospitalization of each of the patients, they had been visited by the chief of surgery, Dr. Jascalevich, even though none of these people were his patients. Frequently he was the first to respond when the patient's troubles were discovered. He had visited each patient at least once. No ordinary procedure at Riverdell or elsewhere required the chief of surgery to call on colleagues' patients unless asked to do so. Except in one case, he had not been asked. Sometimes he had issued his own orders on the patient, including the initiation of intravenous feedings, which he would do himself. To issue orders on another doctor's patients was extraordinary except in dire emergency, and I.V.'s were ordinarily started by nurses or house physicians on doctors' instructions.

By 5 o'clock that afternoon, Lans and Harris had looked at each of the relevant files. The pattern of similarities was apparent. The beginning of the series of deaths seemed to coincide with the arrival of Stanley Harris on the Riverdell staff, less than a year before. Until just before Nancy Savino's death in October, 1966, there were only two surgeons with privileges at Riverdell—Mario Jascalevich, and Robert Briski, who operated less frequently. At that time, the hospital directors had determined that Riverdell could comfortably support four surgeons, and that the staff increase was in fact necessary to provide sufficient coverage for patients' needs.

Jascalevich, as the surgical chief, had a profitable arrangement. He got most of the referrals from the twenty-seven doctors with Riverdell privileges, which generated about $75,000 a year for him in fees from his Riverdell practice alone. He also had additional income from work at two other New Jersey hospitals. When the directors admitted Stanley Harris to the surgical staff in March of 1966, Jascalevich for the first time had major competition. Despite his difficulties in relating to the other staff members, the chief surgeon was normally quiet and somewhat introverted, hardly an aggressive personality. Uncharacteristically, he had expressed strenuous objections to the plan to let the new young surgeon share his territory.

Once the decision was made, Jascalevich switched gears. He approached Harris and initiated discussions about joining together as partners in a group practice, to maintain the monopoly. Nothing came of this and their discussions broke off, but not before Jascalevich had circulated a premature memorandum to the medical staff announcing their new affiliation.

The stakes were high. A surgeon's economic well-being is dependent upon referrals from other physicians. Now, an aggressive, bright young competitor was on the scene, willing to work hard.

Lans and Harris knew how competitive most surgeons could be—it was one of the facts of life of the medical community. Surgeons regard themselves as the top of an elite profession. Like all doctors, they earn admission to medical school by competing with other undergraduate students; then they continue to compete for the few available surgical residencies which assure them of the highest professional income. Charges for surgery in 1966 ranged from $250 to $2,500; the average operation at Riverdell in 1966 probably netted the surgeon a fee of $500 to $750 for an hour or two's work. A busy surgeon might expect to handle two, three, or even four operations a day. An annual income in six figures was not unusual.

Whether or not large financial rewards are involved, the frequency of surgery is in suspiciously direct proportion to the number of surgeons available. Communities with twice as many surgeons have twice as many operations per capita. According to a 1976 survey done for the U.S. House of Representatives Committee on Interstate and Foreign Commerce, New Jersey's rate of surgery is more than twice the national average. In the same Congressional report it was found that there were 2.38 million unnecessary operations in 1974, costing the American public $3.92 billion. Ralph Nader sets the figures higher: 3.2 million unnecessary operations costing $5 billion. The majority are hysterectomies, tonsillectomies, and appendectomies. Studies indicate that American women submit to a quarter of a million unnecessary hysterectomies each year; the number of unnecessary tonsillectomies, primarily on children, totals 1.5 million. Along with the surgeon's fee in each of these cases, there is the bill for anesthesia, with all of its attendant risks, a charge for the operating room, related laboratory work, and the other general expenses of hospitalization. In some places, the referring physician is asked to assist the surgeon so that the "assistant" can also send a bill. Sometimes the assistance is legitimate and sometimes it can be a form of fee splitting. It has become evident in recent years that prepaid health plans—whose surgeons are not rewarded on the basis of the number of operations they perform—have half the incidence of surgery as when fee for service is involved. The ordinary risks of surgery are great, and even if these statistics on useless operations are exaggerated by as much as 100 percent, we face a situation in which physicians and surgeons, some out of greed and some out of incompetence, are willing to subject 2 or 3 million American men, women, and children to the risks and pain of unnecessary surgery. Frequently, the victims of this horror never become aware of the lack of necessity for their operations.

While the public has remained largely ignorant of these facts, doctors are very much aware of the statistics and their implications. The advantages of being chief of surgery in a proprietary hospital are, therefore, quite apparent.

Lans and Harris felt compelled to bring the cases to the prompt attention of the hospital's board of directors so that a full inquiry could be conducted to determine the meaning of the pattern of unexplained deaths in Riverdell Hospital.

CHAPTER II

Skeletons in the Closet

Kinderkamack Road wends its way in and out of Oradell, New Jersey, through the trees and lawns of a number of the bedroom communities for commuters to New York City, only a half hour's drive away. The four-lane blacktopped road, with frequent traffic lights, is surrounded with the usual array of retail stores, automobile showrooms, garden apartments, real estate offices, and fast food outlets found in nearly every American suburb. Number 576 is Riverdell Hospital, at the end of a short, circular driveway leading up to the neat, single-story, red-brick Georgian structure, trimmed in white and looking like an elongated local post office. If one lived in that part of Bergen County and was facing hospitalization, it would seem a pleasant place to be, convenient for the people who would visit you. The atmosphere inside is cheerful, efficient, and unhurried, with rooms more attractive than those found in most other hospitals of our day.

Hospitals in America fall into one of three easily defined categories: "public," owned by governmental agencies; "volunteer," owned by not-for-profit or charitable organizations; and "private proprietary," like Riverdell, meaning that somebody owns it to make a profit. No matter who owns them, money problems dominate all hospitals, as they share the challenge of living within a budget and paying the ever-increasing costs of interest, wages, professional salaries, maintenance, and very expensive equipment. Like the owners of a hotel, the proprietors of every hospital are concerned with their occupancy rate. Most expenses of running a hospital are nearly constant, no matter how many or how few patients are in residence. Empty beds lose money for the hospital. Beds must be kept full of patients who pay. Patients are referred to hospitals by doctors who have staff privileges at those hospitals and whose fees are paid by the same patients, or more frequently by their insurance carriers. The fact that hospital costs are rising at twice the rate of inflation is largely due to the fact that 90 percent of hospital bills are paid for by third parties (government or insurance companies), so that neither the physician, nor the patient, nor the hospital is motivated to control these expenses.

When Riverdell was opened in 1957, there was no shortage of hospital beds in Bergen County or elsewhere in the area surrounding New York City. At that time, experts were beginning to recognize that excess hospital capacity was causing rapid increases in the cost of delivering health care. Blue Cross rates skyrocketed because the Blues wound up paying the bills for most of the patients, as well as a number of other hospital expenses billed directly by the hospitals. America luxuriates in an overabundance of hospital beds. There are at least 100,000 totally empty hospital beds in the United States at all times, and an additional 250,000 occupied by patients who would be treated at home if there weren't so many extra beds and the pressure to fill them. Recent efforts by governmental agencies have been directed toward eliminating excess beds in order to increase the utilization of the remaining beds.

Riverdell itself is owned by five doctors. In 1959, Allan Lans and Dr. Edwin Fireman, a general family physician, were invited to join three other Bergen County osteopathic physicians: Dr. Marvin Wisch, an ophthalmologist; Dr. Irwin Rhine, an ear, nose, and throat specialist; and Dr. Jay Sklar, an internist, who, together with Dr. L. Melvin Elting, a surgeon, had raised the capital to create Riverdell two years previously. It gave them the double benefits of a good, convenient place to care for their patients and the extra income derived from the hospitalization of their patients, over and above the normal fees paid them. They had another reason: practical necessity. When Riverdell was built, medical doctors controlled all accessible hospitals in the country and were committed to keeping osteopaths out.

A century ago, major distinctions did exist in the philosophy and training of osteopaths and medical doctors. Osteopathy is a theory of medicine which holds that the human body is endowed by nature with all of the agents necessary for the preservation of health and recovery from disease, and keeping these agents in proper balance is the key to good health. The osteopathic medical schools taught most of the same curriculum as medical colleges did, although some of the subjects were approached from a different philosophical viewpoint, and manual manipulation of the body was once emphasized as a treatment to be perferred over medication.

In recent years, the philosophical distinctions have become less relevant. There are only a few osteopaths who still treat patients exclusively with manual manipulation and today the two branches of medical art offer their students nearly identical training at major osteopathic colleges across the country. In 1957, however, most M.D.'s were unwilling to accept the qualifications of their osteopathic brethren.

At the time Riverdell Hospital was built, D.O.'s and M.D.'s were meeting identical requirements for a license in New Jersey, as well as in every other state in America. The federal government, in its funding of medical programs, gave the two branches of medicine the same recognition. However, local M.D.'s maintained their boycott as a means of reducing competition.

In our lifetime the medical profession has steadily lowered its professional standards until they approach those of the marketplace. Recent publicity has revealed the money-making methods of hundreds of Medicaid mills, helping to dissolve the popular misconception that because doctors are "professionals," with supposedly high standards, they are always more concerned with making people well than with making money. Frequently, that is just not so.

As a place where D.O.'s and M.D.'s practiced medicine together in 1966, Riverdell was ahead of most hospitals in the country. Osteopaths, few in number, had no reason to exclude M.D.'s, and a number of progressive M.D.'s, recognizing that Riverdell was both convenient and well-run, happily sought and obtained staff privileges.

In October of 1966, however, the distinctions between D.O.'s and M.D.'s were totally irrelevant to Allan Lans, D.O., and Stanley Harris, M.D. It was their common medical knowledge and experience that had enabled them to share their common conclusion about what was happening to patients at Riverdell during the past year. Convinced of the serious nature of their problem, they chose to share their burden. It was evident to them that the matter had to be handled by the hospital in which the problem arose. So, early on the morning of October 25, Allan Lans asked the four osteopaths who were his fellow hospital directors to meet with him and Harris at 9:30 that evening to discuss a matter of critical concern—the hospital's growing surgical mortality rate.

The group of doctors who comprised the board of directors of Riverdell had shared an intensely unpleasant experience after they decided to suspend one of their colleague's hospital privileges in 1962. The suspended physician happened to be Dr. Jascalevich's predecessor as chief of Riverdell's surgical department, and the events which surrounded the board's action in 1962 made such an indelible impression on the doctors that the shadow of that occasion influenced their reaction to the crisis in 1966.

Dr. L. Melvin Elting had been a moving force behind the creation of Riverdell Hospital in 1957. When his colleagues suspended his privileges in 1962, Elting was the hospital's largest single shareholder, a former president of its board, and the only physician privileged to perform surgery there.

Somehow Dr. Elting, an osteopath, had managed to gain the experience of a one-year surgical residency at a regular medical hospital. Osteopathic surgeons were rather rare in 1966 because so few graduates of osteopathic schools had the opportunity to obtain surgical training. Like a great many other surgeons, Elting operated without benefit of either surgical board certification or fellowship in an appropriate surgical specialty college.

Most people have no occasion to consider the significance of specialty credentials, but in New Jersey and elsewhere any licensed physician is authorized to perform even the most complicated surgery regardless of his surgical training, experience, or lack of it. For example, a licensed physician who spends his entire thirty-year professional career doing research, or who never reads a medical journal, can legally perform open-heart surgery if he feels inclined to do so and has a willing patient and a place to work. While the example is far fetched, it serves to dramatize one of the tragic facts of American medicine. The American College of Surgeons estimates that one-half of the surgical operations performed in this country are actually done by "doctors who are untrained or inadequately trained to undertake surgery."

Board-certified surgeons are those whom the American Board of

Surgery—or, for osteopaths, the American Board of Osteopathic Surgeons—has certified as able to practice surgery after the doctor has passed some supposedly rigorous examinations, oral, written, and clinical. The physician must first qualify to take these tests by completing the full training offered at approved surgical residencies, which includes the requirement of performing a significant number of operations under supervision.

Another useful criterion for evaluating a surgeon's competence is fellowship in the American College of Surgeons—or, for osteopaths, the American College of Osteopathic Surgeons. Admission as a fellow (F.A.C.S.) is based upon training qualifications similar to that which the boards require, but there is no requirement that the surgeons submit themselves to any actual testing.

As a founder of Riverdell Hospital in 1957, along with Dr. Wisch and Dr. Rhine, with whom he was also engaged in a group medical practice known as the New Milford Group, Elting had negotiated a contract for himself to be the exclusive surgeon at Riverdell, and chief of the surgical department. In exchange, Wisch and Rhine had been awarded similar exclusivity in their own particular fields of specialty.

Because he had already lost his privileges to operate at Dumont Hospital, the county's only other osteopathic hospital, Elting had reason to be more anxious than his colleagues to establish Riverdell. In a sworn statement filed in connection with a lawsuit in 1963, Elting said he had lost his privileges at Dumont as a result of "professional disputes and jealousies." But in an affidavit sworn to by Dr. Rhine in connection with the same lawsuit, other reasons for Elting's dismissal by Dumont Hospital were presented in great detail. The pertinent portion of Dr. Rhine's statement says that Elting's dismissal was

> . . . based on a surgical malpractice, a cut ureter in the course of a hysterectomy operation, which was called to the plaintiff's [Elting's] attention at the time that it happened and provoked only a jesting commentary—"Now you can't see it"—as the plaintiff covered the injured organ with a fold of peritoneum and sutured the patient. This appears from the proofs filed in an action in this very court entitled "*Elting* vs. *North Jersey Osteopathic General Hospital Association*" (Docket No. C-973-56),

in which injunctive relief, seeking reinstatement, was denied to him and which suit was ultimately dismissed.

The legal action which is referred to here, and in which all of the sworn affidavits described here are contained, was initiated in the Chancery Division of the New Jersey Superior Court by Dr. Elting against the Riverdell directors after they suspended Elting's privileges in 1962 (*Elting* vs. *Frieman, et al.,* Docket No. C-1457-62). The story that the court papers lay bare is that when the Riverdell board suspended Elting for thirty days, he refused to accept the discipline; he then brought the action to recover damages and to require them to reinstate him completely and restore his exclusive contract to perform surgery.

The Riverdell directors stated in their answer that Dr. Elting had performed a vasectomy to sterilize a male patient in March of 1962 without first obtaining the consultation that was required by the hospital's rules, although the necessity for such a consultation had been called to his attention prior to the operation. It was that incident that led the board of directors to suspend Elting's surgical privileges for thirty days. In the end, the incident led the parties to the courthouse in an attempt to resolve a series of long-standing differences.

When Elting refused to accept his suspension, the directors, according to Dr. Wisch's affidavit, reevaluated Elting's previous surgical activities. A cursory investigation of Elting's clinical charts revealed that within a span of some twenty-eight months "Elting's surgery had resulted in nine eviscerations," one of which resulted in a malpractice action which Elting's insurance carrier was required to settle. ("Evisceration" is a medical term meaning that the surgical incision opens up after the operation is over.)

In the same court papers, an affidavit of Kenneth H. Judy, M.D., a board-certified surgeon who, among other qualifications, was a professor and chairman of the department of surgery at the Seton Hall University Medical School, testified that the nine cases of eviscerations of abdominal incisions constituted "a rate that is dangerously high and considered prohibitively non-acceptable, regardless of the number of operations performed during this period and regardless of the type of patient operated upon."

Dr. Wisch testified that the Riverdell directors became aware of four other surgical mishaps, as well as two pending malpractice suits, one of which involved a cut ureter, precisely the type of mishap which allegedly led to revocation of Elting's Dumont Hospital privileges in 1956. Wisch also swore under oath in his affidavits that when the board reviewed the appendectomies performed by Dr. Elting from 1959 to 1961, they found a startling result: "The pathological reports indicate that 50% of Dr. Elting's appendectomies were misdiagnosed and resulted in the removal of normal appendices."

The legal battle between Elting and the Riverdell directors involved a variety of issues and also recorded many aspects of the managerial problems which beset the hospital in its formative years. In 1960, Elting's colleagues had removed him as president —another manifestation of the long and complex dispute which resulted in the 1963 case.

Elting, in his legal action, asked the court to afford him a variety of different forms of relief. Among the more relevant aspects, he said that the defendants (his cofounders and fellow board members) had violated his contract as exclusive surgeon at Riverdell Hospital, and that they had illegally removed him as president, denied his hospital privileges, and diluted his shareholdings and his voice in the direction of the hospital. He asked the court to award him damages and to restore his original place as Riverdell's exclusive surgeon. The Elting lawsuit was eventually settled out of court, with an arrangement for Riverdell Hospital to purchase Elting's shares and his agreement to drop his effort to be reinstated.

(Although somewhat peripheral to the story of what happened at Riverdell in 1965 and 1966, the story of Dr. Elting's career as revealed in the sworn affidavits filed in court during the 1963 dispute took on an ironic significance more than a decade later. In the fall of 1976 Dr. Elting coauthored *The Consumer's Guide to Surgery,* a book in which he advises the American public how to go about protecting themselves against incompetent surgery.)

With respect to the events of 1966, no one can fairly appraise the actions of the different Riverdell board members concerning the allegations of Lans and Harris without fully understanding the long years of controversy and distraction that these same doctors had survived only a few years before. The Elting affair left a residue of tension among the board members, with the result that their decision-making process became more deliberate and cumbersome. Disputes arose frequently over management philosophy, and more time was consumed with meetings than their busy practices should have permitted.

The physicians' previous difficulties with Dr. Elting provided a logical basis for their current behavior. For doctors whose normal work does not contemplate the intensive involvement and activity of preparing for litigation, such a lawsuit became an unbearable strain. The experience naturally colored their attitude on any matter which portended involvement with lawyers and courts of any kind.

None of the doctor-directors had any extensive administrative experience, but Riverdell Hospital was now a big business, generating millions of dollars in annual revenues. For some, management of the hospital provided the same source of ego satisfaction that nourishes the captains of industry.

Mindful of the arduous debates among the directors over easier issues, Alan Lans prepared himself well for the board meeting of October 25, 1966. Lans brought with him the hospital files of the eight cases that he and Harris had reviewed. Harris knew six of the cases intimately because the deceased had been his surgical patients. The two doctors reviewed the records again while awaiting the arrival of their colleagues. The matter would be further complicated by Harris's competitive position with Jascalevich and his embarrassment at the mortality rate among his own patients. Lans recognized the magnitude of the resistance that he and Harris would have to overcome in order to convince the board of directors to deal with the problem.

A Boston University survey once asked 214 doctors if they would be willing to testify in court for a patient whose surgeon had removed the wrong one of his diseased kidneys. Only 31 percent of the specialists and 27 percent of the general practitioners interviewed said they would be willing. This finding indicates that most physicians turn a blind eye to evidence of a colleague's incompetence. It is a conspiracy of silence.

Dr. Robert L. Derbyshire, former head of the National Federation of State Medical Boards, and a recognized authority on this subject, put the proposition succinctly: "There's a great reluctance on the part of doctors to interfere with another doctor's reputation and means of livelihood. The philosophy apparently is that a man's reputation is more important than the welfare of his patients."

In general, a doctor has very little fear of losing his license to practice. The fear of "getting involved" is far greater. Statistics reveal how rarely a license is suspended or terminated. Over the last 13 years, of the 320,000 physicians throughout the United States, an average of only 66 lost their licenses each year.

The Hippocratic Oath, established by the father of medicine to guide his disciples, still functions today as the universal basis of medical ethics. In the revised version currently approved by the American Medical Association, the doctor's first duty is established as loyalty to his colleagues. The oath begins with these words:

> You do solemnly swear, each man by whatever he holds most sacred,—That you will be loyal to the profession of medicine and just and generous to its members . . .

The oath concludes with a promise of "prosperity" to those who are loyal to it.

In one form or another, all of these facts, circumstances, and considerations were either on or under the table at Riverdell Hospital, as the directors pulled up their chairs at 9:30 P.M. on October 25, 1966, to discuss the unexplained deaths in their hospital.

CHAPTER III

Case Histories

Harris and Lans reviewed all of the details of the cases of Nancy Savino, Eileen Shaw, and Margaret Henderson, and the relevant hospital records were passed around the room for each director to examine if he wanted to.

Dr. Harris then asked the directors to review the case of Emma Arzt. She was a seventy-year-old retired librarian who had come to Riverdell for a gallbladder operation about a month before on the recommendation of Dr. Bernard J. Topfer, her family physician.

Mrs. Arzt had been undergoing various tests and examinations at the hospital for five days before her surgery on September 22, 1966, when Dr. Harris removed her gallbladder and extracted a fatty tumor from her head. As in the other cases under discussion, Mrs. Arzt's surgery was considered uncomplicated and, in the parlance of the hospital charts, "uneventful." The record shows that her first postoperative night was "comfortable," and that she was being nourished intravenously.

On the morning of September 23, at about 8 A.M., the dressing from Mrs. Arzt's surgery was reinforced because of a red discharge that was noticed by the attending nurses. She became "cyanotic and ceased breathing" soon thereafter, according to her progress record, which Dr. Harris now passed around the table to the hospital directors. At 10:10 A.M., Dr. Jascalevich responded to the emergency call, and it was he who gave Mrs. Arzt artificial respiration and a heart massage before hooking her up to a respirator. By the time Dr. Harris arrived, she had started to breathe on her own, and Harris attended her intermittently until 2:10 that afternoon, when she began perspiring profusely and stopped breathing again. After a ten-minute effort to revive her, she was pronounced dead.

No autopsy was performed on Mrs. Arzt, and her death was attributed to "circulatory failure."

Another ulcer patient had undergone a very similar experience in August of 1966. A fifty-seven-year-old accountant, Frank Biggs was a regular patient of Dr. Hubert M. Stavrand, an internist with Riverdell privileges, who had asked Dr. Briski to operate in order to relieve the patient's suffering from a duodenal ulcer. Dr. Briski operated on August 23, 1966, and performed a subtotal gastrectomy (removal of part of the stomach).

No complications were noted relative to the surgical procedure, but Mr. Biggs did have some postoperative difficulties and a couple of uncomfortable nights until August 28, when, according to the hospital records, he reported that he had a much better night and felt good in the morning for the first time since his operation. Considering what he had been through, Mr. Biggs was having a good day. According to the notation on the hospital chart by one of the nurses at 8:00 in the evening, he had no pain and good color.

Just a little more than an hour later, the patient, who had been receiving medicine intravenously since the operation, was discovered by his nurse to be having difficulty breathing and suddenly cyanotic. Dr. Jascalevich and Dr. Ortega, who were nearby, both responded to the nurse's call and administered heart massage and a respiratory stimulant. They were unsuccessful, and at 9:30 P.M. Mr. Biggs was pronounced dead.

In this case a very complete autopsy report was prepared by the Riverdell pathologist, Dr. Markley, who performed the autopsy fourteen hours after death and prior to embalming. His report states on the one hand that "there is no anatomical lesion that points directly to the cause of death," and then goes on to state that ventricular fibrillations (a fast heartbeat) "might" be the immediate cause, or that "perhaps" there was a clue to a liver abnormality. One fact the pathologist did state with certainty: "The events of the preceding two or three days gave no warning."

Stanley Harris looked across the table at Marvin Wisch. He asked him how certain they could be about the cause of death of his patient Ira Holster, on whom Harris had been asked to operate last July.

Just like several of the other patients, Mr. Holster had expired during his first postoperative day, July 29, 1966, when he seemed to be doing well after surgery, although in this case the surgery was of a serious nature.

Mr. Holster was sixty-four years old and was suffering from a duodenal ulcer and some other related disorders. Harris had performed a vagotomy and gastrojejunostomy, suturing the stomach to the small intestine after severing the vagus nerve, a relatively unusual procedure for relieving the ulcer. At the same time he removed the patient's gallbladder.

Mr. Holster's hospital chart showed that through an intravenous tube the patient was receiving Demerol to relieve pain, when Dr. Wisch visited him at 8:30 A.M. and ordered an alcohol bath because Mr. Holster was perspiring profusely. Dr. Wisch noted on the chart that Holster told the doctor he was feeling better. At 9:55, less than one and one-half hours after Dr. Wisch left him, the patient suddenly ceased breathing. His death was attributed to an acute coronary occlusion, and there was no autopsy.

While Dr. Harris was speaking, Dr. Jay Sklar remembered the incident of almost a year before involving his own patient, Carl Rohrbeck.

As a child Mr. Rohrbeck had immigrated to the United States with his parents from his birthplace in Germany. He served his new country in World War I and became an American citizen. In 1965 he lived in Teaneck, enjoying his pension as a retired employee of the New York City Department of Public Works.

Dr. Sklar thought that Mr. Rohrbeck was healthy enough to consider elective surgery to repair a ventral hernia, so on his seventy-third birthday, he entered Riverdell Hospital for the operation. Repairing a hernia is normally routine surgery, and experts agree that even people of Rohrbeck's age can be considered good surgical risks, especially if, as in Rohrbeck's case, their general health is good.

Carl Rohrbeck was never operated on. Dr. Sklar had arranged for Dr. Jascalevich to perform the operation, which was scheduled for the early morning of December 13, 1965.

Sklar recalled that morning very well. While he was in the dressing room, preparing to assist Jascalevich, the surgeon came to him at about 7:30 A.M. and said that he had canceled the operation. According to Sklar, Jascalevich told him that he had "a premonition" and that he did not want to operate on this patient.

Sklar had given his patient the usual preoperative examination after he checked in the previous evening and had found him to be in fine condition. The notes on the hospital chart show that Rohrbeck's heart and lungs were normal.

Upon hearing Jascalevich's surprise announcement, Sklar went to Rohrbeck's room, listened to his heart and lungs with his stethoscope, and then took his blood pressure, while Carl asked him, "What's holding up the show?" Finding nothing unusual, Sklar went back to see the surgeon, whose action in unilaterally canceling the operation on Dr. Sklar's patient was so extraordinary in terms of professional courtesy and hospital practice. He was expected first to discuss any such action with Sklar, as the admitting physician. Sklar told Jascalevich, "I just don't understand you, this isn't the Dark Ages, you have to give me a better reason. I want you to take another look at him."

Jascalevich agreed and went back to the patient's room while Sklar waited. When he returned to Sklar, Jascalevich told him again that he would not operate. Sklar stood speechless while Jascalevich turned away to call for his next case. Sklar was just about to tell Jascalevich that Rohrbeck was the last patient he would ever send him, when a nurse came into the room and announced, "Dr. Sklar, your Mr. Rohrbeck just died."

Sklar ran to the dead patient's bedside, where he found that Jascalevich had started an intravenous feeding tube going on Rohrbeck when he visited him a few minutes before. Completely mystified, Dr. Sklar ordered an autopsy.

The autopsy was done by Dr. Lawrence J. Denson, Bergen County's assistant chief medical examiner. Dr. Denson found that all of the deceased's vital organs were normal except for "marked arteriosclerosis with total occlusion of anterior descendary branch" of the left main artery, which led Denson to enter on his form report under the section for cause of death: "pending further examination, appears to be coronary occlusion." (The fact that this determination was at least somewhat tentative in Dr. Denson's mind is borne out by his sending the patient's liver and kidneys to Edel Laboratories for analysis, all of which were reported as normal.) Sklar also remembered one of the nurses at Riverdell had told him that Dr. Denson had requested that the I.V. tubing and bottles and any medicine given to the deceased be sent along with the body, but he never heard what became of that material.

The incident was a completely isolated one when it happened in 1965, and Sklar felt that there was nothing further to be done. He had no reason to recall the matter until the discussion with the directors precipitated by Lans and Harris.

The Riverdell directors were forced to face unpleasant insinuations that night. Even more objective men could easily have found the implications difficult to accept. These doctors had to balance the incomplete facts at hand against their need to protect their own reputations and that of the hospital they cherished and owned. With the supporting evidence so circumstantial, and lacking any firm indication of the actual causes of these deaths, much less an eye witness, it was understandable that a Riverdell Hospital doctor-owner-director would assume the best, not the worst. Damage to the hospital's reputation would surely be matched by damage to the practice of every member of the hospital's medical staff.

The difficult deliberations went on until early the next morning. Dr. Lans remembers that voices were raised in both anger and anguish. The discussion exacerbated emotions and damaged some relationships forever.

For everyone present, and for some who were not, lifelong careers were on the line. Men whose ethics and entire training had spawned a cult of silence were facing an unprecedented responsibility. It was too much. From their conversation, it became evident that the directors would not take any action.

CHAPTER IV

"Someone Is Killing My Patients"

Allan Lans's voice carried a sense of great urgency when he called my office late one afternoon in 1966. He said he needed to come to see me early in the evening to discuss a problem that required my immediate attention. Soon afterward we found ourselves alone in the small den which doubled as my office at home.

Allan's face was drawn. I had never known him to look or sound so disturbed. With his eyes closed, under a frowning brow, he whispered a sentence that has remained with me ever since.

"Matt—Someone is killing my patients."

Allan had been my close friend for ten years. I had known him since undergraduate days, but his statement required a lot of explanation. I could scarcely grasp, let alone accept what he was telling me. Allan did not appear to notice my reaction.

He began by going back seven months to the loss of Nancy Savino, whom he constantly referred to as a "little baby." Allan also filled me in on the details of the death of Eileen Shaw, just two days earlier.

"There was no reason for that lady to die. We wouldn't even call her a surgical risk. She wasn't my patient, but I heard the whole story from Harris and the staff and I knew something was wrong.

"People don't just die. There is always a reason." He paused momentarily, and said softly: "Sometimes it's more apparent than other times, but never without a reason.

"This time there was no reason. She was getting better. It was just like the Savino baby, she was getting better, then suddenly, she was dead. No warning. Nothing . . . nothing."

I sat there stunned and silent. I was being asked to accept as fact a multiple murder in the sterile security of a modern hospital.

Dr. Allan Lans

Allan broke the silence with the second most dramatic statement of the evening: "A doctor killed them."

"Allan, that's crazy. What the hell are you talking about?" I said, feeling my stomach churning.

Frowning, he told me how he and Dr. Harris had discovered eight surgical mortalities during the past seven months in which the circumstances of death were unusual and the ascribed causes unsatisfactory, how they became convinced that these patients were victims of premeditated murder. Allan emphasized that Harris was a knowledgeable colleague and had come to the same conclusion independently.

He described the other cases in general terms, but he was specific about how unusual it was for the chief surgeon to administer to other people's patients and how Jascalevich had been at the bedside just before or just after each death.

"Allan, how could such a thing happen?"

"I don't know. If a doctor wants to kill someone there are many ways to do it without leaving a trace, but I don't know how—I just know that he's got to be the one. He's always there and there's usually no reason for him to be there."

It was still hard for me to grasp. Perhaps because of my training as a lawyer, I needed a more rational explanation.

My first thought was that perhaps another doctor had concocted the whole thing to cover some fatal flaw.

"I thought of all that," Allan explained. "But, I was there when Harris operated on the Savino baby, I saw his work and it was superb. She didn't die from the surgery. Besides, that wouldn't explain the people that Briski lost, or Sklar's patient, Mr. Rohrbeck."

He remained firm and sure of his diagnosis. None of my alternatives changed his view. As he added more facts about each case, the pattern of events supporting his theory became clearer. We reviewed the available information again and again. He had an answer to every question.

Finally, I asked the obvious question: "But why would anyone do such a thing?"

Allan went into the economic facts of a surgeon's practice and suggested that if he was a psychopath, the threat of losing that much income could conceivably set him off. Psychopaths are not detected through their ordinary behavior, according to the college professors with whom we had studied.

I remained dubious. In all my experience as a lawyer—including two years on Governor Averell Harriman's staff, during which I had processed a great number of extradition and clemency applications in New York State—I had never encountered or even heard of criminal behavior of such magnitude.

Allan stopped long enough to drink a third mug of the black coffee that was sustaining us through the late hours. It had grown late enough for the quiet to be penetrated by the distant bumping and clicking of a long freight train making its way up the tracks along the Hudson. Then he went further. "The most incredible thing is the reaction of my partners."

I said nothing, but my Corona emitted a barely audible hiss as I pushed it into the few drops of cold coffee at the bottom of a saucer. I waited for him to continue. I knew of his fellow hospital directors only slightly from a few meetings, but Allan had frequently told me of their arguments and his frustrations in dealing with his colleagues.

"Matt, they are impossible. We had a meeting last night until 2:30 in the morning. They listened to everything that Harris and I had to say and they did nothing. They think that Harris is a troublemaker and I am being ridiculous. I'm disgusted and Harris is mad as hell—he's never seen them in operation before. A couple of them think that what we say is possible, but they're scared to death. They don't want anything to embarrass the hospital."

Throughout that long evening, I reacted by reviewing every conceivable alternative to Allan's theory. I was more than the devil's advocate—for, despite Allan's arguments discounting whatever alternatives I raised, I had serious doubts about his conclusions.

On the other hand, I was determined that as a friend I should to do everything possible to help Allan get to the bottom of this situation. We decided to investigate Jascalevich discreetly ourselves, to find out more about his activities, his background, or anything else that might tend to shed more light on his behavior. We agreed to commit ourselves to this task over the next couple of days, and hoped we could come up with something that might be convincing one way or the other.

I also pointed out to Allan the legal problems in this situation. We had to avoid defaming the reputation of anyone who might be innocent, and the evidence at hand was far from conclusive. No matter how convinced Harris or Lans was, the law required proof beyond a reasonable doubt.

I also cautioned Allan about potential liability for instituting the prosecution of another person maliciously or without probable cause. Truth is the best defense to either action, and as long as the complainants, acting in good faith and seeking justice, restricted their allegations to the facts and only made them to the proper authorities, leaving out conclusions or accusations, they would be protected. Allan had his own keen sense of justice and he readily understood all this.

The Bergen County prosecutor was the proper authority to investigate such suspicions. It was his duty to determine if there was sufficient evidence of a crime for a grand jury to find the probable cause necessary for an indictment.

Obviously, the case would be more meaningful to the prosecutor if it were presented by the entire hospital board, so we agreed that Allan and Harris should go back to the board again and inform them of their personal determination to go to the prosecutor, hoping that their resolve might force the board to support them.

CHAPTER V

A Private Investigation

I was oddly exhilarated when Allan left me just before 2:00 that morning. What he had told me was a real-life mystery of enormous proportions, and I was feeling the responsibility that went with it, as well as the challenge. Finding an effective method for developing more objective information was the first order of business.

The hospital directors were clearly in no mood to pay the expense of a private detective, so I tried to think of an inexpensive alternative. There was also a need for confidentiality required to protect the reputation of the hospital and any suspect, while shielding the survivors' families from any further anguish, an especially important element in case my friend's theory should turn out to be erroneous.

The idea of enlisting the interest of a good newspaperman, an experienced investigative reporter who could be trusted to work quietly, motivated by the reward of a good story, occurred to me while driving to Manhattan the next morning. To find the right person required very special contacts and judgment, and I knew one person who could be relied upon for help.

During most of 1966, I had managed Howard Samuels's campaign for the Democratic nomination for governor of New York, and had become good friends with Paul Buiar, who was in charge of Samuels's public relations. Buiar, a former AP reporter, is one of New York's most effective people. He knows how to keep a confidence, he has an intimate knowledge of the New York press corps, and he has superb judgment.

I called Buiar as soon as I got to my office, and late that afternoon went down to his dingy office at the campaign headquarters in the Commodore Hotel, where he was then running the press relations for Frank O'Connor, the ex-district attorney of Queens

County who had beaten Samuels for the nomination. With Buiar's ever-present radio routinely masking conversations from eavesdroppers, I spelled out our problem.

As I retold the story myself for the first time, I realized as the words came out that the tale was really incredible. I suddenly became apprehensive. Buiar is an unusually blunt man; but although I hesitated at enough places in the story to give him the opportunity to express himself, his silence encouraged me to go on. I finished, and I knew I had him hooked when he said, "How can I help? What can I do?"

I asked him about several good reporters to whom he had introduced me during the campaign, but he rejected all of them. He suggested that the best man would be Bill Federici of the New York *Daily News,* who in Buiar's view was the most knowledgeable crime reporter in New York, if not the country. The *News* was then most famous for its crime coverage, and Federici had just distinguished himself with his coverage of the murder of Senator Charles Percy's daughter in Illinois and the unusual case of the Star of India jewel theft from the Museum of Natural History. At the time, he was also covering the Coppolino case. So, in my presence, Buiar called Federici.

"Bill, I got a guy here who I know very well and he can be trusted. He's on to a story that's bigger than anything you ever heard of and it's in your line. I suggest that you join us for lunch tomorrow and if you have anything else on it's worth breaking it for this."

One of Buiar's special talents is to know where everyone likes to eat or drink. So, to be sure that Federici would accept the invitation, he picked the bar of the Tudor Hotel on East 42nd Street, only a half block from the *News* offices. Federici took the bait, and my hopes grew.

We met at the entrance to the small, dark room with high ceilings. The noisy lunchtime crowd contributed to the publike atmosphere and we quickly blended in. Federici, a dark and wiry man with eyes that constantly seem to be anticipating things about to happen behind him, talked about all sorts of famous criminals, cops, lawyers, and prosecutors, and he talked so fast that he was able to make twice the impression in half the time.

After bringing us up to date on his activities of the last few months, the crime reporter left some time to hear what I had to say. I summarized the story for him, leaving out all of the names, except to let him know that it was taking place in nearby New Jersey, expecting that proximity might help to motivate his interest.

I was wrong. Federici had too many other things on his plate to spend his time doing spade work on something that seemed more like fantasy than fact. In retrospect, I think he was humoring us, but he said that with all the other big things he was on to, he wanted to wait till there was something more definite before he could get into it himself. He would be happy to put me in touch with a detective he knew in the New York City Police Department who would be willing to work on the case on his own time. I knew that would give me access to police records, and a good cop with New York City chutzpah and a gold badge could certainly extract information that no private investigator or a reporter could easily get access to.

"If anyone can get what you need here it's this guy," Federici told us. He told me about one of the most famous robberies in the history of the New York City Police Department, and named the detective responsible for solving it.

Federici said, "He's the one who cracked the case, and he's the best detective in New York." He would have him call me, and I thanked him for that. Federici agreed to say nothing to anyone else.

I walked Paul back up 42nd Street to the Commodore, feeling a little disillusioned that the most creative of the working press was so willing to let go of what might be the crime of the century, and wondering if I should be a little more skeptical of the story I was telling. As consolation, I had a way to proceed, with good resources if I could find a way to finance it.

Detective Hank Murphy, as I will call him here,* arrived at my office by appointment the next day wearing his Broderick Crawford face and "Detective Story" suit. He was a big man, who appeared to be in his early forties, exuding all of the "street smarts" that one expects of an experienced New York City Police Department detective. Another man accompanied Murphy. He was aver-

*I had promised him that his identity would never be revealed if he helped us, and his name is irrelevant.

age in size, dark, with black curly hair, and at first glance looked rather unkempt. A second glance confirmed that he was downright dirty, wearing a red and black flannel shirt over filthy dungarees, and he seemed somewhat ill at ease with his two-day growth of beard and black fingernails, all of which contrasted with the gold carpet of our rosewood and chrome corporate offices. Murphy introduced him as "my partner in private work and the best burglar in New York."

Having my own burglar was a thought that had never before entered my mind. Actually, it was an appealing idea, especially a burglar with a gold shield in his pocket, and I quickly envisioned him crawling out of a suspect's transom with a copy of a diary recording his innermost thoughts about each of the cases in question at Riverdell. (Years later I read in the newspapers that my burglar had been convicted of using his gold badge while "investigating" accounts payable as a collection agent for a private corporation.) For the third time in two days, I told the story about my doctor friend's problem, and I outlined the idea we had of trying to get some independent information about the background and other activities of Dr. Jascalevich. The way to begin would be to go back to wherever else we knew he had been previously to ascertain if there was anything concealed in his background.

The nature of police work is such that a cop gets jaded after a few years, and the more he has to deal with criminals, the more suspicious he gets of everyone else he meets. As I unfolded the story, the two West Side detectives were looking at me just as they would look at a suspect caught with his pockets full of loot.

It was apparent that these men were not going to be motivated by any desire to share in the glory of some triumph of justice. They did that every day. Turning to Murphy, I said, "Tell me what you think you can do and how much it's going to cost."

Murphy spoke for his organization. "First of all, you always need two men. That way one covers for the other, because sometimes when you're on to something, and there is a tour change or overtime on the job, and one guy has to work, the other can stay on the case."

I was less than convinced by this line of reasoning, but was in no position to argue. Murphy went on. "First we check out all of the regular sources of information, criminal records, immigration,

FBI, etc. That's basic and you never know what we might come up with. Maybe he's done something else that you would want to know about. After that, we check out the other places he worked before in order to find out what other people know about him, and if he ever had any trouble."

I told him that I would be able to get some information from the medical directory and could ask my friends at Riverdell to get a list of the other hospitals or institutions Jascalevich had ever been connected with.

They knew what would have to be done, and their terms were simple: $8.50 per hour per man, plus out-of-pocket expenses, and $15 a day for the use of their car—all cash, no checks.

I told them that I would have to see if I could find a way to finance such an investigation and would get back to them in a few days. I didn't bother to tell them to keep this to themselves, because they obviously kept everything to themselves anyway.

It was Friday night when I called Allan at home to tell him what I had been up to since our conversation earlier in the week. He sounded more despondent than ever, because he and Harris had met with the directors again the night before and they got nowhere. Allan was intrigued with the idea of hiring our own detective, and I felt that it would be worthwhile to do so before going to the county prosecutor, because it might lead to something more concrete and create stronger insulation against any liability. Allan said he was willing to come up with some money for this purpose if he could get Harris to share the expense. He would see him on Monday and find out if he was willing to do so. It would be expensive, but we could turn the investigators off if they didn't come up with anything soon.

I didn't hear from Allan again until Wednesday night, November 2, and by then a lot had happened.

CHAPTER VI

Eighteen Empty Bottles

The morning after our long discussion Alan called each of the directors and asked them to meet again that evening. Once more they gathered in the hospital conference room, but their discussion was a repetition of the previous session. In two days their positions had hardened, and they were even more convinced of the correctness of their original decision.

The threat of one member of the group to go outside on his own seemed to have no impact. As Allan remembers it, his colleagues couldn't believe that either he or Harris was really prepared to do it, because they had never encountered such a thing happening among doctors. The meeting served only to intensify acrimony and frustration, leaving everyone feeling more burdened than before.

It was nearly midnight when the group disbanded, and, except for Stanley Harris, the doctors left the hospital. Harris went back to the dressing room to change into the street shoes he kept in his locker.

Sitting there all alone on the long wooden bench between the steel lockers, and feeling more frustrated than at any other time in his life, he remembers seeing the name "Dr. Jascalevich" on the label of one of the steel cabinets. A Master lock hung through the hole at the bottom of the chrome handle, and to Harris it represented another barrier in the path of justice.

Recently, a thirty-four-year-old New Jersey anesthesiologist named Coppolino had become famous because he was about to be tried for the murder of his next-door neighbor, an army colonel whose wife had allegedly been having an affair with the doctor. Television and newspapers of the day were full of the story because the doctor had been accused of killing his victim with an injection of succinylcholine, a muscle relaxant which anesthesiologists use in connection with certain surgical procedures. Harris, like everyone else, had read about the details of this case, and during the many hours of thought he directed to the deaths at Riverdell, the possibility had occurred to him that there might be some similarity to the Coppolino case.

The frustrating lock on Jascalevich's cabinet took on new meaning for Harris, and in the late afternoon of October 31, while most of the other Riverdell doctors were treating patients back at their offices, Stanley Harris, clad in a white coat, went to the administrative nurse at the hospital and told her that he had left his locker key in the jacket of his suit in his own locker. She gave him her passkey.

Harris made sure he was alone in the dressing room when he inserted the passkey into the lock on locker number 4 and opened the cabinet.

For a surgeon's locker, it was an unanticipated picture of disorder, looking like a medical garbage can. He found a pile of small pharmaceutical boxes and bottles. Some surgical instruments were also on the locker shelf, some bottles of vitamins and a variety of hypodermic needles, including one 10-cc plastic syringe which was loaded with a colorless fluid. Several of the pharmaceutical boxes were identical, and labeled "Tubocurarine—10 cc." Most of them were empty, as were eighteen small bottles bearing the same label as the boxes.

Harris tried to leave everything in precisely the same disorder as he found it. His hand was sweating as he closed the metal door. Harris remembers that as the latch clicked into place he felt lonely and awed. To suspect murder is one thing; to find weapons is another. Harris shuddered.

Badly shaken, Harris left the hospital as quickly as he could, and drove straight to his office, disregarding the 30-mile-per-hour speed limit on Kinderkamack Road. He called Allan Lans and the two of them discussed the significance of what Harris had found.

Tubocurarine, like succinylcholine, the drug allegedly used by Dr. Coppolino, is a pharmaceutical name for the generic drug curare.

Curare is sold under different trade names by different pharmaceutical manufacturers. But curare is curare, and by whatever name, it serves essentially the same purpose. Most doctors are familiar with it as a muscle relaxant. Carefully controlled dosages are injected before surgery. It relaxes the muscles, and thereby reduces the amount of other anesthetics that need to be administered for surgery. It is also used to stop normal breathing, so a surgeon can work near the patient's lungs when the patient is put on a respirator. Although its medical value was discovered in 1938, the first synthetic form of curare wasn't developed until after World War II. Today it is found in the locked pharmacy cabinets of most hospitals.

Curare in its various forms has a number of other medical applications. Because it artificially induces muscular flaccidity, it has been used to relieve spastic paralysis. It is also useful when treating fractures or dislocations, because it can reduce the tendency of muscles to pull during setting. As a general anticonvulsant, curare has been used to treat tetanus and to minimize convulsions during electroshock therapy. The amount of the dosage is critical. Too much curare absorbed too quickly can relax the body into eternal sleep.

The deadly nature of the drug has recommended it to mystery writers for decades, and ever since Sherlock Holmes described its use on several occasions, the bodies of curare victims have occasionally been found in movies, magazines, and other detective stories. In real life, Francis Gary Powers, the ill-fated U-2 pilot of the Eisenhower era, recently revealed that he carried a concealed curare dart on his reconnaissance flight over Soviet Russia.

The fascination of curare derives as much from its primitive origins as from its much heralded efficiency as a traceless instrument of death. For hundreds of years, South American Indian tribes have employed the drug for hunting food and killing enemies. These primitive people discovered that when curare penetrates a wound it stops breathing by paralyzing the respiratory muscles and quickly causes the death of either animal prey or human enemy.

Just like pharmaceutical manufacturers, each of the various tribes of South American Indians who developed the weapon gave their own brand a different name. In Guyana, the Macusi tribe call theirs "Urali," and they made the resinous, aromatic, dark-brown sticky mass from the climbing vine *Strychnos toxifera.* They mixed this extract with other plants, black ants, red ants, and the poison fangs of some favorite snakes. The tall, light-skinned and sometimes blue-eyed Zaparos who live in open thatched huts along the Curary River on the Peruvian/Equadorian border are probably responsible for the present generic name of curare or curari.

Other tribes applied such names as "Wourari," "Ourari," "Urirarery," and a number of variations thereof, but they all used it the same way, dipping the sharpened end of a blow dart, arrow, or spear into the poison before sending it into their victim's hide. For that reason, curare has also been referred to as "flying death."

Like other doctors, Lans and Harris were thoroughly familiar with curare's use in surgery. They knew it is used by anesthesiologists, and not by surgeons. They knew how dangerous it could be. Finding it in Dr. Jascalevich's locker, they could conceive of no proper explanation for his having it there. Even an anesthesiologist would not keep such material in his own locker.

Lans was concerned by Harris's violation of Jascalevich's locker and his privacy. He remembered that the fact that Harris could do such a thing had momentarily become almost as important as the significance of what he found. There seemed to be something wrong about it, and even more so because Harris was all alone when he did it.

Allan told me of his conversation with Harris. "Stanley, I don't know how you could do such a thing all by yourself. People might think that you put the stuff there."

But Harris was consumed with the meaning of his discovery. "Allan, that really doesn't matter, they will have to believe us now."

Lans persisted, mindful of the importance of the evidence and the need to preserve its integrity. "We have to find a way to corroborate your story in order to establish that Jascalevich knew the stuff was there."

They decided that the most important thing to do was to get further confirmation, and Allan called the president of the hospital board, Dr. Edwin Frieman, asking him to come to the hospital at 5:00 P.M. When Frieman arrived, Lans and Harris took him into the administrator's office, and told him what Harris had done. Frieman listened in silence, and when he had heard it all, he asked to be taken to the locker himself. They went to the dressing room and there the three doctors opened locker number 4 again. Lans and Frieman saw that its contents were exactly as Harris had said they were. They saw the empty boxes of tubocurarine.

Before closing the locker, the doctors removed one bottle of curare which they would later use to dramatize Harris's discovery to their colleagues. The three doctors went back to the administrative office, closed the door, and told Eliot Weiner, the hospital administrator, to call the three other directors to his house, a few blocks from Riverdell, for another meeting just after supper.

Once the other directors heard about the discovery and Frieman's confirmation of it, and saw the bottle of curare, they all started firing questions at once. Their doubts of the past meetings were quickly dispelled. The directors knew they would now have to act.

One of them said he had to see for himself and the others thought that would be a good idea. They went back to the locker with Weiner's Polaroid to take some pictures of the contents. After their personal confirmation, the directors decided that they should go to Hackensack and find the county prosecutor. It was agreed that they would meet at the hospital at 10:30 the next morning.

The fact that Harris had opened the locker by himself still concerned Allan Lans. He told his colleagues that he would like to see what happened when Jascalevich opened his locker the next morning. By observing Jascalevich at his locker, he felt he would be able to dispel anybody's doubts about whether or not Jascalevich was aware of the locker's contents, and he could attest to Jascalevich's familiarity with the contents. If there was something amiss or something that was not his, Jascalevich might give some indication.

In hospitals, doctors ordinarily work in accordance with an established routine, which is usually familiar to their colleagues. Therefore, when Jascalevich's Chevrolet pulled into the blacktopped Riverdell parking lot at 7:20 A.M., Lans was already sitting on the bench in the dressing room fiddling with his necktie from a position which gave him a clear view of locker number 4.

In his quick manner, long familiar to Lans, Jascalevich came into the dressing room to prepare himself for surgery. He opened the locker with his back to Lans, who was watching intently. The contents of the messy locker were visible to Lans, and, of course, to Jascalevich. From his vantage point, Lans could see several of the boxes and some glass bottles on the shelf. The contents of the cabinet were in Jascalevich's full view. Jascalevich, facing into the locker, according to Lans's observation, took out a white hospital coat and changed, hanging his suit jacket in the locker. The entire procedure took less than five minutes, but Lans recalls them as the longest five minutes of his life. The surgeon finished, locked the door of the cabinet, and, noticing Lans for the first time on the way out, he nodded his usual curt greeting.

Lans saw what he had come to see. He slid his necktie back up, put on his plaid sport jacket, and went to the administrator's office, where Harris, Frieman, Sklar, Wisch, Rhine, and Weiner were waiting. Jascalevich's lack of any visible reaction was enough to dispel any doubts about the legitimacy of Harris's discovery.

At 11 o'clock in the morning of November 1, two cars bearing the board of directors of Riverdell Hospital drove into the massive parking lot at the county office buildings in Hackensack. The doctors found their way to the county prosecutor's wing of the aging Bergen County Courthouse, where Guy W. Calissi, the part-time county prosecutor, was busy in the second floor grand jury room presenting a routine felony case. When Calissi heard that there were five doctors waiting outside, he agreed to see them for a moment in the hall.

Lans remembers how ridiculous he felt among his five colleagues, all trying to squeeze out the complex set of facts to the harried official who said he had only a couple of minutes to spare.

The only time a smile comes to Allan Lans's face when he talks about the entire affair is when he recalls that scene in the hall of the courthouse, as Calissi was encircled by the babble of doctors from Riverdell, all feeling very uncomfortable, much out of their element, and all trying to talk at once about multiple murder.

The courthouse hall was a busy place, and the portions of the doctors' story that Calissi could hear sounded like something to deal with in private, so Calissi excused himself momentarily, adjourned his grand jury proceeding, and invited all the doctors to come into his private office. There they told him the whole story in detail, showing him the bottle of curare and their Polaroid snapshots of the locker and its lethal contents.

CHAPTER VII

Enter the Prosecutor

When the five directors of Riverdell Hospital came to see County Prosecutor Guy W. Calissi, his reputation was already well established in Bergen County. To the Riverdell doctors, however, on November 1, 1966, he was an unknown quantity. Until that day there had never been an occasion for their universe to cross with his.

As his reward for supporting Robert Meyner's successful election campaign, Calissi, a three-term Democratic mayor of Wood Ridge, was appointed county prosecutor by the new governor on June 30, 1954. For Calissi, the appointment was the highlight of a decade of political and community service. He was to hold that office for sixteen years, under three different governors.

In 1966, neither proximity to more sophisticated New York City standards nor a population of nearly one million relatively affluent suburbanites had yet demanded that Bergen County should pay its chief law enforcement officer a competitive salary or that his full-time attention should be required to the job. Calissi was permitted to supplement his $10,000-a-year salary, and it appears that he took every opportunity that power and prominence brought his way.

Besides maintaining a private law practice (which a change in the law has prohibited since Calissi left office), the county prosecutor found the time to hold several other public jobs. While prosecutor, he was also the borough attorney, responsible for the civil legal affairs for the municipalities of Paramus, Dumont, and Maywood, all at one time.

When important corporate interests looked across Bergen County for the right Democratic lawyer to serve their business needs, they had reason to conclude that the one-man powerhouse who ran the prosecutor's office just might have what they needed. They were right. Certainly, Calissi was the county's leading Demo-

Formerly Bergen County Prosecutor, now Judge, Guy W. Calissi

cratic attorney, if you measure such things in terms of the number of public offices held at the same time or the total amount of public salary paid per annum. If your measurement was influence, there were very few who could compare with Calissi.

On occasion, Calissi was rather candid about the interrelationship between political office and private practice. When he was questioned by reporters for the Bergen *Record* about the propriety of his role in representing major shopping center developers in Paramus, only four months after he had stepped down as the Paramus borough attorney, and while he was still the county prosecutor, Calissi told the newspapers, "I think it's ridiculous not to assume they hired me because I know certain people—it's better to go before someone you know, whether you get a no answer or a yes answer. That's been the case from time immemorial. But whether it's sinister depends upon the person."

Despite his many considerable interests and activities outside of the prosecutor's office, Calissi was able to keep his staff of six part-time attorneys and seven full-time investigators working effectively. County prosecutor Calissi was a hard worker, capable of relentless round-the-clock efforts to identify and convict perpetrators of major crimes. During his three terms as county prosecutor, there was no hint of scandal.

Those who observed his performance closely during his years as prosecutor regarded Calissi as an honest man who erred only in that he may have been too timid in prosecuting some cases. Calissi's very proper philosophy of prosecutorial responsibility was made clear at his first swearing-in ceremony in 1954, when he said, "One of the simplest things in our legal procedure is to make a complaint. Those who violate the law must pay the penalty, but those against whom complaints with no substance have been made must be protected."

The Riverdell doctors' first meeting with Calissi was a tense one. Under the best of circumstances, dealing with the county prosecutor on official business is no ordinary experience, and the story that the doctors were putting before Calissi was potentially the biggest case that anyone in that room had encountered.

The prosecutor asked his first assistant, Fred Galda, to join with him and two of his investigators as the hospital directors each took a turn at supplying pieces of the complex set of facts. They started with the details of what Harris found in locker number 4, and how the death of Eileen Shaw had eventually driven him to open that locker. They told Calissi what curare was and all the doctors agreed that it has no place in a surgeon's locker, nor were any of them aware of any legitimate use of the drug at Riverdell.

Lans related the details of little Nancy Savino's death in March, and Sklar told the story of what had happened to Mr. Rohrbeck almost a year before. They told the officials about a dozen other cases which they thought should be reviewed because of the unusual nature of the postoperative deaths in the particular cases. They emphasized their point by relating Harris's observation that in many of these difficult-to-explain cases, problems had occurred around 8 o'clock in the morning, when Dr. Jascalevich was on the premises, and in several cases he had been known to have visited the patients, even though it was procedurally unusual for him to have done so. They described the frequent symptoms of chest pain, shortness of breath, and patients turning blue, all of which could indicate the presence of curare.

Galda asked questions about Harris first coming to the hospital, about his background and his relationship to Jascalevich. From his questioning, the doctors were made to feel that perhaps their own motives were suspect. Galda appeared distrustful of them, but Calissi was more sympathetic.

Galda "played the heavy" for Calissi that day. It was a technique they had developed over many years of working together. They had come up through the same machine in New Jersey politics, and Galda's appointment as his first assistant was the first selection that Calissi made when he took office.

There was a certain absurdity in their relationship, because for ten of his years as first assistant prosecutor, Galda was also the mayor of Paramus, and in that capacity it was he who had appointed Calissi as the Paramus borough attorney. So, while Galda worked for Calissi in the prosecutor's office in Hackensack, Calissi was working for Galda in Paramus Borough Hall.

When the doctors finished their story, Calissi told them he would look into the matter and would be calling on each of them for formal statements. He told them that he would arrange to seize the locker's contents before the end of the day, and they were instructed to say nothing to anyone until the next morning, when he wanted them to invite Jascalevich to a board meeting to inform him of the discovery of his locker's contents and to demand his explanation. Calissi promised to have one of his detectives overhear that meeting.

The doctors went back to their work, and Dr. Frieman, as president of the board, told Eliot Weiner, the hospital administrator, to set up another board meeting at his home for the next morning, and to invite Jascalevich to attend.

When the doctors left, Calissi told Galda to put everything else aside and prepare an application for a search warrant to be brought before a Superior Court judge for the necessary approval before the court closed.

At 5:00 that same day, Calissi, Galda, and three county detectives brought their search warrant to Riverdell Hospital. They delivered it to Weiner, who then escorted them to the locker where the law enforcement officers took their turn at opening Dr. Jascalevich's locker. They found exactly what had been described to them, and the detectives took photographs before placing the entire contents into large manila envelopes labeled "Evidence—Office of the Bergen County Prosecutor." As each of the seventy-one items was deposited into one of the envelopes, and a description and an assigned number were inscribed on a separate inventory form.

Before the first day of November was over, one of the county detectives was dispatched to Riverdell with a subpoena from the prosecutor for any tissue, slides, autopsy report, and hospital records on Eileen Shaw.

During the balance of that week, the detectives would find themselves calling repeatedly at the hospital at different times with a number of subpoenas, each for another set of hospital records.

CHAPTER VIII

More Case Histories

Now the Riverdell directors had to determine exactly which of their cases were of sufficiently suspicious nature to warrant turning them over to the authorities. The dead were already buried, and for each patient a death certificate had been required, indicating the attending physician's determination of the cause of death. That's how it's done—but now the doctors who signed those certificates were confronted with the question of which of their own judgments should be reconsidered.

There was just one exception: Dr. Lans had never been able to bring himself to fill in any cause of death that would satisfy him in Nancy Savino's case, and her death certificate still lay in his desk drawer—incomplete.

Dr. Frieman, as president of the hospital board and chairman of its mortality committee, along with Lans and Harris, became an informal committee to make the selections. Some of their selections were obvious; others were not. The doctors could only give Calissi their best judgment, with the understanding that an abundance of precaution would require them to include some cases in which the deaths were normal, but the ascribed causes were not as clearly established as they would have wanted.

Some twenty files were brought to Calissi's attention, but after they were reviewed, Calissi and the doctors decided that only thirteen of the cases clearly deserved his investigative attention.

Seven of the most obvious cases have already been described in detail: Nancy Savino, Eileen Shaw, Margaret Henderson, Emma Arzt, Ira Holster, Frank Biggs, and Carl Rohrbeck.

Among the six additional cases was that of Edith Post, who died on May 17, 1966. She was a sixty-two-year-old patient of Dr. Stavrand and she was operated on by Dr. Briski. Dr. Briski had surgically repaired her perforated diverticula (mucous membrane which pokes out through the large bowel) on the afternoon of May 15, after an exploratory laparotomy (an incision to open the belly to permit the surgeon to look inside for diagnostic purposes), which consumed about an hour on the operating table. At 6:30 A.M. on her second postoperative day, the nurse who visited her indicated on the hospital chart that the patient was feeling fine. There were absolutely no preliminary signs of distress when she died at 7:45 A.M. the same day—just after she was visited by Dr. Jascalevich, who had been invited to consult with Dr. Briski. It seems that Mrs. Post had suddenly developed severe chest pains and shortness of breath. Dr. Briski had the hospital pathologist, Dr. Lawrence Markley, do a complete autopsy, and one again, his conclusion was inconclusive. He identified pelvic peritonitis, but he did not attribute the death to that cause. His summary said, "What remains is the possibility of cardiac arrhythmia and asystole as a terminal event." The cause of death that Dr. Briski inserted on the certificate—"paralytic ileus"—was obviously based on one of the observations of the pathologist, which the pathologist himself had not related to the cause of death.

Eighty-year-old Mary Muentener was another of Dr. Briski's patients who died unexpectedly at Riverdell Hospital. On August 28, 1966, three days after Dr. Briski had removed her gallbladder, and the day before Dr. Jascalevich left for a brief vacation, Mrs. Muentener suffered a sudden respiratory failure. The elderly woman was revived. She survived until September 1—the same day that Dr. Jascalevich returned from his vacation. At 7:45 that morning, the hospital chart notation says she was "conscious and alert," but only twenty-five minutes later, when a nurse came in to take her blood pressure, she was unable to do so—Mrs. Muentener was dead. In this case there was no indication of Dr. Jascalevich's presence. No autopsy was done, and her death was ascribed by Briski to "acute cholecystitis," or acute gallbladder disease.

There were two other deaths at Riverdell that Calissi's office kept on its list. One of the dead was Paul Grisel, a seventy-one-year-old on whom Dr. Harris performed a subtotal gastrectomy (removal of part of the stomach) on August 1, 1966. This was another instance where the patient seemed to be recovering smoothly from an uneventful operation, until the third postoperative day, August 4. Grisel's I.V. was running when the nurse attended at 7:00 A.M. and noted on the chart that Grisel "Seems cheerful this A.M." Suddenly, at 8:20 that morning, everything changed. According to the way the hospital chart records the expiration of one more life at 8:35 A.M., the patient appeared "lethargic," "color poor," and "ceased breathing." There was no autopsy.

Finally, the earliest case the prosecutor's people kept on their active file was the only one of the situations that actually involved the death of a person on whom Dr. Jascalevich himself had operated. Her name was Louisa Romano. On October 2, 1965, Dr. Jascalevich had operated to remove an annular carcinoma of the colon. She had been referred by Dr. Harvey Lifset, an M.D. internist who assisted Jascalevich in the surgery. Her expiration was deemed significant because, like so many of the others, it was sudden and unexpected. The hospital chart reveals that when she was visited at 8:00 A.M. on October 8, Mrs. Romano was feeling good enough to want to get up. At 11:00 that morning, Dr. Jascalevich himself came by and restarted a dextrose and water I.V. After an 8:30 P.M. visit by Dr. Jascalevich, who examined her and made no other entry on the chart, the record says that at 9:00 the patient was "listless" and complaining of being "very tired." She died two hours later. There was no post mortem.

There were two more cases on the list for Calissi's investigators, but in neither of these had the patient died. Yet because these cases also fit the pattern that had become tragically clear to the doctors at Riverdell, they felt obliged to call them to the prosecutor's attention.

The first involved another patient of Dr. Stavrand who was also operated on by Dr. Briski in the summer of 1966, a woman in her sixties. The other case was especially interesting because the patient, Pasquale Benvenuto, was discharged from the hospital on October 30, 1966, just a week after Eileen Shaw's death, and the day before the doctors decided to seek help from the prosecutor's office. Mr. Benvenuto was seventy-four years old when Dr. Harris performed routine and uncomplicated elective surgery to repair a hernia on October 19. During Benvenuto's recovery, while he was in a four-bed semiprivate room, he experienced a sudden respiratory arrest. His life was saved by the quick response of Dr. Arthur F. DeMarco, the anesthesiologist, who was called promptly by the attending nurse. Subsequently, one of the nurses told a doctor that she saw Dr. Jascalevich in Mr. Benvenuto's room just prior to the incident, although none of the patients in that room was being cared for by Jascalevich. Because he had been sleeping, Mr. Benvenuto himself had no idea whether anyone had been near him prior to the incident.

What had brought this case into focus for Dr. Harris, who called attention to it, was that he heard that about an hour after Mr. Benvenuto's respiratory failure had occurred, Dr. Jascalevich called the hospital to inquire about Mr. Benvenuto. Harris was never able to find anyone at the hospital who had told Jascalevich about the case before his telephone call.

CHAPTER IX

Detective Work

In telling their story to the prosecutor, the Riverdell directors had surmounted a gigantic barrier. It meant going beyond the borders of their own profession for help in dealing with another doctor. To deal with a law enforcement agency under circumstances that tested their own credibility and jeopardized their own reputation and that of their hospital was distasteful for these men. Their careers were at stake and their world was going to be exposed to a degree of scrutiny that they had never contemplated.

Dr. Lans bore an additional burden, because, as his fellow directors saw it, he had precipitated their uncomfortable situation. Lans remains convinced that some of his colleagues would have preferred that he had been neither so conscientious nor so responsible. But circumstances had dictated their course, and this affair, unlike so much of their professional lives, was no longer in the control of physicians. That fact made them uncomfortable.

It was Wednesday, November 2, when we spoke over the phone and I found Allan consumed with fatigue and worn down by the emotional impact of the events of the past few days, culminating in the morning visit to the prosecutor's office and then the board meeting at which Jascalevich and the directors had their initial confrontation. Besides all that, the full complement of Allan's regular patients persisted in being ill with problems that sopped his remaining physical and emotional energy.

"It was like a spy movie," Allan told me. "Calissi had two detectives hiding in the closet with a tape recorder. There was a concealed microphone in Weiner's dining room, and we were supposed to act like it was a normal meeting. Matt, we're not used to such things.

"When Jascalevich got there, Frieman told him that there was some kind of an investigation going on and Sklar said that we all had our lockers opened. They said that the police took what he had in his locker because all those powerful drugs were there, and that we were confused and wanted to know why he had that stuff.

"And Jascalevich—he was his constantly cool doctor-self, he didn't even seem peturbed. He told us he was doing experiments on dogs at Seton Hall—there is a medical school there—and that afterwards he always brought the stuff back to his locker at Riverdell.

"Nobody really questioned him in any great detail. We were all kind of nervous with those detectives in the closet, and we didn't really know what else we were supposed to say, but we couldn't imagine why he would bring empty curare vials all the way back to Riverdell if he was working at Seton Hall in Jersey City. That's about a half-hour's drive from Riverdell.

"Jascalevich asked us if anything else was taken and Sklar told him that there were some other things, but it was all kind of deliberately vague.

"Matt, I can't believe that all this is happening—sitting there, knowing that the room is bugged, thinking about that little baby and all the other dead patients—and Jascalevich just acting like it's not any concern of his.

"Calissi hasn't told us what he plans to do. He hasn't said whether he's going to arrest Jascalevich or not.

"It's making me sick, and I don't know if that prosecutor knows what he's doing. Last night they came with subpoenas and took all the material in the Shaw case, but nothing from the others. I don't know why they need subpoenas—we would give them whatever they wanted.

"I'm not even sure they believe us. They haven't told us anything and they don't say what they are going to do next—or what we should do. Just go home and leave it to us boys.

"Besides, Calissi has this chief assistant named Galda. He's been very nasty, and sometimes he treats us like he thinks maybe Harris made up the whole story to cover himself.

"I keep thinking about all those patients and their families. These are real people, and I know many of them. It's all so terrible."

I had anticipated that Allan would be relieved now that the whole thing was in the prosecutor's hands, but instead, it was getting him down. He was beginning to find the entire process discouraging. As he saw it, the matter demanded an immediate resolution, and because there were no results yet, he didn't see that happening. Calissi's office had not impressed him. They seemed disorganized, and now he was afraid that the prosecutor might just "screw it up." He was confounded by the fact that they never asked for everything at once, even though the hospital had supplied them with the complete list of "suspicious" cases which he and Harris had assembled and Frieman had reviewed.

Allan's frustration was growing, and there was Jascalevich, still working in the hospital. They would have to deal with him every day, nobody knew for how long.

There was now all the more reason to get our own detectives operating. That was the only thing we could do, besides cooperating with Calissi to whatever extent he permitted.

"This is an opportunity," I told Allan. If our guys come up with something we can give it to Calissi; besides, they ought to be able to get us some idea about what the prosecutor is really doing. It's a complex case and it will need accurate scientific evidence, so it must be handled very carefully, or else it can be ruined."

Allan saw it the same way. He told me that Harris had agreed to share the expense with him, and so I should get our detectives started.

As soon as we ended our conversation, I called Detective Murphy. He agreed to come over to my office at the end of the day.

This time he came alone. I brought Murphy up to the moment on the developments since our last conversation. He needed some cash in advance to cover expenses, and I agreed to get that for him in the next couple of days. We spent about an hour reviewing the details of the situation. The fact that the doctors had now gone to the prosecutor had an obvious effect on Murphy: it was a real case now, more serious, and I found his response somewhat reassuring.

Before Murphy left, he promised to be in touch as soon as he had something to report, and he cautioned me that he needed some time, probably at least a week or maybe more. Fortunately, he had some time off starting the next day and he was going to be able to begin immediately.

I gave him $300 of my own money as an advance against his

expenses, to assure that the start of his work would not be delayed.

According to Murphy's time records (which he later submitted to me with his bill), he and his partner worked very intensively over the next nine days. He called me several times to let me know of the progress they were making.

First, he initiated routine requests for criminal records through regular police and FBI channels. Nothing of value showed up from these sources, except the confirmation that Jascalevich had no recorded criminal past.

By the end of the week, Murphy had made a contact with someone in the Bergen County prosecutor's office. He never said who it was, but I assumed it was one of the detectives. To my surprise, they didn't give Murphy any very precise information about their investigation; but he did find out that ten people, almost the entire investigative staff, had been deployed by Calissi, and everything else in the office had been put aside. He ascertained that inside Calissi's office there was a clear division of thinking about whether or not the entire Riverdell story was true. It seemed that the split was between Galda and Calissi himself, although we couldn't be sure, as the information was somewhat sketchy.

I could not determine whether details were not forthcoming from Murphy's source because the Bergen County people were so professional that they wouldn't share their information, or because they just didn't know what they were doing and hadn't come up with anything to share. Perhaps Murphy knew something that he couldn't share with me because he felt obligated to his source—another policeman. Any one of those alternatives seemed possible at the time.

Nevertheless, our private detectives developed a considerable amount of information. According to their report, Mario Jascalevich was born in Poland on August 27, 1927, although the medical directory and Jascalevich himself always gave his birthplace as Argentina. This discrepancy troubled me for some time, but eventually I came to believe that it was most likely an erroneous report.

Murphy found that Jascalevich had entered the United States from Buenos Aires, Argentina, at Miami, Florida, on March 16, 1956. He gave us his immigration card number, and also said that

Jascalevich was naturalized as an American citizen on April 24, 1961.

Murphy determined that on January 20, 1962, Jascalevich was married to Nora Caperan. The marriage was performed by a judge in the City Hall of West New York, New Jersey, and the witnesses to their marriage were Mary and Henry Caperan, who I gathered were the bride's parents. Two days after the wedding, on January 22, 1962, Jascalevich and his wife purchased a home at 435 60th Street in West New York, which also became his office.

Murphy had obtained a couple of medical directories, and from these he had assembled a complete record of when and where Jascalevich was licensed, where he had taken his postgraduate medical training, and a list of the other hospitals where he had staff privileges. The detective reported that in 1961 Jascalevich was licensed as a physician in both New York and New Jersey.

On the theory that if we were indeed dealing with a psychopathic killer, it was probable that he would have been doing the same thing wherever else he had the chance, Murphy went to each of the hospitals where Jascalevich either had privileges or had taken postgraduate training.

At the Jersey City Medical Center, Murphy reported that they would make no comment about him other than acknowledging that he was on staff.

At Christ Hospital in Jersey City, they acknowledged that he was on staff and said he was highly recommended.

At North Hudson Hospital in Jersey City, they acknowledged that he was on their courtesy staff, but would give no other information.

At Polyclinic Hospital in New York City, where the doctor had been a resident from 1956 to 1960, Murphy found that he had earned very high praise from the director of medical education, department of surgery.

Murphy had done everything he was asked to do in attempting to check on these references, and it soon became clear that nothing was going to show up to indicate that Jascalevich was not well thought of, nor was anyone going to whisper any secrets about him wherever else he had been professionally involved. By the nature of this summary, its results were not conclusive, but they represented the extent of what we could obtain without any official authority.

Our detectives also accumulated some interesting, but probably irrelevant, information about the doctor's wife, Nora. Apparently she was a talented pianist who had come to the United States from Buenos Aires in 1957 at the special invitation of the University of Iowa, where she taught piano. She also had scholarships from the Juilliard School and the Rothko Foundation. In 1958 she was selected to represent Argentina at the Brussels World Fair, as a concert pianist. She had some other accomplishments in this regard, having given a concert at the Brooklyn Academy of Music on Sunday, October 14, 1962, and a broadcast over WNYC radio as part of a salute to the United Nations. The detectives also found out that she once made a record of Latin American piano classics under the Spanish Music Center label.

This gave us only some minor insights into the surgeon's background, but the entire effort of our private detectives revealed only one fact of any conceivable significance.

Nora's mother, Maria Theresa Girard-Ryder, had lived at the same West New York address as the doctor until she died on July 27, 1965 at age 65.

On her death certificate, Dr. Mario Jascalevich is listed as the attending physician. He ascribed her cause of death to a "cerebro vascular accident—arteria hypertension," which in layman's language is commonly referred to as a stroke. On the death certificate, Jascalevich indicated that he had attended her from January 1953 until her death. There was no explanation of how or where he was attending her before he came to the United States, or whether he was licensed to practice elsewhere at the time, perhaps in Argentina.

At the end of the second week of his work on our case, I asked Murphy to make it a point to spend time with his Bergen County contacts. He began to get some bits and pieces of information out of them.

During the last part of November, Murphy called me at my office at 3:30 one afternoon and asked if I could meet him at the end of my day. He had just come back from a long, and apparently quite liquid, lunch with one of the people who had worked on the case in New Jersey, and Murphy had a lot to tell me. Because he had to go to work himself at 4:00, he could see me only if I would come to his squad headquarters at about midnight.

Murphy met me in the lobby of the old fortresslike police headquarters which was just off Broadway on the West Side, somewhere near 72nd Street. He had just finished a four-to-twelve tour. We walked over to his favorite West Side watering hole near the headquarters building. There we sat, in surroundings clearly familiar to Murphy, but just as clearly unfamiliar to me; and after he finished exchanging greetings with half the regulars and all of the help, we talked over his day's work, beginning with the events "on the job" during the last eight hours. I remember that conversation, because he told me how he and his partners would identify and apprehend "car jumpers," people who walked along Broadway or the side streets breaking into parked cars and emptying them of valuables. Eventually, we got to what really interested me, his lunch some twelve hours ago.

Murphy said that his New Jersey colleague confided that an unusually long report had been prepared by Mr. Galda himself. The investigator from Calissi's office had no conclusive answer about the results of the investigation, but it seemed that he was very impressed by the fact that on at least one occasion, in his presence, Galda had shouted at the Riverdell directors, accusing them of giving him contradictory statements. He thought he was being helpful by suggesting to Murphy that his clients ought to have a powerful local attorney "to put them in a more favorable light," and suggested they should hire a certain state senator who was then the leader of the Republican party in Bergen County. I failed to see any relevance to this "advice," but it left me with a clear feeling that perhaps the Riverdell doctors' motives might be suspect in the prosecutor's eyes.

On the other hand, Murphy was also told that the prosecutor's office was suspicious of Jascalevich's explanation for the curare vials in his locker and of the dog experiments at Seton Hall.

The New Jersey detective mentioned to Murphy that there was definitely no evidence in the Shaw case, because the available tissue was already embalmed.

The source's only conclusion, vague as it seemed to be, was that Calissi had not been able to come to a decision and that the case was perplexing, once again reflecting the split in thinking in the prosecutor's office.

From this conversation, which turned out to be my detective's final report, I surmised that the New Jersey investigation was foundering. It seemed to have no sense of direction, and I wondered if I had the whole story. Our second-hand source of information was reticent, restricted, and of limited value.

There had to be more to it.

CHAPTER X

Dead End

"Calissi gave up—he dropped the case completely, just like that?"

I was repeating Allan's words, and he was confirming that I had heard him correctly. I couldn't believe it.

We were so unprepared for that happening. Both of us had always assumed that if Calissi ever came to the conclusion that the investigation should be ended without taking action, at least there would be some warning; at least he would call the doctors in and ask them if there was anything else they had left out; at least he would tell them why, or just ask them to review the information he had and comment on it. That's what we expected.

But it didn't happen that way. One afternoon in the third week of November, Calissi's office called the hospital and left word for Dr. Lans and Dr. Frieman to stop over to see the prosecutor at the end of the day. When Lans and Frieman arrived, Calissi saw them by himself, without his usual entourage of assistants present. He said, "Ive gone as far as I can and I don't have a case. There is nothing else that I can do. There is nothing else that you can do. It's over. Just go home and forget about it."

Allan told me he was stunned. He thought that Frieman was surprised, but very much relieved.

"Did Calissi indicate whether he thought any crime had been committed?" That was my first question.

"No, he didn't indicate anything," Allan said. "He just said we should go home and forget about it, but he did seem pleased with himself, because he had agreed with Jascalevich and his lawyer that Jascalevich would resign from the Riverdell staff after a decent amount of time passed."

Allan paused to emphasize the point by shaking his head in disbelief. "Ed Frieman was very pleased about this and he took it as an indication that nobody would sue anybody else, which is what my colleagues are worried about. There's nothing to be done? Jascalevich can go practice anywhere? What good is it all? What can we do?"

We were deeply discouraged as we sat together in Allan's house; total frustration stifled any useful thought for the better part of an hour. Neither of us was prepared to accept Calissi's decision as the end of the matter. We tried to look for some meaning in the situation.

Although we had already embarked upon the course of running our own independent investigation, so far that had not generated any useful information. The idea of finding some history of misconduct elsewhere had already reached a dead end, and the dead end had already run up a large bill from the detectives, almost $2,000—another personal penalty on Lans and Harris for assuming the burden of doing the right thing.

The only alleviating factor for us, however minor, was that through our detectives we knew that during the past two weeks Calissi's staff had worked hard on the case; but we had no good idea of what they actually did, how effectively they did it, or even if they shared our suspicions.

Allan asked me, "Is there any other place for us to go, to get Calissi reversed, to make him go further, to get to the bottom of it, to get some explanation?"

There was no federal jurisdiction that I could see, no way to get the FBI involved, even if their investigative capacity was superior. We had to discard that idea.

We had no evidence of corruption or incompetence on Calissi's part, therefore no reason to appeal to the governor who appointed him.

There was nobody else to go to. It was up to the prosecutor. That was the American way—under our system of criminal justice, only the prosecutor (or district attorney, as he is usually called) can decide if he should present a case or not.

Tyranny comes from opposite directions: prosecutors have been known to convince a grand jury of crimes that never happened, and they have been known to fail to present crimes that clearly did happen. Sometimes such failures are due to lack of evidence sufficient to convince the grand jury, and the prosecutor must make those judgments. That's his duty. The only redress a complaining citizen has in such a case is to go to court to compel the prosecutor to act or to ask the governor to remove him for inaction. Either way, it's the citizen's burden to prove incompetence or venality, and the presumption is that the prosecutor is neither venal or incompetent.

Our only constructive thought at that moment was to continue our own efforts to supplement the prosecutor. If we could come up with something new, something he didn't have, we hoped he would have to listen to us again.

Because Calissi had told the Riverdell directors absolutely nothing about his investigation, we could only surmise that his work had to be either inadequate or unsophisticated. We were unaware of any satisfactory explanation for the curare in Jascalevich's locker. By the nature of the suspected crime, sophisticated, reliable, and highly technical scientific capacity would be required to trace the drug in the remains of the dead patients in order to solve such a case. Our logic dictated that it would be impossible for Calissi to have handled all of these complex aspects properly in such a short time.

I asked Allan if he knew whether or not the presence of curare could be detected in a human body after death. The breadth of his response surprised me. He said that it was the sort of drug that metabolized rather rapidly once it got into the system—that is, it would break down into its component parts and would be likely to be totally eliminated or disappear after a couple of days, but that was about all he could say about it. We really needed to consult an expert.

The question was how to find that kind of talent. I remembered that during the trial of Dr. Coppolino earlier that year, the chief medical examiner of the City of New York had testified about the alleged use of succinylcholine, a drug similar to curare, as a murder weapon, and that there had been a great deal of publicity about his testimony and his cross examination by Coppolino's famous attorney, F. Lee Bailey. The doctor's name was Milton Helpern.

Allan said, "Sure, it would be great if we could talk to him—but how can we arrange that? This case has nothing to do with New York City."

"Neither did Coppolino," I replied. "But apparently he is free to testify as an expert in other jurisdictions. Let's give it a try. At the least, he may be able to give us some direction. Let me see if I can find a way to see him and to get him interested."

CHAPTER XI

Expert Advice

The intersection of First Avenue and 30th Street is atypical of most of bustling New York City. There, the street actually appears to be broader than elsewhere because the nearby buildings are set back a little more, and generally they are not as tall as they are in so many other parts of Manhattan. As a result, the neighborhood benefits from a little extra cheerfulness provided by the little extra sunlight that comes through. Even the traffic seems to run along at a more leisurely pace. In between the East River and First Avenue is the New York University Medical Center, and among its decrepit buildings the City of New York has located a very modern city mortuary, and the Office of the Chief Medical Examiner.

The cheerfulness of the setting relieved the apprehension that attended my first visit. I had been conditioned by years of movie going to expect a darker and far more morbid atmosphere.

Once again, my good and valuable friend, Paul Buiar, had been able to find the right contact for me. Through his associate, Nick Cavatero, I had a proper introduction before coming to see the famous Dr. Milton Helpern. Realizing by now how bizarre my story could sound to someone hearing it for the first time, I thought it important to protect my credibility by having someone open the door to Dr. Helpern with such assurances as Nick had provided for me when he told Helpern that I "could be trusted." I imagined that after all the publicity he received for his Coppolino testimony, the chief medical examiner of the world's largest city must hear from more than his share of "kooks," and so I was also concerned that it might be very hard to get to see him.

When I arrived at 11:00 in the morning of Thursday, December 15, all I knew about Dr. Helpern was that he was New York City's chief medical examiner (and what that meant wasn't clear to me), that he was respected as one of the nation's leading experts in forensic medicine, and for that reason he had been selected by the prosecutor in the New Jersey murder trial of Dr. Carl Coppolino as the people's major expert witness in a case which involved the alleged use of a drug something like curare as a murder weapon. Soon I would find out a great deal more about his credentials.

Meeting Milton Helpern in his office was an experience in itself. Once cleared by the policeman-receptionist in the antiseptic, marble-walled waiting room, I was ushered into "The Chief's" outer office, where his very private secretary (who, I later learned, was in fact Mrs. Helpern) guarded the door to what I can't resist referring to as "the inner sanctum" (for reasons which will only be apparent to those readers who are old enough to remember radio drama).

Shortly afterward, the door beside Mrs. Helpern's desk opened, and "The Chief" himself filled the doorway, dressed in a grey suit, white shirt, and nondescript tie, under exactly the sort of long, starched, white hospital coat that anyone should expect to find on a chief medical examiner.

Helpern ushered me through his office and into an adjacent conference room dominated by a great oil painting that covered an entire wall. The nearly life-sized painting, in full color, depicts an autopsy in progress. The head of the cadaver in the picture is almost in your lap as you face the picture, and the body is carefully split open down the full length of the middle. Depicted are four white-coated men gathered around the drainboard table, and one of them is obviously a very much younger Dr. Helpern himself. Another man, the oldest among them, has the rapt attention of the others by holding up for inspection a very realistic and very bloody organ, which I suppose could be more precisely identified by most other visitors to that office. Along the other wall are some cabinets and shelves containing selected bones and bottled organs floating in preservatives, which appear to be the subjects of pending studies.

Dr. Helpern listened carefully, without a trace of incredulity. Nobody could have been kinder or more understanding. He said that he was especially sympathetic to Allan's plight as a practicing physician who bore the burden of working under such conditions imposed by the situation that I described. I was relieved to see that he did not seem to find it at all difficult to imagine that our worst fears might be justified.

He, in turn, told me some details of the Coppolino case. While I was pleased, I was also amazed to be taken into his confidence so quickly. He went so far as to confide aspects of his forthcoming testimony at the second trial which was coming up in Florida during the next few months, in which he would turn out to be the star witness whose testimony would send Dr. Coppolino to jail for life.

Dr. Helpern surprised me again when he embarked on a long diatribe about the incompetence of medical examiners and county coroners throughout the United States. He said that most of them had no training or qualifications, but that didn't stop them from giving erroneous opinions and reaching erroneous conclusions. He said that there weren't more than a handful in the entire country who knew anything at all; and indirectly he made it very clear that among this handful, except for the people he had personally trained, most of the so-called experts themselves had little to commend them and most knew nothing when compared to himself.

I had gone into the meeting with Helpern concerned about whether or not I could get his attention and his advice. Now I was getting even more, some fascinating stories of many of the actual cases that he had been involved in, and surprisingly, extensive and candid comments derisive of most of the practitioners of forensic medicine. While all of this was unusual, if not completely out of order, I had known people like him before, so I accepted his attitude. Dr. Helpern gave me his earnest commitment to help in any way he possibly could, and that was what we needed most.

I asked Helpern what he needed from us and what he could do to determine if the patients died from curare poisoning. He said that he should first ascertain if they had actually died from the causes ascribed to their cases, and to do that he would need the relevant portions of the hospital charts and all of the autopsy reports that I could get for him. He would also like to have any slides or samples of tissue that might be remaining from any of the autopsies. He would have to know what evidence was available before determining what could be done with it. Helpern agreed that I should convey his offer of help to Guy Calissi, the

Bergen County prosecutor, in the hope that by doing so I might encourage the prosecutor to keep the case open.

Before I left, Dr. Helpern gave me his private office number and his home number, and said I could call him at any time. His enthusiasm was a great encouragement to me.

I thanked him and left, happy that he hadn't offered to show me around the facilities.

As soon as I got back to my own office, I ordered lunch at my desk and called Allan Lans to report on the morning's success. He was jubilant over the prospects, the glimmer of hope that Dr. Helpern's interest might bring to our situation.

Allan suggested that we finalize our planning over dinner on Saturday night. We would all bring our wives, and the evening would also be an occasion to celebrate the enlistment of our important new ally. He said he would also invite Stanley Harris, so that I could get to meet him first hand.

My first impression of Stanley Harris, even in the relaxed atmosphere of the restaurant, was that of an intense, intelligent, and aggressive man—much more like the premedical students Allan and I knew at N.Y.U. in the Bronx than what I would have expected from a Yale man. He shared the full measure of frustration and anxiety that Allan had been suffering, and, out of his own barely disguised sense of desperation, he seemed to be pushing hard for me to do something. Harris seemed to be oblivious to the fact that I was merely acting as a friend of Allan's and an unpaid volunteer. He was obviously a man at his wits' end and very committed to determining the cause of the unexplained deaths. The two doctors agreed to gather up whatever records they could find and to search for any tissues or slides that might be around the hospital, but neither of them was sure if any existed. They knew where to look, and divided the list of possible locations.

For some reason, a moment of that evening lingers in my memory. After we left the restaurant, we said goodbye to both of the doctors alongside their cars, with M.D. plates, parked on the street in a no-parking area, and Barbara and I walked to the garage where I had paid to park mine.

During the next week, Dr. Helpern's secretary, as she preferred to call herself, telephoned and asked if I could stop down to see Dr. Helpern on Friday, December 23, at 2:00 P.M. When I got there, the doctor introduced me to his colleague, Dr. Charles J. Umberger, a Ph.D. (not an M.D.), who was the chief toxicologist in Helpern's office. Helpern said that Umberger was also a key witness on succinylcholine in the Coppolino case.

Helpern revealed that Dr. Umberger had been approached directly some time ago by prosecutor Calissi's office to examine some tissue in the Shaw case. The document that he held in his hands was the autopsy report on Mrs. Shaw. Helpern had been completely unaware of Umberger's connection with Calissi until he happened to mention my visit the previous week—apparently, Umberger had been moonlighting with a New Jersey laboratory that Calissi's office used. Helpern was very critical of the Shaw autopsy report, which he said was incomplete and inconclusive, a good example of the professional inadequacy he had previously discussed with me.

Umberger explained that he was attempting to break down the tissue he had with a series of tests utilizing the spectrograph. As the tissue was treated with different solutions, they would change color and the color itself would indicate positive or negative for the presence of curare. However, he did not yet know whether the test was going to work because of the presence of formalin, the solution that had been used to preserve the tissue sample. Helpern also assured me that as soon as the analysis was completed he would let me know the results.

The revelation of these ongoing tests raised new questions in my mind about Calissi's conduct of the investigation. I wondered why Calissi had told the Riverdell people that he was finished with the case before he had received the results of Umberger's tests.

By the first week in January, the pertinent portions of each of the hospital charts had been assembled and recopied by Lans and Harris. The complete set covered nine of the cases in which the patients had died, plus the two who had survived. Allan had also found the slides from each of the autopsies that were done at Riverdell by the hospital pathologist. It was January 5 when

I sent Dr. Helpern the summaries of the records, and a few days later Allan dropped off the pertinent slides at Helpern's office.

That same day, I called Mr. Calissi.

CHAPTER XII

Meeting Mr. Calissi

I had no idea how Calissi would receive me, or if he would do so at all. It is easy for a prosecutor to hide behind a wall of secrecy, so there was a considerable risk that Calissi could consider me meddlesome or resent my presence in the situation. I felt that it would be best to save my effort to persuade him to cooperate until we met face to face.

Calissi's receptiveness would be critical to the continuation of our effort, and I knew that he would have every right to throw me out of his office. It is proper for prosecutors to refuse to discuss a pending case even with the people who have a legitimate involvement; and from Calissi's point of view, I was an outsider.

After introducing myself on the telephone as a lawyer who was a good friend of Dr. Lans, I asked for an opportunity to meet with him for a few minutes to discuss some aspects of the Riverdell matter. Although he was rather curt on the telephone, he was willing to see me the next day and even took the trouble to ask if I knew the best way to reach his office. The directions he gave me are still on the back of an envelope in my file.

All the way to Hackensack I rehearsed my opening statement to Calissi. I knew that I would have only one shot at convincing him to deal with me, as I had no official status.

The first good sign was that Calissi saw me immediately on arrival, and the second was that we were alone in his office with none of his staff present. He had a large, cold office which was sparsely furnished with the usual issue of municipal government furniture. As expected, his walls had the familiar splattering of political honors and photos of the man himself with various New Jersey luminaries; and I used these pictures to break the ice. While looking them over, I let Calissi know that I shared his Democratic party background and was active in New York State politics, having just managed a gubernatorial primary campaign. Although he was somewhat closemouthed at first, Calissi relaxed and quickly became more open and even quite friendly.

My pitch, as outlined in my preparatory notes, was straightforward: "Mr. Calissi, I very much appreciate your willingness to see me. I'm an attorney; however, I'm here not as a lawyer, but as a good friend of Dr. Lans, who has kept me closely informed about the entire case, and I've been trying to help. He's very concerned about doing the right thing, and I know he has.

"Sometimes I get the feeling that doctors have difficulty in communicating in such matters, and I know that they are rather confused about the results of the case so far.

"Through some friends, I have been in touch with a man whom I'm sure you have heard of, Dr. Milton Helpern, the chief medical examiner in New York City, and we have discussed the case. He is most interested in it and is willing to be helpful in any way he can—and he's authorized me to tell you so.

"It's my feeling that perhaps he could be helpful in interpreting some of the medical records or autopsy reports, and in reviewing whatever alibi Jascalevich has for keeping the curare in his locker."

Calissi understood me very quickly. He told me that he was very suspicious of Jascalevich, but that he had nothing to go any further with. He acknowledged that he knew of Helpern's reputation and that he would be most eager to have whatever benefit his thinking might add to the picture.

I was relieved when Calissi said that any help that I could provide was going to be welcome. Calissi was very direct, and it was obvious that we were getting on well and had already achieved a good level of communication.

I told the prosecutor that Helpern had asked me to arrange for him to obtain whatever additional tissue, slides, or reports the prosecutor was willing to let him see. I was hoping that Calissi would respond by agreeing to have his people deliver such material to Helpern, or at least to let Helpern examine it in Calissi's office.

But Calissi did better than that. To my eternal surprise, he handed me a thick sheaf of papers: "Here is a copy of the transcript of the testimony Jascalevich gave us. Let Helpern read it and see what he thinks of it. You read it too, and let Lans and Harris see it. Just keep it confidential." Obviously improper, this was a gift beyond my expectations.

Then came the second home run.

Calissi got up, and without a word he opened a door at the side of his office and stepped out. In a moment he reappeared carrying a cylindrical cardboard canister which he handed to me. "There are all the slides that I have. They are labeled. Ask Dr. Helpern to take a look at them. I'll send you the autopsy reports next week."

I was dumbfounded. I never expected, nor considered it appropriate, that the prosecutor would hand me his physical evidence or even let me see the sworn testimony of the target of his investigation.

I did not consider that he really wanted to take me into his complete confidence, but instead, I took it as an indication that he had given up on the matter. In either case, I took the testimony and the evidence gladly, eager to see what it would reveal.

It was about 3 o'clock on Friday afternoon, and as soon as I got down to the lobby of the county courthouse I called Heather Cowan, the world's most efficient secretary, and asked her to stand by to do a major photocopy job as soon as I got back to the office. I wanted to be sure that Lans and Harris would have a copy of Jascalevich's testimony to read over the weekend.

In the trunk of my car I locked up the canister that contained the autopsy slides made from the last bits and pieces of Eileen Shaw, Frank Biggs, and Nancy Savino.

PART II

Dr. Mario Enrique Jascalevich

CHAPTER XIII

Explanations

Some forty days had passed since Allan Lans had first confided his suspicions to me. In many respects, his charges seemed far easier to doubt than to believe.

Without the other side of the story—the explanation, alibi, or whatever else it should be called—I was unable to come to any personally satisfactory judgment of Dr. Jascalevich's conduct. Until that unexpected instant when Calissi handed me the transcript, I had not conceived of how we could ever be able to analyze the situation fairly.

It was Armistice Day, November 11, 1966, when Jascalevich came to the prosecutor's office in Hackensack. James E. Anderson, the surgeon's attorney, made a point out of the fact that his client was there voluntarily. He had asked for the opportunity to come in to be interviewed. Although ten days had passed since the Riverdell doctors had interrupted Calissi's grand jury presentation to get him to launch the investigation, Dr. Jascalevich had never been questioned. Apparently, Fred Galda had already asked Mr. Anderson for some limited bits of information, but nobody had asked for any explanation for the curare that had been found in the doctor's locker.

At 10:30 in the morning the interview began. In addition to Calissi, Jascalevich, and Anderson, the official stenographer recorded the presence of Galda, Ralph Polito, another assistant prosecutor, and three of Calissi's investigators: detectives Vahe Garabedian, Edward Kastner, and Ernest Frahm. There was no representative of the county medical examiner, no medical expert among the questioners.

According to the opening remarks of the transcript, Dr. Jascalevich had been at the prosecutor's office once previously—along with the doctors on the Riverdell board. At that time he was advised of his rights and told to get himself an attorney. All of this was acknowledged by Mr. Anderson, who asked Calissi to clarify the nature or scope of the instant investigation before taking Dr. Jascalevich's statement.

Calissi, whose cordiality toward the surgeon leaps from the initial pages of the transcript, explained that his office had been advised of several unexplained or unusual deaths at Riverdell and a high rate of postoperative mortalities. He said there was suspicion that the deaths were caused by a drug like curare. On the basis of that information, Calissi said, Jascalevich's locker had been opened and its contents seized. Calissi reviewed the inventory that his staff had prepared, which listed all of the items that were taken from Jascalevich's locker, and described each item briefly.

Upon hearing the list of those items read aloud, Jascalevich spoke for the first time that morning when he asked if he had correctly heard the description of a "blue box" containing a vial of tubocurarine.

"I never used this material myself," Jascalevich said, and he explained that he had never seen a blue box in his locker.

Calissi stopped for a moment, to ask Jascalevich if he was saying that he never used tubocurarine. Jascalevich explained: "No, tubocurarine in a blue box, my tubocurarine which is solely supplied to me by General Surgical Supply in West New York, is a product of Lilly Laboratories and comes in a whitish box. . . . I have never used a blue box containing it, but I may tell you this, and this comes out of observation, pardon me, a blue box contains tubocurarine made by another company. There is one called—one laboratory called Burroughs & Wellcome, and this laboratory supplies tubocurarine to Riverdell Hospital."

Before Jascalevich's sworn testimony began, Anderson asked Calissi if the Riverdell directors had told him that Jascalevich had requested a meeting of the board to discuss the surgical mortality rate just prior to the time when the doctors came to see Calissi. Calissi said that he understood that such a meeting was indeed requested, but it was called by the directors themselves, and not by Jascalevich.

Then the surgeon raised his right hand and took the oath that subjected his testimony to the penalties of perjury.

He gave his full name, Mario Enrique Jascalevich; and in response to Calissi's friendly questioning, explained that his "heritage" was Italian on his mother's side and Yugoslav on his father's side, his father coming from that portion of Yugoslavia near the Italian border. The doctor told the Italian-American prosecutor that he was brought up in Buenos Aires, but "in the Italian pattern of education and culture."

Dr. Jascalevich said that he had attended college and medical school in Buenos Aires, graduated in 1954, and came to the United States about a year later.

Once again the doctor was shown the inventory of items seized from his locker, and he agreed that everything on the list had been in his locker except for the two blue boxes, items number 6 and 17, empty blue boxes of 10-cc vials of tubocurarine, and then, under oath, he repeated his disclaimer about never using tubocurarine that came in a blue box.

Then the prosecutor asked Jascalevich to explain the purpose of having these items in his locker. The surgeon responded: "The purpose of me having these items in my locker were to utilize them for my experimental surgery series on dogs at Seton Hall. . . .

"I started my experimental surgery, my experimental surgery, in 1963 under a grant of the American Cancer Society."

The doctor had brought with him the March 1966 issue of *Surgery,* a professional magazine, containing an article by himself which he said had resulted from additional experiments he did in 1965–66, and he distinguished these from the experiments done in 1963–64 under a $500 grant from the American Cancer Society.

(Although Jascalevich told the prosecutor that the March 1966 article described experiments done on dogs at Seton Hall in 1965 and 1966, the article itself was submitted for publication on January 6, 1966. Furthermore, the article does not refer to dog experiments. It refers to "clinical experience," which in medical terms means experience with patients. In January of 1967, Jascalevich submitted another article to *Surgery* magazine, which was published in September of 1967, and which describes his dog experiments of 1963–64 under the American Cancer Society grant. The article says that he used twenty-five dogs.)

Calissi asked Jascalevich to describe the procedure for obtaining dogs for experimentation, and he went over that aspect of the surgeon's story again and again. Because of its potential significance to the entire picture and the insight it offers regarding some of the doctor's attitudes, most of it is set forth here. (Throughout this chapter, extensive exerpts of the transcript are included to afford the reader an opportunity to hear exactly how this interview was conducted and the quality of the surgeon's responses, so that the full flavor of the inquiry can be recaptured objectively. Some of the answers may seem garbled or imprecise, and some of the questions incomplete; but that is the way they actually were. Some difficulty with the English language also seems apparent in Jascalevich's responses.)

Q. BY MR. CALISSI: "Now, in order to obtain dogs for experiments, doctor, what procedure must you go through?"

DR. JASCALEVICH: "Well, there are two ways. Of course, one is the official way. Let me put it this way, see if it's better. If you have a grant, if you have the money to obtain these dogs there is no problem, the money is there. If the projects are out of your own pocket, out of your own enterprise, of course, a less expensive way should be searched, and my experiments in 1963 cost me nothing really because they were backed by the American Cancer Society. . . .

"The other method to obtain is well, to go after working hours and to work on dying animals that have been worked by previous investigators during the day, by giving a small tip to one of the several sweepers and animal care attendants."

Q. "Where is this, at Seton Hall now?"

A. "Seton Hall."

Q. "Same place; you conducted no experiments anywhere but at Seton Hall on dogs. Is that right?"

A. "Absolutely."

Q. "The only place?"

A. "That's right."

Q. "And when you started your experiments, after the experiments for the American Cancer Society, you obtained dogs that were already dead, from some of the employees of Seton Hall. Is that what you are saying?"

A. "No, sir. For the American Cancer Society—"

Q. "You got live dogs?"

A. "Live dogs, exactly."

Q. "I'm talking about after that experiment."

A. "They were dying dogs."

Q. "Pardon?"

A. "Dying dogs. They had been already experimented upon by previous investigators during the day."

Q. "Who said they were dying dogs?"

A. "Well, they are at the end of so many investigation procedures done on them that really very little the poor creatures have to support more, to die. They have been already operated. They have been already cannulated. There have been different experiments that the previous investigators did. . . ."

Calissi asked Jascalevich how he obtained the "dying dogs."

A. "Well, after 5 o'clock, when the head of the—the man in charge is gone and the employees are still there sweeping and cleaning the place, it is rather easy to offer anyone a tip and sometimes by simple request even without money to do some work on this, on these animals."

Q. "You mean you would see a fellow sweeping the floor or cleaning up and ask that person for a dog?"

A. "You could ask, right. . . ."

Q. "Why is it necessary for you to ask a janitor or a porter, or someone doing menial work, for a dog?"

A. "Because, sir, if I have to pay for a dog in the regular manner it's very expensive. It cost me $30 to get just one animal to prove, to work on some instruments I had. The animal—the man that received the money is Mr. Riggi, the man in charge of the animal experiments, and I gave the money to him and he assisted me."

Q. "How much did you have to give these people doing menial work to get the dying dogs?"

A. "Just one or two dollars."

Q. "One or two dollars. Did they go into the cage wherever they kept the dogs and brought the dogs out?"

A. "No. The animals are already on the table, sir."

Q. "Pardon me?"

A. "They are already tied on the table. The experiments of the day are finished already."

Q. "They are alive but tied on the table?"

A. "They are alive. They are just as the investigator left them. . . ."

Q. "Are you sure that these particular dogs that you say you experimented on after 1963–1964, that you got from the people doing menial work around the place, were dogs that were tied up and dying on the table?"

A. "Right, sir. . . ."

Q. "Have you ever destroyed any dogs, doctor, when you finished with them?"

A. "Very few times. Most of them were destroyed by the attendant, but I never witnessed that."

Q. "Some of your dogs were destroyed by reason of the operation or procedure that you were following?"

A. "It is not such an explosive thing as to destroy the animal."

Q. "Kill."

A. "Or kill the animal. The animal when I left most of the time was still alive."

Q. "You just told Mr. Anderson some of them you disposed of."

A. "Some of them I did, but the others were disposed of by the animal attendant."

Q. "These people that you gave these one or two dollar tips to, what specifically is their job or was their job at the time, do you know?"

A. "They used two different uniforms. One was a white coat and the other is more or less a bluish-grayish coat. I don't know their responsibility in the place. It seems to me that they are cleaners, they should clean the place once the jobs of the morning, the jobs of the day are finished."

Q. "Do you know the names of any of these people?"

A. "I recall one of them, we used to call him Lee."

Q. "Lee? How about anybody else, any other names?"

A. "Well, Mr. Riggi assisted me but that I had to pay."

Q. "No, I'm talking about those people you gave tips to."

A. "No, Lee is the only name, but there were at least three or four colored fellows."

Q. "Colored fellows, all colored?"

A. "All of them colored."

Q. "You gave them tips and they gave you these dogs and you experimented on these dogs in 1964–1965?"

A. "Exactly, sir."

Q. "And in 1966?"
A. "In '66."
Q. "Did you experiment with them in '66?"
A. "In '66, certainly, sir."
Q. "How often would you go to the Seton Hall medical laboratory for the purpose of experimenting on dogs?"
A. "Well, the research in my case, I'm not a pure researcher, I'm in practice, so that is something I time according to my responsibilities in my private practice, but it would usually be a Wednesday because I'm off, Wednesday afternoon, after 5 o'clock usually, and many times I went there were no dogs and I had to return."
Q. "How about during the day on Wednesday when it's your day off?"
A. "No, sir."
Q. "You never went there during the day?"
A. "No, sir."
Q. "Why not?"
A. "Well, during the day the man in charge of the department is there."
Q. "You couldn't get the dogs?"
A. "You couldn't get the animal. . . ."
Q. "How about Wednesday afternoons?"
A. "Wednesday afternoon is off for me."
Q. "You never experimented on Wednesday afternoon?"
A. "Usually after 5 o'clock."
Q. "Because you could get the dogs for nothing?"
A. "Because you could get the dogs for nothing."
Q. "That is the reason?"
A. "Yes."
Q. "You made $50,000 last year at Riverdell Hospital net after 25 percent you had to pay the hospital?"
A. "Yes."
Q. "At that hospital, and you made a very handsome salary or income last year?"
A. "Yes, sir."
Q. "Is that correct?"
A. "Right."

Jascalevich was about to begin describing his animal experiments when Calissi briefly returned once again to the subject of the disposition of dogs, and he asked Jascalevich,

Q. "Were there any other experimenters or doctors or other people in the laboratory with you at the time that you were conducting these experiments?"

A. "No, sir."

Q. "Never?"

A. "No, not that I recall having."

Q. "Never any other person was conducting an experiment or working in the same room with you all during the time that you were conducting the experiment from 1963?"

A. "Yes, right."

Q. "To date."

A. "No, sir, not that I remember having met any doctor or any professor from the school, no, not that I remember, but there were many dogs, I should say. . . ."

Q. "Wait a minute. You got one dog or two dogs when you went there?"

A. "Only one dog."

Q. "Only one dog. All right."

A. "Only one dog and I think I would probably—I worked on something like six dogs in 1965, probably some nine dogs in 1966, so it makes a total of some fifteen dogs. That means fifteen trips."

Q. "I'm not talking about—15 trips?"

A. "Really probably during thirty or forty or fifty trips I would have a chance to meet somebody."

Q. "But in the fifteen trips you met nobody?"

A. "Right, sir."

Q. "Nobody at all?"

A. "Right, sir."

Having a clear picture of how the doctor obtained the dogs for his work, the interrogators finally turned to a new series of questions to elicit descriptions of the doctor's different experiments.

Jascalevich then described four different series of experiments which he also conducted in 1965–66. He told Calissi that the only drugs he used in any of these were Seconal or Nembutal. He said they were used for anesthesia only. Jascalevich gave Calissi his records describing some of these experiments.

In order to be sure that he would be able to calculate correctly and follow the entire series of experiments, Calissi specifically asked the doctor if there were any drugs besides Nembutal or Seconal that were used in any of the experiments discussed so far. Jascalevich answered, "No other drugs."

Finally, Jascalevich came to describe the series of experiments in which he said that curare was used. For these experiments, the doctor produced original drawings entitled *"The Posterior Liver Biopsy,"* which the prosecutor marked as Exhibit M-6.

Jascalevich explained that in the experiment it was necessary to insert a needle into a very precise spot in the liver—and that in order to do so, he utilized curare to arrest breathing and the resultant movement so as to facilitate inserting the needle correctly.

At that point, the doctor created some considerable confusion among his interviewers when he revealed that he was doing these liver biopsy experiments on the very same dogs that he used for the other experiments. He said that he did these biopsy experiments throughout 1965 and 1966 and that he would do four or five experiments simultaneously on the same dog—first one experiment would be completed, then another, so that while he had first stated so decisively that curare was not used in the first experiment, curare was certainly used in the last experiment on the same dog, on the same day. As Jascalevich explained it, "I would say curare has been always used at the end, for one simple reason, curare inhibits the respiration of the animal and so shortens the life of the animal so that will be the end, the last experiment I should do. First I use the animal for the other nonkilling experiences and this is the one that carries the possibility that precipitates the death of the animal most probably."

After the details of his experimental procedures were disclosed, along with the dates when they occurred, Calissi pressed Jascalevich in order to explore when precisely he had purchased the curare. Jascalevich's response was that he purchased the drug only in 1965 and 1966, for the liver biopsy experiments, and that he didn't buy any for the experiments he did in 1963 and 1964.

The doctor said that his only supplier was General Surgical Supply, across the street from his office in West New York, New Jersey, and that he didn't recall the brand name. Jascalevich wasn't sure if the drug was tubocurarine or tubarine, but he was sure that it came in a 10-cc ampule, made by Lilly Laboratories and packaged in a white box. Calissi pressed him on this point—attempting to ascertain if he ever obtained any of the drug from the pharmacy at Riverdell Hospital, or otherwise used any of Riverdell's supply. Jascalevich was positive that he never did and said that that was why he was so surprised by the blue box that they found in his locker.

Jascalevich explained that he had a glass cabinet at Seton Hall which was available to him for storage. At first he said he kept his curare and tools there; but later on, when asked about it the second time, he said that because the Seton Hall cabinet was glass and without a lock, he could not use it to keep anything as dangerous as curare, and so he brought his curare supply back to Riverdell for safekeeping, even though it was 15 or 20 miles away.

The prosecutor asked him how much curare he could use on each dog. The doctor said that it would usually take one vial, but sometimes more if he missed the vein, in which case he would use a second vial.

Jascalevich was not precise about how much curare he needed for each dog, and when asked specifically, he was unable to define which muscles of the body curare affected first. His position was that these were details that an anesthesiologist would know, and that he only knew that the drug would provide the "quiescence" that his experiments required.

The doctor also explained the presence of the empty vials, boxes, and used syringes in his locker. He said that even though the syringes were disposable, he saw no reason to throw them away when they could be used again, and for that reason he saved them. Sometimes, he told Calissi, he even brought some of the used syringes from his office practice to use them in his dog experiments.

He told the investigators that it was his practice to save the empty vials and the boxes the curare came in because the possibility always existed that a particular batch was weak or out-dated, and that would affect his experiments, in which case he would need to identify the batch of the drug from the package so he could complain to the supplier. But he admitted that he did not mark the boxes in any way—just saved them because the batch number, lot number, and expiration date were recorded on the box.

The degree of clarity in this portion of Jascalevich's testimony left much to be desired. The following excerpt from the transcript illustrates how imprecisely these questions were answered:

Q. "So you decided you would take the empty bottle of curare?"

A. "Yes."

Q. "Which had been used?"

A. "Which had been used."

Q. "Which would not endanger anybody, because there is nothing in the bottle, right?"

A. "Let me tell you this. Sometime I return with a half bottle."

Q. "I'm talking about an empty bottle."

A. "Oh, yes."

Q. "An empty bottle, right?"

A. "Yes, you're right."

Q. "When you used the 10 cc of curare on the dog the entire vial or ampule was empty?"

A. "Right."

Q. "You still found it necessary to take that particular small bottle—empty curare bottle, I should say—and—"

A. "Right."

Q. "—and take it to a locker at Riverdell Hospital, which is what, 15 or 20 miles away from the place where you are experimenting?"

A. "Right."

Q. "And put it in your locker?"

A. "In my locker."

Q. "Why?"

A. "Well, it's very important to keep for the researcher this material. The material will give you the batch number, the lot number of the drug, and the expiration date of the drug, any other question that may come up later in the research. It's very important to know what is the drug that you worked with, which was the expiration date, whether you worked with the right drug or not in the sense of whether it was active enough, any further question about the quality of the drug, is important to keep the original vial."

Q. "When you gave curare to these dogs there was nothing so mysterious about what curare was going to do, was there, that you had to keep the vial?"

A. "I'll say this, something very interesting. Sometimes in my research, something that comes very much apropos of this, sometimes in my research, I think it was during 1966, I noticed that I wasn't getting any—very poor respiratory inhibition with my drug. So I called back my supplier and I told him, 'Look, I notice that my drug isn't working or is not giving, it is not having enough action.' He told me that this is the usual we get."

Q. "Who did you talk to there?"

A. "One of the three men that direct the laboratory."

Q. "The laboratory where?"

A. "My supplier. It's called General Research Laboratory."

Q. "You talked to somebody?"

A. "Right."

Q. "And you told them the curare they sold you was no good?"

A. "I told them it wasn't working right, it wasn't working, did they give me something different or what. 'No, doctor, we did not.' And I think the matter was terminated there."

Q. "Wait a minute. As a result of this conversation you had with these people who were supplying you with curare did you take the lot number bottle back to them and say—"

A. "No, I didn't."

Q. "You didn't do that?"

A. "No, I didn't do that."

Q. "What did you do with that bottle or those bottles you used that you say didn't work?"

A. "I just took it for granted I thought probably I got a bad batch or a poor drug and I continued working with it. I didn't proceed further into this inquiry which terminated with that conversation with my supplier."

Q. "Let me see if I understand what you are trying to tell me, doctor. You have to forgive me."

A. "I'm very pleased to answer."

Q. "We are talking about medicine and research and I am a lawyer and I don't propose to know too much what you are talking about."

A. "Please."

Q. "And I think I'm intelligent enough to understand if I can get it in maybe monosyllabic terms."

A. "That's all right."

Q. "You're telling me, I think, and if I'm wrong correct me, that you save the empty bottles of curare and put them in what you call the dirty locker at Riverdell Hospital because you wanted to keep those empty bottles to be able to go back and determine what batch they came from?"

A. "Right."

Q. "And whether or not there was anything wrong with the batch or what the reaction of that batch was. Am I right about that?"

A. "Exactly, sir."

Q. "Is that correct?"

A. "Exactly right."

Q. "Now, my question to you now is this. When you injected or administered curare to these dogs there was a reaction, that you inhibited the respiration of these dogs?"

A. "Yes."

Q. "Is that correct?"

A. "Right, sir."

Q. "And you continued to experiment for this posterior liver biopsy after you inhibited the respiration?"

A. "Yes, sir."

Q. "What more did you want curare to do for you at that stage of the proceeding in your experiment?"

A. "This was the purpose, to inhibit the breathing and perform this procedure which takes just a few minutes because it is very fast to get through a needle through the back, and then open the belly and see where did you land."

Q. "So the curare did its job. Is that correct?"

A. "The curare did its job. As a matter of fact, I have here a picture of some of my dogs in which you can see a 'hit target, hit target, no, hit target, hit target question mark, hit target.' In here 'miss, miss?' In other words, this was the purpose."

Q. "But what I am trying to find out, doctor, is this with regard to this experiment, the posterior liver biopsy, you gave curare to the dog and the dog then either died by reason of the 10 cc that you gave them, right?"

A. "Right."

Q. "Or they were moribund. Is that right?"

A. "Exactly."

Q. "Is that right?"

A. "Right."

Q. "What else did you expect the curare to do?"

A. "Nothing more."

Q. "Nothing more. Now, why was it necessary for you then to save the empty vial or ampule of the curare that you used for that purpose?"

A. "My investigation is methodic and I think it's the one of every researcher that if possible every data should be kept, nothing should be thrown away and again I say the keeping of this permitted me some reflection on the effects of the drug, whether I was missing the target, because actually I didn't get enough result, enough result with my drug, I didn't have enough respiratory inhibition, or was missing the target because I just was in the wrong place."

Later on in the course of the morning's testimony Calissi tried again:

Q. "Again, if you don't mind, I would like you to tell me why it was necessary for you to keep the empty bottles."

A. "Yes. The empty bottles and carton boxes were kept so as to have a control on lot number of the drug and expiration date of the drug."

Q. "Well, did you note that in any of your notes and experiments, the lot number of the drug?"

A. "I didn't have need of that because I kept the empty vials. That's why I kept it."

Q. "How would you know which empty vial you used on what dog?"

A. "No, it is not that way of putting it."

Q. "It isn't that way of putting it?"

A. "Because sometimes we use the same dog, the same vial, so it wasn't that kind of a detailed study."

Q. "What do you mean, it wasn't that way of a detail study? I don't understand what you're talking about."

A. "Then I didn't understand your question. Would you?"

Q. "My question was how would you know which empty vial of curare was used on what dog?"

A. "Well, in these notations of mine, which I don't have, I had a control."

Q. "Now you say you had a control?"
A. "Yes."
Q. "What did the control say?"
A. "I had a list, I had a listing."
Q. "Of what?"
A. "Of my dogs which I worked."
Q. "What else?"
A. "The approach I used."
Q. "What else?"
A. "And I have some notations about reaction of the dog."
Q. "What else?"
A. "And notes about the procedure itself, again if I missed or hit target."
Q. "What else?"
A. "I think that's all what I know of these."
Q. "Did you put down the number of the batch?"
A. "Of course, that first, yes."
Q. "You put down the number of the batch of the particular bottle you used of curare?"
A. "Of the particular bottle, but I still, I kept the empty vial and the empty box as a control."
Q. "No, I want to know whether you put on these experimetnal notes of yours the number of the lot and the number of cc."
A. "The number of cc I wrote down, sir."
Q. "How about the number of the lot of the bottles?"
A. "The batch number?"
Q. "The batch number, did you write that down on your experimental notes?"
A. "I don't know, sir. I didn't write them because I had the control."
Q. "You didn't write them?"
A. "Because I had the control of the boxes, of the box that I had on the empties."
Q. "How would you know what empty vials you used on specific dogs?"
A. "It was not my purpose to go to such a detail in evaluation of my experience. For instance, thanks to having this control I was able to call back the laboratory and tell them, 'Look, I notice that what you sold me lately is not working properly.' "
Q. "What control? I could tell as a lawyer that if I give 10 cc

of what is supposed to be curare to a dog, and the dog runs around the house and doesn't react, that there is something wrong with the supply of curare that was sent to me. I don't have to have any control for that, do I?"

A. "You need the control in the sense that it may permit you to locate—as a matter of fact, I may tell you this, which is also important, in this conversation which I had with the laboratory, I pointed out that I noticed that the fluid was sort of yellowish and would be turbid. That was anothing thing that I noticed. I went back, as a matter of fact, to my paper bag and went over the carton box to see the expiration date to see if I had been using lately any dead drug and I couldn't have done this if I wouldn't have kept the original boxes and bottles."

Q. "What happens to curare when it gets old?"

A. "I don't know."

Q. "You don't know?"

A. "I don't know."

Q. "How long is curare—"

A. "I would say this, that the anesthetist at Riverdell Hospital told me the other day that he keeps curare in the Frigidaire. This I didn't know."

Q. "That is not my question. My question is you don't know how long it would last?"

A. "I don't."

Calissi failed to get any more satisfactory explanation of Jascalevich's "control" system.

In the course of this interview, Jascalevich also revealed to the prosecutor that on the Wednesday previous to the interview—November 2, the same day he learned that his locker's contents were seized by the prosecutor—he had gone to Seton Hall in search of his missing surgical instruments in order to see if they had been left there. Because he was going to be there anyway, the doctor said, he decided to see if he could run an experiment, and he asked the animal keeper, Mr. Riggi, if there were any dogs available. Jascalevich said that Riggi reminded him that because of some changes in the hospital administration there were no more dogs available, which Jascalevich admitted was a situation that he had been aware of since last August. According to Jascalevich, Riggi suggested that he should go to Pollack Hospital in Hudson County and ask for Dr. Timothy J. Regan, who was in charge of such things there and might be able to help.

Jascalevich told the prosecutor that he then went to Pollack and introduced himself to a Dr. Reagan, who proceeded to check him out by telephone, and then introduced him to a Dr. Burke, who was in the midst of concluding experiments on two dogs. Burke offered to make his dogs available to Jascalevich when he was finished with them. Jascalevich's testimony does not make it clear whether or not he actually did any experiments that day.

Before the morning's interview was over, Jascalevich also gave his own version of the meeting with the directors on November 2. The surgeon said that he had called the meeting himself in order to discuss the mortality rate at the hospital and what he referred to as "the explosive issue of the caesarean section case." He explained that when the directors told him about his locker being searched, he informed them that it was his "dirty locker," as he called the one which had the materials from his experiments, and that they were unaware that he had a second locker where he kept his instrumetns.

After two and a half hours of steady questioning—at about 1:00 P.M.—Calissi suggested a fifteen-minute break to allow Jascalevich to confer with his counsel.

At 1:24, after the brief recess, the prosecutor turned his attention to the circumstances of the deaths of several particular patients.

First, he asked Jascalevich about the death of Nancy Savino. Jascalevich pointed out that Nancy was not his patient. He said that she was operated on by Stanley Harris. He made the point, rather emphatically, that he believed that she was probably the first instance of Harris's losing a patient at Riverdell, and that she might have been the very first case Harris had operated on there.

Calissi inquired about how Jascalevich, as chief of surgery, reviewed a new surgeon's qualification. In response to that question, Jascalevich said, "The problem that the director of surgery has when a new surgeon comes along is what to do, to give a credit to his papers and diplomas and to give him full privilege, this is one way of approaching. The other is to despite his qualifications to say, 'I'm going to operate with you for a time, half a year or one year or whatever and see what your results is. And if you are operating well, then you can operate.' These are two the two divergent, two ways of approaching a new man."

Q. "So what did you do with respect to Dr. Harris?"

A. "On this man, and it's my policy, I reasoned this way, if you tell a man you're going to assist him for six months or one year is a way, is a trick that can be used by any surgeon to put a tourniquet and control a new man and not allowing him to operate and criticize him and put him nervous and put him on the spot.

"My opinion is rather, let the man show what he can do and stop him when his pyramid of complications reaches a certain point. This is my point of view, laissez faire, let the man do.

"All right, we let him do, and the mortality count as I call is when we have reached a certain number that was really—that needed a discussion."

Q. "Were you ever in the same room when Dr. Harris was operating?"

A. "Of course."

The prosecutor pointed out to Jascalevich that only a short time ago he had circulated a memorandum throughout the hospital indicating that he was going into partnership with Harris, and that the memorandum was rescinded by Harris. Jascalevich merely verified that incident, but he was neither asked for, nor did he offer, any more detailed explanation.

According to the surgeon's testimony, he first became aware of the Savino case when he was called from the operating room to attend to her on an emergency basis on the morning of her death. This is how Jascalevich described what he found:

"So I went from the operating room . . . rushed into the room and there it was, this creature, with the priest at the foot of the bed, the intern, Dr. Ortega, on one side, and, I will be precise, holding the left hand, if you allow me to say so, on the left hand of the patient, and on the right hand the nurse in charge who was Mrs. Nelson. These are the three parties I met in the room with the girl in the center. They gave me the stethoscope. I examined the girl. The girl was dead. The intern was crying, and to complicate even the priest was going to become my patient I think the day after, I had to remove his stomach, and I became, I recall, very mad why they called this man before an operation so important, why not to call somebody that covers him. In other words, this poor guy in pajamas, because he was a patient, giving the extreme unction. . . . So this is the picture of the situation. . . . I pronounced her dead. I went back to the operating room. Again they call me to the room. . . . I went to the room, but no, it was dead. I think the intern was emotionally inclined, thought that he heard some heart sound. The girl was dead."

After describing the situation, Jascalevich was asked to comment on the cause of her death. He responded, ". . . So this is a sudden death. Now, the cause, the autopsy is labeled as a physiological reaction."

Q. "What does that mean?"

A. "Physiological reaction means that a cardiac arrest that has occured, that the heart has stopped."

Q. "That in a four-year old girl?"

A. "It can happen at any age, it can happen at any age. It is not attributed—"

Q. "You mean that a girl could die suddenly as explained in this chart without—"

A. "Without a cause, obvious."

Q. "Pardon me?"

A. "Without an obvious cause, without any autopsy."

Q. "Without any autopsy?"

A. "Oh, of course, I would say that in the experience of any pathologist, a man of experience, there will be cases of sudden death at any age for undetermined causes, and this is the way they label it, usually, undetermined cause, probably physiological. Physiological means this. It means the patient can have an allergic reaction, an allergy to something that is dripping into his body, like, for instance, infusion that is dripping, the medication just given, or the sedation makes a sudden what is called immunetary [sic] reaction, mortal, this is in this man. It is one way—"

Q. "You mean like intravenous that is going into this child could have killed her? Is that what you are saying?"

A. "I would say any medication has an allergic potentiality, any medication. This is one of the causes in which you can have a death and in the autopsy you don't find a reason. The other is a condition called a very early myocardial, very early coronary, to put it in layman's terms, so early that it hasn't been given the chance to leave an imprint on the heart, on the muscle of the heart, so tiny and right at the spot where you have the main center that contracts, that sends the information to the heart to contract, so strategically placed, that attack, that the patient dies and you can't find anything in the heart and still he died of a heart attack. There is two. There are many reasons for which, there are conditions called auto-something that is rather new that we are waking up to the possibility of, auto-allergy, allergic to yourself for some reason, medications, operation, manipulation, or whatever. All of a sudden the patient develops an allergy to his own system, to his own materials and tissues, that we call autoimmunity, kill yourself. These are three of many causes.

"So it is certainly not a rarity, the negative autopsy, no matter what age is the patient. Of course, we always like to have a positive diagnosis, and you know very well my anxieties with the caesarean section, the last one. At this moment, we are bringing up the first one. The last date at the hospital apparently another mystery of death, no cause for death, a caesarean section in a young woman."

Jascalevich's commentary on the Savino case had led him to a discussion of the circumstances of Eileen Shaw's death. Actually, it was Jascalevich who brought it up. (Reading this for the first time, I found Jascalevich's story totally unsatisfactory and assumed that Calissi's reaction had to be similar. I was eager to know if a knowledgeable medical person reading the transcript would feel the same way.)

A. "It's an example in this sense that this lady up to yesterday was a mystery."

Q. "Which lady was a mystery?"

A. "The caesarean section, the cause of death we didn't know, but reexamination, microscopic studies show what happened to this lady."

Q. "What happened to this lady?"

A. "She had a huge liver full of fat tissue and most probably the manipulations of the surgery or whichever were the maneuvers, had broken up pieces of fat tissue in this liver and seeded her body with it and the pathologist was able yesterday finally after two weeks—I don't know when she died and we have been going through a tremendous anxiety about this case—he found a cause."

Q. "Yesterday?"

A. "Remarkable emboli, he give it to me. He give me, give the report to me because he knows how anxious I was."

Q. "This is—"

A. "The caesarean section that died at the hospital a week and a half to two weeks ago, I don't recall."

Q. "You got a report yesterday, you are telling me?"

A. "Right."

Q. "From whom?"

A. "From the man that did the autopsy. . . ."

Q. "Did you call him?"

A. "Let me see, he called me."

Q. "He called you yesterday?"

A. "Yes, because he knows I have been very worried about this case. It's this case that motivated my call for the mortality conference at the hospital."

Q. "Where did he call you?"

A. "I was at the hospital."

Q. "And he called you and you spoke to him?"

A. "And I spoke to him. His name is Dr. Markley. . . ."

Q. "You had called Dr. Markley yourself a couple of times prior to this, had you not, trying to find out the cause of death?"

A. "Sir, I have been very concerned about this case, this young woman that dies after a caesarean section. As head of the department I have been on my toes with this case. This is tops, my tolerance about the morbidity and mortality of a surgeon in my department. There would be many causes for my anxiety. I should go into detail, I don't want to be misunderstood as to the call. The call yesterday came from Dr. Markley. He didn't get me at the moment.

"They left a message for me to call him back. When I called him back he gave me number one, he gave me a report about a different case and then I asked him, 'How about that caesarean section, did you finally reach to any conclusions?'

"So actually he didn't call me to give me the report. I told him, 'How about that case?' Because I know that his man Markley is an excellent pathologist, he has been breaking his head to try to reach a diagnosis in this woman and since our first conversations I had my idea that this large, gigantic fatty liver had something to do with her death."

Q. "What did he call you about?"

A. "So he called me to give me a report about a different case."

Q. "What case?"

A. "About a different case that we have at the moment at the hospital, a report, pathology report, so I asked him when we finished talking about that case, 'How about the caesarean section, did you get any conclusion?'

" 'Oh, yes,' says he, 'finally I got it. There was multiple fat emboli and I have,' and he mentioned, 'I have the literature that this is not the first time, fatty, huge fatty livers can seed the body with fatty emboli, little fat clots all over the kidneys.'

"He mentioned particularly kidneys and he said if she got it in the kidney she got it all over. So this is the cause of death.

"I said, 'Wonderful, I'm glad that we did find a cause of death for this lady; would you please transmit this finding to the surgeon?' "

Jascalevich indicated that he had seen Eileen Shaw prior to her surgery, because a sterilization procedure had been suggested in connection with her caesarean section, and under the hospital rules, Harris required the approval of another consultant. While Calissi failed to ask him specifically, it was implied in Jascalevich's testimony that because he had been consulted, it was perfectly natural for him to stop by and check on the patient's condition that morning.

He said that he found her in what he called a "shocky condition," with low blood pressure, perspiring in cold sweats.

In response to very specific questions by Calissi, Jascalevich denied that Eileen Shaw was having any trouble breathing.

Q. "When this woman, Eileen Shaw, that is the name of the patient I believe. Is that correct?"

A. "Yes, sir."

Q. "Was first seen by you after her operation, you were in the doorway and she was having trouble breathing, was she not, she had a pain in her chest?"

A. "I had a patient downstairs that morning and I went to do rounds."

MR. ANDERSON: "Yes or no to that question, please."

Q. "Was she having trouble breathing and did she have a pain in her chest at the time?"

A. "No, the problem was rather changes in her color, the cold sweats, the thready pulse, the low blood pressure. She did not show any signs whatsoever and difficulty in breathing at the moment when I rushed to Dr. Harris's phone—to the phone to call Dr. Harris, rather. It was when the entire picture developed in which there was a respiratory difficulty, there was an increase in that shocky condition, a restlessness, a state of unconsciousness, but not in the beginning."

Q. "Not in the beginning?"

A. "Not in the beginning, it would have been—"

Q. "Did she ever complain of a pain in the chest to you while you were in her presence?"

A. "Not at any moment."

Q. "Not at any time?"

A. "Not at any time."

Q. "Did she complain to you that she had trouble breathing?"

A. "No."

Q. "Never?"

A. "Never."

Q. "You recall this case clearly?"

A. "Sir, I recall to the best of my recollection. I don't recall the patient having told me, 'Doctor, I can't breathe,' or, 'Doctor, I have a tremendous pain in my chest,' I don't recall."

Q. "I'm not talking about tremendous pain. I didn't use the word tremendous."

A. "Pain in the chest. I don't recall. Actually this lady couldn't even talk, slowly went—very fast—into a state of—she couldn't, I don't think she could have mumbled a word, a coherent word."

Jascalevich told the prosecutor that he called Dr. Harris to tell him that the patient was in difficulty, and how he followed Harris's instructions and participated in the efforts to treat her.

According to the surgeon, even before she died, the doctors had reason to suspect an embolus as the cause of the patient's difficulties. Jascalevich's discussion of that embolus rambled on extensively.

When he had exhausted this subject of Eileen Shaw's death, Calissi turned to the Rohrbeck case and asked Jascalevich to describe his recollection of that situation.

Q. "And you came in on the morning of this operation and was scrubbing with Dr. Sklar?"

A. "Right."

Q. "And you advised Dr. Sklar that you had a premonition of some kind that you didn't want to operate?"

A. "It was no premonition. It is my custom to go to see my patient before surgery the morning of surgery to have a short talk, to make evaluation, explaining what they can expect from surgery, what the pain means, how they should behave right after anesthesia. I think this helps tremendously, and I went to Mr. Rohrbeck and he wasn't looking good to me."

Q. "What was the matter with him?"

A. "He looked to me having some—he was pale, had a fast pulse. I sat him up, listened to his chest and I detected in this man on listening to his chest signs from the lungs which were not normal. We call it very early congestion of the lungs. So I advised the operating room that I am not going to operate this case and I am going to talk with Dr. Sklar about it. As a matter of fact, there was a big—I had a little bit of an exchange with Dr. Sklar because I did something probably wrong, I called first the operating room telling them I wasn't going to do the case, I didn't want them to prepare everything; I should have called first the referring physician and tell him about it.

"Anyway, when Dr. Sklar arrived I told him about my feelings. He went to examine the patient and came back and told me, 'I don't think he's so bad, I think you could have done this case,' and I told him, "Well, I don't. I think we should wait, do some tests, this is not an emergency, this is a hernia, it's a procedure of certain magnitude and this man may die on the table, we better cancel the surgery and do those further tests.' "

Q. "Did you put what you found wrong with this man in the clinical chart?"

A. "I don't recall, can I see?"

Q. "Sure."

A. "No, I didn't, although Dr. Sklar wrote, 'After receiving preoperative medication'—well, this is—"

MR. ANDERSON: "What did he say?"

A. "This is a facet I didn't know in the case, you see this? 'After receiving preoperative medication' again we go to the problem of reaction to drugs, immunitary or allergic drugs. This is completely new to me that.

" 'After receiving preoperative medication and being examined by Dr. Jascalevich and Dr. Sklar and some doubt being given as to the patient's looks this case being cancelled.'

Q. "Who wrote that?"

A. "Dr. Sklar, looks like Dr. Sklar's signature."

Q. "What did you put in the chart?"

A. "I didn't put anything in the chart. . . ."

Q. "You heard these noises in his lungs. Is that correct?"

A. "Yes, but of course that's my point, Dr. Sklar is an internist, and a man of ability, he is the man supposed to handle better the stethoscope than mine, but I'm the surgeon and it was my responsibility to cancel the case and I did."

Q. "So Dr. Sklar went up to examine his patient, came back again, and said he didn't find anything wrong with him?"

A. "Well, he thought that he didn't find contraindication to the surgery, but I told him the kind of surgery that we needed here, extensive surgery, very hazardous one. I thought at best this man needed at least some degree of a workup; that this cannot be admitted on a certain day and operated the day after, that we needed some workup. There was no need in rushing into surgery and my premonition was right, the man had a coronary."

Q. "Let me ask you something, did you tell all this to Dr. Sklar down in the scrubbing room?"

A. "Not only that but to the anesthesiologist."

Q. "Did you tell Dr. Sklar what you are telling me now?"

A. "Exactly, sir."

Q. "Not what the premonition was, what your professional opinion was?"

A. "I gave my professional—it wasn't premonition, this would carry this into the field of magic and imagination. We got to a point. I told him this man has wet rales in his lungs, very fine wet rales."

Q. "How do you spell *rales?*"

A. "R-a-l-e-s."

Q. "What does that mean?"

A. "It means water in the lungs, the beginning of water in the lungs. When you're about to get a heart attack this is the way you end, you start to develop a very first incipient sign that the pump is failing and the pump fails by water clogging. First signs before the pain in the chest, before the electrocardiogram, before anything, this is one of the incipient first signs."

Q. "And you can—"

A. "You can hear it."

Q. "—you can hear water in the lungs?"

A. "You can hear it."

Q. "With the stethoscope?"

A. "Of course, the doctor translates that and we call it rales, crepitant rales, crepitant rales."

Q. "You heard this?"

A. "I heard this, and what is most important, on both lungs. I told Dr. Sklar, because sometime when you get it in one lung it means pneumonia or it means a little bit of mucus from the bronchi from coughing, but when you listen in both lungs that means, that means the heart, unless you—"

Q. "You told this to Dr. Sklar?"

A. "Right."

Q. "When you went downstairs?"

A. "Right."

Q. "Or when you were downstairs with Dr. Sklar scrubbing up with him?"

A. "Right."

Jascalevich described how while he and Sklar discussed the cancellation of the operation, they got a call to come to Mr. Rohrbeck's room, where they found him dead. Jascalevich said that he had a coronary, and that the autopsy showed that.

Q. "And you attribute the death to—"

A. "To a coronary."

Q. "—a coronary?"

A. "A man that starts with the rales in the lungs and has sudden death, has 99 percent of a chance to have a coronary, and I think the autopsy showed a coronary."

Q. "What you told me was discussed between you and Sklar is everything that you remember pretty clearly. Is that right?"

A. "Very clearly, because this is a case in which I'm sorry that the man is dead but I have shown my—I'm glad that I behaved this way, and it shows again one of the many times I show at the hospital that I am not going to operate on cases that are not duly—that were not duly prepared or there should be no rush into surgery. Every case should be well examined. Every case should have justified surgery and should be ready for that surgery. There is no rush. There is always time for consultation. There is always time for evaluation. Mr. Rohrbeck is typical of how you can avoid an operating death in the operating room."

Before the day's interview was concluded, assistant prosecutor Fred Galda came back to the Rohrbeck case momentarily to discuss an important medical point that Calissi had apparently overlooked.

MR. GALDA: "Dr. Jascalevich, we have talked about the Rohrbeck file and your findings or some indication that there were rales or something in the soundings that you heard at that time that you made your examination. Do you recall whether or not you ordered any drugs or anything to be administered to this patient, anything whatsoever?"

A. "No, sir, no drugs. There was no chance to do any resuscitation of this man."

Q. "I mean prior to the resuscitation."

A. "But, of course, the man was—nothing by mouth, so the only thing we did was to give him an intravenous feeding of some water and sugar and vitamins, or water and sugar only, until we can reach some decision what to do with this man. That's the only medication he received. I can't recall. And the preanesthesia, pardon me, the preanesthesia which we disclosed through Dr. Sklar's note, the preanesthesia is the morphine and atropine, this is the drug given really, the drug because water and sugar you don't call a drug."

Q. "Would you know who ordered the intravenous, whether it was you or Dr. Sklar?"

A. "No, it was me, sir."

Q. "It was you?"

A. "It was me."

Q. "When you give intravenous to a patient, in effect aren't you giving water to a patient?"

A. "Water, sugar, vitamins."

Q. "Well, if one were contemplating or thought there probably were coronary problems or the rales, you considered that we now have water about to go into the heart?"

A. "Yes."

Q. "Wouldn't you be compounding that particular problem?"

A. "Only if that infusion ascends at tremendous speed and force. If it is just to keep slowly dripping, just to give him nothing by mouth until we reach some decision, no harm can come to him."

The only other one of the specific cases discussed with Jascalevich during the interview that day was the death of Margaret Henderson.

Jascalevich said that she was the first patient to be operated on at Riverdell by another new surgeon, Dr. Livingston. The chief of surgery told the prosecutor that Livingston had come to Riverdell with excellent credentials and was free to operate without supervision.

In the Henderson case, Jascalevich said, he had been asked by Dr. Livingston to consult with respect to the diagnosis, and that he had disagreed with Livingston's conclusion that an exploratory laparotomy was called for, preferring to do further tests before surgery. Nevertheless, despite Jascalevich's recommendation, Livingston called in Dr. Harris for another opinion, and the two of them decided to operate on Mrs. Henderson.

Jascalevich attributed the death of Mrs. Henderson to a hepatitis liver, or acute hepatitis, but there was not very much discussion of the diagnosis.

At the end of the interview, Fred Galda asked a number of questions to fill in a few gaps in the series of questions. One point that had evidently bothered Galda was why Jascalevich had made a point of looking for a dog to experiment on on the very day that he found out that his locker had been seized. Jascalevich's explanation was that he was unaware of the seriousness or of the official nature of the matter at that time. He thought it was merely an internal investigation by the hospital administrator, and that he only discovered how important it was a few days later, when the hospital administrator returned his surgical equipment in an envelope that bore the official label of the Bergen County prosecutor's office. Jascalevich had left his surgical equipment with Galda, who had requested it at the beginning of the investigation.

Taking of testimony from Jascalevich ended at about 3:30 that afternoon. Calissi said to Jascalevich and his lawyer, James Anderson, that he would call and reschedule the taking of the balance of the statement.

He never did so.

I had a number of reactions when I first read this transcript. First of all, I was amazed that an experienced prosecutor could fail to ask so many of the obviously pertinent questions for which I would have wanted answers. For another thing—despite my lack of medical knowledge—it seemed to me that many of Jascalevich's responses were either evasive or confused, and I wondered if he was using his difficulty with the English language to obfuscate matters deliberately. One could not be sure.

Because Calissi had neglected to have a medical expert present to assist in formulating questions, I was eager to learn how an experienced physician would react to a number of the issues raised in the testimony.

PART III

CHAPTER XIV

Other Perspectives

Saturday night and Sunday morning I read and reread the transcript. Through his own words I was beginning to know Dr. Jascalevich for the first time.

My capacity to evaluate the testimony was limited by a lack of the medical competence needed to deal with the details of the surgeon's explanations.

While Jascalevich's logic was apparent in some aspects of the interview, for the most part the transcript left me feeling utterly confused. Especially bothersome was his description of his means of obtaining dogs for experimentation. Could meaningful medical research really be initiated this way? I had a vivid mental picture of the eyes of those dying dogs, exhausted, gradually butchered by one white-coated experimenter after another.

The doctor's explanation of his handling of the empty and unmarked curare bottles, carrying them all the way back to Riverdell, also left me wondering about such medical methodology.

On the other hand, Jascalevich's explanation for each of the deaths that he had been questioned about seemed to be extensive and thoughtful. I wondered if this experienced surgeon, whose experiments were indications of superior qualifications, could perhaps be just that much more knowledgeable than either Lans or Harris.

By the time I was ready to leave for Allan Lans's house, my copy was filled with all of the arrows, asterisks, circles, and underlining that I needed to remind myself of the points that had to be reviewed with Allan and Stanley Harris.

It was just after 8:00 that evening when the three of us assembled. During the last two days, the two doctors had also devoured the transcript.

The opportunity to read Jascalevich's statement had obviously lifted the spirits of my two medical confidants. To them, the transcript was a vindication of their earliest suspicions. They carried on an animated discussion while I systematically recorded the points they made on long yellow legal pads. Each of us had a different perspective, but we were able to shift through our reactions systematically in order to summarize every aspect of all six hours of the testimony while eliminating some fascinating irrelevancies.

The notes that I made that day have been in my file ever since, so it has not been difficult to review all of the significant points we had agreed upon.

Stanley Harris was outraged by what he had read. He called Jascalevich's testimony "preposterous," and found the lack of any revelation of Calissi's own reactions somewhat frustrating, because he wanted Calissi to be outraged too.

Harris's first point was that there was no value to an experimenter keeping the empty vials of curare if he didn't note which ones were used on which dogs and in which particular experiment. In Dr. Harris's view, and based on his own experience, the fact that Jascalevich didn't do this cast a dark shadow on his explanation.

Harris had also tried to calculate, from Jascalevich's own statements, how many dogs had actually been used in the number of experiments the surgeon had described. Harris thought that the number of dogs Jascalevich said he used in experiments which required an injection of curare did not jibe with the number of empty bottles that were found in the doctor's locker. It was clear to all of us that Calissi's interrogation was completely inadequate in this regard. He had failed to pin the doctor down on the precise number of experiments in each category in order to be able to compare that information with the number of empty bottles.

Harris questioned Jascalevich's explanation of his liver biopsy experiment. As he explained it to me, and Allan Lans agreed, there was no point in conducting such an experiment on a live dog, if the dog was going to be left to die from the curare dosage anyway, because the alleged purpose of the experiment was merely to determine the accuracy of the surgeon's ability to hit the correct spot on the liver. Such an experiment could be done just as effectively on a dead dog. Besides, both Lans and Harris argued that it would not be valuable to use a dog in the first place, since a dog's liver is in a different place than a human's, and so a human cadaver would be the more appropriate place to test such a device or the skill needed to utilize it.

I made my notes rather feverishly as the doctors rapidly picked over the testimony. Then we went over each point a second time, just to be certain that my understanding was clear.

Both Lans and Harris had been at the meeting at Eliot Weiner's house when Jascalevich was first told about the prosecutor's seizing the locker. Neither of them believed Jascalevich's denial of his own awareness of the official nature of the investigation.

The point in the record that made Harris most angry with Jascalevich was the statement he made in response to the prosecutor's question about whether he had ever observed Harris performing an operation. Actually, the question to Jascalevich was, "Were you ever in the same room when Dr. Harris was operating?" Jascalevich had responded, "Of course." Harris said that this was just not so, that Jascalevich had once stopped in momentarily just before an operation, but according to Harris, he left before the operation began, and that was the only time he had ever even been in the operating room at the same time with him. Allan Lans shared much of Harris's outrage over this discrepancy, as he had neither seen nor heard of Jascalevich's being present at any of Harris's operations.

There even appeared to be a discrepancy in Jascalevich's story about where he was when he was called to Nancy Savino's bedside. Harris told me that he had heard from Mrs. Nelson, one of the nurses, that she thought Jascalevich had been found across the hall from Nancy Savino's room, and *not* in the operating room, as Jascalevich had testified. The hospital chart which Lans and Harris had reviewed indicated that Jascalevich had arrived on the scene prior to Dr. Ortega, who, according to Jascalevich's story, was already in the room when he arrived. Dr. Harris had also gone over the details of Nancy Savino's death with Nurse Nelson. The nurse's recollection, as Harris conveyed it to me that evening, was that Nurse Price was the last person to see Nancy alive and that was at 7:30 in the morning. Mrs. Nelson also said that she saw Jascalevich making rounds at 7:15, and that when Barbara Kenderes, the technician, found Nancy not responding at 7:45, she came to Nurse Nelson, who told her to get the first doctor she could find

—and she thinks that Barbara found Jascalevich across the hall. Mrs. Nelson had also described Jascalevich's actions to Harris differently than Jascalevich himself described them. Contrary to Jascalevich's story, Nelson told Harris that Jascalevich did nothing to attempt to resuscitate her—just pronounced her dead.

Besides that, Jascalevich testified that he examined Nancy Savino with a stethoscope, and both Lans and Harris told me that Jascalevich never carried a stethoscope. However, when I went back over the testimony, I saw that this point was not significant, because Jascalevich had said, "They gave me the stethoscope"—he never said it was his stethoscope.

Jascalevich's description of his activities on that day when he discovered his locker had been opened was also very bothersome to Stanley Harris. He found much of it to be incongruous. Why would Jascalevich be looking for a dog at Seton Hall when he already knew for some time that the animal facilities there had been closed? Harris also questioned how Jascalevich could have had the temerity to conduct a dog experiment at Pollack Hospital at 5:00 P.M. on the same day he discovered his locker had been opened.

He pointed out that although Jascalevich had testified that in that experiment he used a stapler which he had kept at home, he certainly didn't have his other surgical instruments at that time, because by his own testimony he had only obtained their return from Weiner at 7:00 that evening, which was after the dog experiment was allegedly completed.

Why would Jascalevich be concerned about doing a dog experiment while he thought that his $2,000 stapler was missing and still had to be located? Finally, Harris saw no reason to be doing an experiment to test an old stapler whose utilization was long established and which was already very familiar to Jascalevich himself. Lans too had come up with this same point about the uselessness of experimenting with the old instrument.

Then we started on Allan Lans's list. He had come up with some items that Harris had not.

Jascalevich, Lans pointed out, first said that he operated on dogs only at Seton Hall, but later on he described doing an experiment at Pollack Hospital.

Further, Jascalevich's statement that Nancy Savino's death was due to an allergic reaction made no sense medically to Lans, because an allergic death would not be so sudden and would have been indicated on autopsy.

Allan pointed out that when Jascalevich described Eileen Shaw's difficulties prior to her death, he ignored the fact that there were two episodes, and he felt that Jascalevich deliberately treated them as one.

Perhaps most important of all, Allan disagreed with Jascalevich when he said that rales was a sign of an impending coronary. "That's just not true," Lans told me—and Harris agreed with him. As a matter of fact, both of them agreed that if there was any sign of water in the lungs, the utilization of an intravenous feeding of water, which Jascalevich did, was completely contraindicated.

Allan speculated that since Jascalevich had said that Mr. Rohrbeck was already dead when he and Sklar had arrived on the scene together, the very brief interval of time between their arrival and Jascalevich's last visit to Mr. Rohrbeck indicated that Rohrbeck must have died in Jascalevich's presence or just minutes after he left him.

Dr. Lans and Dr. Harris agreed upon another major point: it is inappropriate for any responsible researcher conducting experiments on live dogs to rely on a system of acquiring them second-hand from janitors. Considering the supposed importance of the experiments, to rely on such an acquisition system would require a miracle of delicate timing which was totally inappropriate to the saving of relatively few dollars, especially for a man whose income was known to be so high.

After we finished reviewing the testimony, we prepared a list of any other items we could think of that might be helpful for further investigation. I had already set Lans and Harris onto the assignment of finding all the available slides or tissues that might be left over from any of the autopsies, because when we had last met Dr. Helpern had stressed the importance of these items.

Allan Lans had a wooden box of additional slides from the Savino case which had been left at the hospital and which Calissi's staff had not picked up. He had also found a parafin block in the Riverdell hospital laboratory in which was imbedded a small piece of remaining tissue from the autopsy of Eileen Shaw. Lans gave these to me to deliver to Helpern, along with the slides from Shaw, Biggs, and Savino that Calissi had given to me directly.

Stanley Harris was certain that the New Jersey State Police Lab in Trenton must have some of the tissue from the Savino case, and he also thought that some wet tissue had been sent there. He believed that there should also be some tissue remaining from the autopsies that were done on Margaret Henderson and Carl Rohrbeck by the Bergen County medical examiner.

Finally, Allan remembered that when the autopsy was done on Mr. Rohrbeck, the staff had also taken the intravenous tubing along with the body, and he promised to make an effort to see if that tubing could be found anywhere in the hospital.

When our session was over that evening, we had looked at every possibility of the whereabouts of any remaining tissue or other evidence that might help to facilitate the inquiry.

On Monday night, after supper, I went through all the notes of our meeting the previous night. Comparing these notes to the transcript again, I composed a memorandum highlighting the different subject areas it covered. The memorandum also listed all the significant discrepancies we had identified.

CHAPTER XV

Expert Opinion

The next morning, Tuesday, January 10, I sent Dr. Helpern the testimony, the memorandum, and the canister of physical evidence that Calissi gave me, along with the box of slides and parafin block Allan Lans found at the hospital. All of it was delivered to Helpern's office by messenger.

After sending the material to Helpern, I called Calissi and reviewed the several missing items that the doctors thought he should be able to obtain from either the state police lab or the county medical examiner's office. The prosecutor seemed eager to cooperate; he assured me that he would find out if this material still existed, and would let me know.

Two days later, Calissi sent me the autopsy reports from the medical examiner's office for the Rohrbeck and Hendersen cases.

When I received that letter, I called Calissi again, to thank him and to find out how he was making out with the search for the additional tissue. I was unable to get him on the phone. I called him several times during the next few days, but for some reason he didn't return any of my calls. So, on January 20, I wrote to Calissi asking once more for the missing tissue.

Meanwhile, Dr. Harris had obtained the autopsy reports for the Post, Shaw, and Biggs cases, and I sent all this along to Helpern with the additional reports that Calissi had sent to me.

During that same week, Lans located the wet tissue from the hospital, left over from the Savino and Shaw cases, and he delivered these to Dr. Helpern's office.

The fact that Calissi had suddenly started to ignore me was troublesome. It appeared to me that he had either lost interest in this entire matter or that he was too busy with other cases to respond to my inquiries; I was also wondering whether I had somehow overstepped my authority by imposing these requests on him. But on February 9, the day after I returned from a week's business trip in Europe, a letter came from Edward Kastner, one of Calissi's detectives, in which he reported that they had no other material available.

We had exhausted all of the possibilities that we could identify and could only await the results of Dr. Helpern's review.

We did not have to wait very long. Only one day passed before Mrs. Helpern called to arrange a meeting with "The Chief," and Allan Lans and I went downtown to see Dr. Helpern the next day.

As we pulled up chairs in front of Dr. Helpern's desk, I could see the transcript open in front of him, alongside the now familiar boxes of slides.

Helpern told us that he had studied Jascalevich's testimony carefully. He shook his head. "Bizarre," he said softly. "Bizarre. I don't understand such explanations for these deaths." He added that rales were certainly not a sign of an incipient heart attack.

Helpern then picked one of the slides out of the wooden box on his desk, and he held it up to the light. I don't remember which of the cases it came from, but I remember very clearly that it was one which the autopsy had attributed to a heart attack. "This person did not die of a heart attack," he explained. The tissue on the particular slide could not possibly have been the tissue of a coronary victim, he noted, and any qualified forensic pathologist should know that.

Helpern took the occasion to repeat his previous denunciation of incompetent pathologists in general, and said that this case was a not unusual demonstration of how the most simple test could be overlooked. Dr. Helpern expressed his serious reservations about the work of the Bergen County medical examiners and the River-dell pathologists.

He then picked up the telephone and asked Dr. Umberger to join us. Umberger came in accompanied by a couple of other men in the familiar white lab coats; I'm not sure if they were introduced or not, but they were colleagues on the medical examiner's staff. Allan and I were impressed that all the resources of Dr. Helpern's office had been put to work on the case.

Dr. Umberger said that he had been working on the Shaw tissue extensively since our last visit. He explained the nature of his experiments, using a spectograph to break the tissue into its component parts, and he had now come as far as he could. Unfortunately, Umberger said, he was unable to reach any definite conclusion. The formalin used to preserve the tissue was preventing him from obtaining a final result. He used the term *masking.* As I understood him, the experiment was done in steps, and each step thus far indicated positively the possibility that curare could be present. However, he had now arrived at a point where he could break it down no further, and the presence of formalin masked any final or definitive result. All he could say positively was that up to the stage of the test that he was able to do, he was unable to rule out the presence of curare, but because of the formalin, he could not go far enough to come to any final conclusion. Unless we could come up with tissue that had not been preserved in formalin, there was no possibility of making a positive identification of the drug, and there was no other way to do it.

Dr. Helpern said it was certainly frustrating, because everything else we had presented made him suspicious that there was something very wrong here. He was very gracious to us and as encouraging as humanly possible. He reiterated his concern and his eagerness to continue to help if we could only provide him with more material to work with. Unfortunately, we had exhausted the possibilities of finding more tissue from any of the cases.

With that conversation our most hopeful avenue of pursuit ended.

Allan and I took a cab uptown and had lunch at a little coffee shop near my office. Amid the lunchtime bustle of shouted short orders, we were very much alone, and a great sense of helplessness overcame us. We had succeeded in getting the most expert advice and attention available in America. That advice tended to support our suspicions, but we were still without confirmation; and now, in the final analysis, there was nothing else to be done. We pondered over every question, every idea we could think of, to determine if there were any other places to turn, any other avenues of investigation to pursue.

The possibility of exhuming bodies to obtain additional tissue occurred to us, but we discarded it because Helpern had not raised it. We assumed that the prosecutor would need a court order, and neither he nor a judge would have enough evidentiary basis to cause the families of the deceased any further anguish without something more concrete to go on. We also assumed that any tissue obtained this way would have been embalmed and would therefore present the same problem to the toxicologist that the Shaw tissue did.

There was only one other possibility that occured to us, however far-fetched. If someone had indeed been responsible for all these deaths, it would certainly indicate a deep psychiatric problem. Perhaps a forensic psychiatrist could shed some light on the subject and provide us with some method for analyzing such a person's personality.

I called Dr. Helpern that afternoon to try out the idea on him. He said that it was certainly worth a try, but he had no idea what could come of it. He suggested Dr. Morris Herman, who was affiliated with Bellevue and Mt. Sinai Hospitals and was a consultant to Manhattan District Attorney Frank Hogan in complicated cases. Helpern offered to make the proper introduction.

Allan and I went to see Dr. Herman the following week. We sat with the psychiatrist in his dimly lit office and reviewed our story in detail. It was a bit awkward. We had no good idea of what we could expect from Dr. Herman as he listened to us with a psychiatrist's dispassion. Not unexpectedly, he said he was unable to come up with anything helpful, unless he had an opportunity to personally examine a suspect. Obviously, we were not in a position to give him that opportunity.

It was the end of February; three and one-half months had passed since Jascalevich's locker was opened, revealing the empty curare bottles. Our effort and that of so many others had been tremendous and the emotional drain horrendous, especially for Allan, who was consumed with deep feelings for the dead patients. Our inability to find justice despite the energy and time we had expended was deeply felt.

We could not find any other stone to turn over. Our only satisfaction came from the fact that we had done all that was within our means to find justice and truth.

At just about that time, Dr. Jascalevich resigned from the Riverdell staff, and the added strain on Allan Lans and Stanley Harris or having to see him, free, every day, would no longer exist. The deep concern that Allan felt for the dead patients and their families was something that he would carry forever, although logic would indicate that the extent of his anguish would be relieved by time. Actually, it never was. His sense of frustration with what he considered to be the mishandling of a matter of life and death, and everything else about the entire experience, was to take its toll on him for years to come. Significantly, his fellow directors were relieved that the matter was ended without publicity. Their hospital, their practices, and their reputations would be preserved.

CHAPTER XVI

Behind Closed Doors

The county prosecutor had done much more than we were aware of in 1966. Many years later we would learn the totality of his effort. Calissi's failure to tell the Riverdell doctors who had come to him for help what it was he was planning to do, or even how he reacted to their tale, should not have been misconstrued by them as either a lack of interest or of intended inaction on his part. The maximum energy of the prosecutor's office, however proficient, had been expended.

When they saw the locker's contents first hand, Calissi and his staff knew that they had a momentous case on their hands. As they drove the short distance back to Hackensack, they discussed the next steps and agreed that they needed professional medical assistance to evaluate the full meaning of what they had to deal with.

When he got to his office, Calissi called Dr. Lawrence J. Denson, the county's assistant medical examiner, and asked him to come over to discuss the case. Calissi gave him only a few preliminary details over the phone.

The investigative records show that Denson came over with three other experts, among them Dr. Charles J. Umberger, the toxicologist. He brought two of his associates from Allied Testing and Research Laboratories, a private laboratory the prosecutor called on from time to time because the county had no laboratory of its own. Although the state police lab was available, its services usually took too long to be useful in such cases.

Calissi was eager to have Denson's ideas on the possible explanation for the contents of Jascalevich's locker, but Denson didn't have any. According to the detectives' notes of that meeting, which took up the better part of the evening, Denson told Calissi that he could not account for a locker full of curare in any way, and none of the other experts present had any explanations to add.

Dr. Lawrence J. Denson

Dr. Denson's advise to Calissi that night was critical to the eventual determination of the prosecutor's investigation. Obviously, in order to establish curare as a lethal weapon in any of the cases, the key question for Calissi was whether or not it could be found in the deceased bodies. If it could be found, how did the experts go about doing so? Some disagreement appears on this point among the recollections of those people who were involved in 1966.

When he was interviewed years later, Dr. Denson said, "I was assistant medical examiner, and I was only involved for the first five hours of the investigation." According to Denson's recollection, the county medical examiner's office wasn't called upon after that. He characterized his own involvement by saying, "It was my feeling that I was quite peripheral to the whole thing."

Dr. Denson remembers that at the time he thought it might be worthwhile to try and exhume some of the bodies, although he thought it unlikely that if they did so they could find curare. On the other hand, Denson did tell the reporters who asked him afterward that he wasn't exactly sure what he told Calissi at the time.

The county prosecutor's view is very different. As a lawyer, not a doctor, he had to rely on whatever medical or scientific knowledge was available to him at the time. Calissi remembers that Denson, among others, advised him against exhumation because there was no hope of their being able to determine if there was curare in the bodies. Even if the prosecutor had sufficient grounds to justify the necessary court order, it was obvious that any effort to exhume bodies would have involved the families of the deceased. To put those people to greater anguish without any useful purpose had to be a major consideration for everyone involved in the decision-making process.

One of the experts suggested to Calissi that if he could find any of the human tissue remaining after the autopsies that had been done in some cases, or even the autopsy slides that might be around the hospital, some analysis might be done, and that he should also have the relevant hospital charts and autopsy reports. As the assistant chief medical examiner, Dr. Denson himself had done some of the autopsies.

Umberger's laboratory people offered to take the needles and any syringes that came from the locker to test their contents to see what might be revealed.

Meanwhile, Calissi and Galda decided to await the results of the next morning's meeting of the Riverdell board with Jascalevich at Weiner's home, on which Calissi's investigators eavesdropped.

As soon as Jascalevich left Weiner's house after the board meeting, Detective John Dunn packed up his wire recorder and carried it around the corner, where he had parked the plain, nondescript black Ford sedan which Bergen County provided to drive himself back to the county courthouse in Hackensack.

Ten minutes later at the prosecutor's office, Calissi and Galda were waiting very eagerly to hear Dunn describe Jascalevich's justification for having a locker full of curare. While he was talking, Dunn was also setting up the machine so the attorneys could hear the surgeon's story first hand. Calissi had two other investigators, Detectives Vahe Garabedian and Raymond Morrisey, listen to the recording. They decided on their next step: to attempt to check out Jascalevich's story before even he told it to them directly.

The next morning, November 2, armed with Detective Dunn's information, Garabedian and Morrisey took the thirty-minute drive over to Jersey City to the New Jersey College of Medicine and Surgery at Seton Hall University, where they located Joseph F. Salerno, the school's administrator. Once they identified themselves to Salerno, the man spoke freely, without even asking them what they were up to.

According to the detectives' report, Salerno told them that he had known Dr. Jascalevich during 1963 and 1964, when Jascalevich had utilized the medical school's laboratory facilities to conduct a research program pursuant to a $500 grant from the American Cancer Society. He recalled that during that research, Jascalevich had used twelve dogs, as well as some human cadavers, and that Jascalevich had paid for the dogs out of his grant funds. That was the extent of Salerno's experience with Jascalevich.

Mr. Salerno suggested that the two detectives should meet Dr. Anthony Boccabella, the head of the department of anatomy, whose office was just across the hall.

Fortunately, Dr. Boccabella was in. He told them that he did indeed know Dr. Jascalevich, because he was an occasional lecturer in the anatomy department at the school. Jascalevich actually came to lecture three or four times a year. As a matter of fact, said Boccabella, Jascalevich had given a lecture at the school just two weeks ago. Besides, said Boccabella, "Jascalevich was here only yesterday."

Garabedian was perplexed, because Jascalevich had spent that particular morning at the Riverdell board meeting which Detective Dunn had bugged. At least he was there until about 11:00 A.M., according to Dunn's account. He asked Boccabella what time he had seen Jascalevich, and Boccabella replied, "It was 1:30 in the afternoon."

Boccabella remembered it well, because he said Jascalevich seemed to be very upset. He was looking for dogs to perform some tests on. He also said that Jascalevich had asked him for a key to one of the closets in the anatomy lab, so he referred Jascalevich to Salvatore A. Riggi, the school's chief animal keeper.

The detectives asked Dr. Boccabella if he could show them that particular locker, and they were escorted upstairs to meet Mr. Riggi. The four of them actually looked at the locker together, but they found that nothing was missing or unusual about it.

Garabedian and Morrisey then took the opportunity to question Riggi. He confirmed that Jascalevich had been there the previous day and had also asked him about the availability of dogs. During that conversation with Jascalevich, Riggi said, the surgeon had mentioned curare as an anesthetic. The animal keeper said it was during that same conversation with Dr. Jascalevich that the surgeon told him that at one time he had been getting one dog each week for a dollar. Riggi told the detectives that it was the first time he had ever heard about such a practice. According to Riggi, up until his visit on the previous day, he had seen Jascalevich "once or twice last year." The detectives asked him if he could remember any details about those visits. Riggi did specifically remember one particular occasion, about a year before, when he saw Jascalevich perform an experiment on a dog with his surgical stapler.

While they were at Seton Hall, the detectives also saw Dr. Timothy Regan, who was doing some experiments there himself. Dr. Regan knew Jascalevich, since he was also on the staff at Pollack Hospital in Jersey City, where Regan was the director of the cardiology department. Regan confirmed that Jascalevich had been at Pollack on the afternoon of November 2 while he was there himself doing a dog experiment, and that he observed Jascalevich work on a dog very briefly. He said in response to the detectives' question that Jascalevich had made no mention of curare.

Robert DeSanles, who worked in animal care, also told the detectives that a man came to Pollack on November 2 and worked on a dog, but he didn't know his name.

At the same time that Detectives Garabedian and Morrisey were conducting their interviews at Seton Hall, Fred Galda, the first assistant prosecutor, was busy interviewing Dr. Jascalevich himself at the county courthouse in Hackensack. When Jascalevich responded to Galda's call, he appeared to be under the impression that the officials wanted him to clear up some matter involving the contents of the lockers at the hospital, which he had understood from the meeting at Weiner's house was the extent of the prosecutor's interest. Jascalevich was alone when he came to see Galda, and he was carrying his "experiment bag," a Horn & Hardart shopping bag containing some of his surgical instruments.

Jascalevich admitted to Galda that the contents of locker number 4 were his, and that immediately after he heard from the board that the locker's contents had been seized, he went to his other locker to check and see if that had also been opened. Galda asked what he meant by his "other locker."

Jascalevich explained that he had two lockers at Riverdell, a fact that neither Galda nor the Riverdell Hospital directors had been aware of. The surgeon told Galda that locker number 4 was used for materials he kept in connection with his experiments, and the other locker was his place for keeping surgical equipment. He told Galda that he had found his experiment bag in his surgical locker and indicated that someone must have moved it there from locker number 4. He also told Galda that he had a box with a clear plastic cover, containing four or five curare vials, which was missing from his surgical locker, and he thought someone must have been into his surgical locker and disarranged it.

Galda wasn't ready to go any further, so he asked Dr. Jascalevich to come back at 12:45 to meet again with himself and Calissi, because he was going to have the other doctors from the Riverdell board present in an effort to examine the entire situation together.

When the board members arrived that afternoon, they were

accompanied by Dr. Harris, Mr. Weiner, and the hospital's attorney. Jascalevich had come back and he was still clutching his "experiment bag."

Calissi told the assembled group that his office was now engaged in a criminal investigation involving a series of deaths at Riverdell Hospital which were unsatisfactorily explained. The prosecutor said that he was considering the possibility that the curare which had been found in Dr. Jascalevich's locker had been used somehow in causing these deaths. He also told the group of doctors that he had already heard enough to believe that "somebody is lying."

Once he heard what Calissi had to say, Dr. Jascalevich told him that since the board members had an attorney present, he felt he should have one too. Calissi assured Jascalevich that he certainly had every right to have an attorney present. He told the doctor to obtain one as soon as possible, and to have his lawyer call Mr. Galda for an appointment to enable the doctor to give a complete statement to the prosecutor's office. As Jascalevich was leaving, Calissi asked him to leave his experiment bag behind.

The prosecutor's staff wanted to begin taking a series of formal statements, so Dr. Lans, Dr. Frieman, Dr. Sklar, Dr. Harris, and Mr. Weiner stayed on to give theirs. Under oath, each one told Calissi's people what he knew of the situation.

The record of the investigation shows that at Calissi's request, Dr. Denson and another assistant medical examiner, Dr. Wilson D. Webb, a surgeon, were all present during the taking of this testimony.

Dr. Lans was the first to testify, making the point that, "Dr. Harris was the one who first brought the question to everyone's attention, about the possibility of there being some peculiar circumstances surrounding the deaths. It was his feeling that Dr. Jascalevich was responsible."

Lans also felt it important to remark, "Dr. Jascalevich himself had expressed concern about the high number of mortalities that Dr. Harris was having, and as a result a meeting had been scheduled to discuss this matter for November 2, but once the curare was discovered in the locker, the meeting was cancelled."

Lans testified that among the strange incidents on the morning of the day that Eileen Shaw died, Dr. Jascalevich had told him and Dr. Harris that he, Jascalevich, had received a call from an attorney named Mooney, who was threatening a malpractice suit relative to the case.

Lans told the prosecutor how he had observed Jascalevich open his locker on the morning of November 1, without any visible reaction, just before they came to the prosecutor with their story. When Galda asked Lans if there had been anyone else in the dressing room at that time, Lans recalled that Dr. Arthur F. DeMarco, the anesthesiologist, was also there, but he did not know if he had observed the situation because Dr. DeMarco was, of course, unaware of what was going on.

Dr. Frieman then followed Lans. He described the call he got from Lans between 2 and 4 P.M. on Monday, October 31, while he was at his office in New Milford, when Lans told him about Harris's opening of Jascalevich's locker and what he found there.

One of Frieman's recollections was that, insofar as he knew, Jascalevich had not been critical of Harris's surgery until very recently, when Jascalevich told him that "he would like to scrub with Harris in order to observe him, as he felt that Harris's surgery may be a little lengthy."

In response to another question, the Riverdell Hospital president confirmed that he had never used curare at Riverdell himself, nor was he aware of anyone else using it.

It was about 3 o'clock when Frieman finished and Dr. Sklar was called in. Sklar related the details of the Rohrbeck case to the prosecutor, and he told him about the "premonition" that Jascalevich had had in that case.

When Sklar finished, Dr. Harris was called in. It was the first time he had been heard from by the prosecutor, because until then, Calissi had only met with those doctors who were the members of the board of directors. Harris had a great deal to say and was very eager finally to have this official opportunity to do so.

He told the prosecutor that so many of the unexplained deaths had occurred around 8 o'clock in the morning, and he described how on a number of occasions he would get a phone call from Mrs. Cassell, one of the nurses at Riverdell, who would say, "Dr. Harris, your patient is not doing well, and Dr. Jascalevich is tending to your patient." Harris told Calissi and his people that the nurse's words would "ring in my mind, over and over."

Harris went on to tell them how he had gone back and reviewed several of the case files—Savino, Holster, Arzt, and Grisel—and that his review of these cases left him even more suspicious. He said that when he found out that in the Shaw case Jascalevich himself had started a dextrose-and-water I.V., he was surprised because physicians usually have a nurse start an I.V., and in any case he had never heard of a doctor starting an I.V. on another doctor's patient unless it was an emergency. After Mrs. Shaw's death, he contacted Dr. Lans because he was suspicious of something. He said he told Lans, "Something was going on. These deaths were not medically determined."

Harris related how when he had first come to Riverdell, some of the staff members had told him that Jascalevich was not giving sufficient coverage, and Dr. Briski, the other new surgeon, was having trouble with some unexplained mortalities. Harris recalled a situation that one of the nurses had told him about, when, after a patient died in her presence, Dr. Briski had actually said to Jascalevich, "What did you give this patient? The patient was alive before you went in."

Harris explained that after they reviewed the files together, "I believed that Lans was sympathetic and he tended to agree with me. That was the reason Lans called a board meeting on October 25, but the only result of that meeting was that when he pointed out the significance of the 8 o'clock timing of so many of the deaths, the board members decided that one of them would always make a point to be around the hospital in the morning to keep an eye on the postoperative cases." After the Shaw case, according to Harris, the board members said that before going to the prosecutor they would want to see the results of the toxicologist's report which they were still waiting for.

Harris told Calissi that after that meeting was over, he made a vow to himself that as an added precaution he wouldn't order any more I.V.'s on his patients in the morning. He further said that the board of directors had also told him that they knew that Jascalevich was interested in instruments and perhaps he was using some sort of a device which could be found in his locker. Some of the doctors thought that Jascalevich had a box where he kept instruments.

Harris said there were a couple of strange things that happened relative to the Shaw case. He told the interviewers of the call that

Jascalevich had claimed he received from Mr. Mooney. He also related that while he was awaiting the toxicologist's report in the Shaw case, Dr. Markley, the hospital pathologist who had done the autopsy on Mrs. Shaw, told him that he had received a call from Jascalevich inquiring about those results, but that Jascalevich had asked Markley not to speak with anyone about his call.

Harris told the prosecutor he was convinced that, "Jascalevich just didn't want anybody else in that hospital doing surgery except himself."

The formal interviews taken that day ended with Weiner's statement. Weiner told them that he had no knowledge of the entire matter until the second board meeting on October 27, which he had been invited to, and that all he could say was that during that meeting he had observed that the board's reactions "ran the gamut from absolutely impossible to possible."

Calissi's detectives were moving in a number of directions. They checked the hospital records in order to determine the names of those people who had shared semiprivate rooms with any of the deceased, and systematically interviewed each of these surviving roommates in order to determine if any of them had ever noticed anything suspicious. None of them was able to provide any useful information.

Beginning on November 5, another team of detectives was assigned to trace the actual sources of the bottles of curare found in Jascalevich's locker. The first stop along this trail was the General Surgical Supply Company at 444 60th Street, West New York, New Jersey, which is located just across the street from Dr. Jascalevich's home and office. The supplier's records revealed that Dr. Jascalevich had purchased twenty-four vials of tubocurarine, a product of Lilly Pharmaceutical Company, on five separate occasions between September 21, 1965 and September 28, 1966, and on September 29, 1966 he had purchased six 10-cc vials. He had also purchased one vial on May 16, 1964. They also showed that earlier in the week, on November 2, Jascalevich had purchased 3 oz. of formaldehyde. (The detectives made a second visit to the supply company a couple of weeks later and learned that the company did not handle tubarine, another curare derivative which was manufactured by Burroughs & Wellcome Company.) They were also told that Jascalevich usually called just before making any of these purchases, because the General Surgical Supply Company did not stock the drug and had to order it for him. The manager at General Surgical Supply Company also recalled that Jascalevich had once told him he was using the drug in connection with experiments on dogs. In response to one of the detectives' questions, the manager told them that they had never received any complaints from Jascalevich. (Jascalevich had told Calissi that he had complained to the Surgical Supply Company on at least one occasion.)

The detectives also began interviewing other people at Riverdell in order to check out the board members' unanimous certainty of recollection that the drug was not used there.

First, they interviewed a former Riverdell Hospital operating room nurse, Enid McKeon, who contradicted the board members' recollections. She recalled that tubarine was used at Riverdell, according to her own knowledge, and it came in a blue box, manufactured by Burroughs & Wellcome Company. She estimated that in her experience, the hospital used about ten vials a year.

The nurse's recollection in conflict with the board members' caused the detectives to decide to search the hospital pharmacy and the operating room. They started with the hospital pharmacist, and interviewed him. He did not think that there was any on hand, and he had been in his job for about a year and a half. When he pulled out the latest inventory record dated October 31, 1966, it showed no form of curare. The investigators were not satisfied, and they prodded him to look through his supplies. While the two county detectives waited, he found four blue boxes containing vials of tubarine, manufactured by Burroughs & Wellcome. The pharmacist was surprised, because he had never ordered any, and he was sure of that.

At the suggestion of the pharmacist, the detectives went to interview his predecessor as hospital pharmacist, and they learned from him that tubarine was used frequently by an anesthesiologist who had left Riverdell during his time. He said that he had always ordered it from Burroughs & Wellcome in Tuckahoe, New York. According to the former pharmacist after this particular anesthesiologist left Riverdell, the drug wasn't used by anyone else.

The detectives went back to Riverdell again, to see if a further search would turn up any more curare. It did. In the pharmaceutical locker they found another tubarine vial and one vial of a similar product manufactured by the Squibb Pharmaceutical Company. The refrigerator in the operating room contained one opened 10-cc vial of tubarine, which one of the nurses told them had been there for at least six months, and that according to her knowledge, it was really not used at Riverdell.

A few days later the detectives interviewed Dr. Arthur F. DeMarco, Riverdell's chief anesthesiologist. He told them that about a year before, he had used tubarine himself on at least one occasion, and he knew that it was kept in the hospital. He also said he knew that a previous anesthesiologist had used it.

To complete their investigation, one of Calissi's investigators put in a call to the old Burroughs & Wellcome Company across the Hudson River in Tuckahoe, New York, and asked them to check their records of sales of tubarine to Riverdell Hospital. The pharmaceutical company was able to confirm that it had made six shipments of its curare product to Riverdell during the years 1960 through 1966, and its lot numbers matched those on the bottles and vials of tubarine that were found in Jascalevich's locker, in the pharmacy, and in the operating room.

Dr. Frieman and Dr. Lans were asked again if either of them was aware of any use of curare at Riverdell; neither was.

That was the totality of the investigators' effort to identify the drug's presence at Riverdell and its use there. There were several significant gaps in these efforts, because a number of people who may have been more familiar with the use of curare by certain anesthesiologists were not interviewed.

Obviously, the extent of each physician's or nurse's knowledge of the presence or use of curare at the hospital depended upon his or her own particular practice or experience. Although it was certainly used at Riverdell occasionally, those who were not involved with its use had no reason to be aware of it.

CHAPTER XVII

A Variety of Medical Examiners

I hope that at some future time people who look back at this story and at these days will wonder about the extent to which justice could be achieved in a civilization that was unable to mobilize all of its scientific resources. In our present state of organization, or disorganization, it is the office of the medical examiner that is designed to be the most effective link in a chain of institutional devices dedicated to the scientific detection of criminal behavior, as well as the discovery of medical mistakes—before they are buried.

Why did it take ten years for the story of what happened at Riverdell Hospital in 1966 to come to public attention, and why was the Bergen County prosecutor's original investigation so inconclusive? To answer these two critical questions requires that we understand one of the most significant inadequacies in the American system of criminal justice. The fact is that when it comes time to deal with that class of complex or out-of-the-ordinary crimes whose solution depends upon medical or scientific knowledge, our system just doesn't work, except under the most ideal circumstances or in a relatively few places. It is for this reason that poison is the most common weapon of the physician-killer.

Little is ever said about the importance of the role of physicians, dentists, pathologists, toxicologists, chemists, medical examiners, or coronors, because when their forensic work is deficient, violent crimes may easily go unsolved or even unnoticed—and they do. And, in many places, society continues to depend on the old-fashioned county coroner.

County coroners were the predecessors of medical examiners. The office of county coroner can be traced back to 1194 in England, when he was a most important representative of the Crown, from which the name *coroner* actually derives. In those days the royal concern for the dead stemmed from the Crown's pecuniary interest in the deceased's estate.

The first functional English coroner, established by the Coroners Act of 1887, was appointed by the freeholders of the county, just as he is in New Jersey today, and in most of the counties in America. Coroners are usually elected or appointed at the county level of government.

For that reason, the post is frequently a patronage reward given to the local mortician who has contributed the most to the party in power, or to the party's favorite physician, without regard to his qualifications as a pathologist or toxicologist. Ranking third among the primary occupations of American coroners, behind physicians and morticians, are, naturally enough, plumbers, perhaps because they are at least familiar with pipes and connections.

The New York City medical examiner's office is uniquely effective, and the key to understanding it is the statute which was enacted to establish it in 1918 by the New York City Council. The councilmen followed the example of an 1877 Massachusetts law, but New York City became the first American jurisdiction to require that its chief medical examiner must be qualified both as a pathologist and a skilled microscopist. The law gives the medical examiner the authority to do autopsies when he deems it appropriate, thus eliminating the need for family consent, which in other communities has thwarted many investigations. The New York City law also prescribes minimum requirements as to what must be included in the autopsy. The city's health code demands that every death be certified and the cause of death reported before burial can take place.

Where criminal violence is suspected, two trained medical examiners must participate in the autopsy, review the findings, and sign the report. Under New York City procedures, the body is dissected during autopsy and each vital organ examined, while tests of blood, tissue, hair, fingernail scrapings, semen, and other appropriate material are routinely made as deemed appropriate to each case. In homicide cases, even the victim's clothing becomes an integral part of the autopsy procedure.

In explaining his own techniques, Dr. Helpern emphasized the importance of thoroughly examining bodies, no matter how decayed, or otherwise odorous; even the parts of bodies that have been partially destroyed require close examination. Helpern said, "It is not a job for the surgical pathologist or the hospital pathologist who is unhappy if an autopsy has to be done more than a few hours after death."

Dr. Helpern had hundreds of grisly stories to report of cases where the real causes of a mysterious death were revealed by careful examination of every aspect of the cadaver despite what may have originally appeared to be more obvious explanations. Dr. Helpern could solve crimes where those called "medical examiners" in other jurisdictions had been unable to do so. Sometimes it was only a matter of practiced thoroughness which enabled Helpern and his well-trained colleagues to find a discreet needle mark in an unlikely site such as an armpit, which had been overlooked by a less experienced examiner. It was such a tiny needle mark in the victim's rump that led Dr. Helpern to the solution of the famous Coppolino case, where a physician had used a curare-like drug to murder his wife.

The fact is that in the overwhelming majority of jurisdictions, this sort of thorough procedure is either nonexistent, or the important job is performed by unqualified people who regularly provide the authorities with totally erroneous explanations because of incompetence, distaste, or lack of genuine interest in the job.

There are simply not enough properly qualified and trained people to go around. At present, there are only 341 board-certified and practicing forensic pathologists in the United States. Board certification was not even established until 1959, and to be eligible to take these boards, a physician requires training in one of the only twenty-five forensic training centers that exist across America. That training includes experience in performing at least 300 autopsies under expert supervision.

There are few places in this world which provide facilities anything like those found in the New York City chief medical examiner's office, with its 160 employees and $3 million annual budget. Under Dr. Milton Helpern's guidance, the degree of professionalism and scientific resources reached its present pinnacle.

Dr. Helpern devoted his life to the improvement of his own highly specialized branch of medicine. He wrote prolifically, lectured frequently, and always exuded an infectious brand of enthusiasm. A sort of mystique grew up around his glamorous role of medical detective, and he played it to the hilt in order to develop the needed support of the city's newspapers and a long string of different mayors, budget directors, and city councilmen. Thus did he maintain the financial support necessary to achieve his high standards of service.

Elsewhere in America, with only a few large metropolitan areas as exceptions, complete inadequacy prevails. Nobody can say how many capital crimes and horrendous medical errors go undetected as a result.

In 1966, Bergen County was relatively rare among American counties in that it did have an office of chief medical examiner; but while the law required that the incumbent be a physician, there was no requirement that he have either the training or facilities necessary to do the job properly.

As a result of major legislative reform in 1971, modern science was made available to New Jersey law enforcement officials through the creation of an Office of State Medical Examiner with authority to supervise and consult in certain aspects of the medical examiner's work in each county, and to provide a statewide facility where needed. But in 1966 that wasn't the case—no statewide medical examiner's office existed and there was no official channel for a county medical examiner to obtain expert assistance when he needed it.

In New Jersey, then as now, the county chief medical examiner is appointed by the elected board of freeholders of the county. The state law describes the medical examiner's responsibilities as similar to those found in most other places. The medical examiner is required to investigate fully the essential facts in every case where a person dies in a suspicious or unusual manner, and a number of particular examples of such deaths are set forth in the governing statute. Included in these situations are cases of violence, casualty, suicide, or otherwise sudden deaths where a person is in apparently good health and unattended by a physician. There is no requirement to notify the medical examiner if a physician is in attendance. The county medical examiner is also empowered to perform autopsies whenever he deems it appropriate.

A major problem, however, even in 1966 in New Jersey, was the lack of qualifications for the official charged with responsibility for determining cause of death in unexplained cases.

The medical examiner's job in New Jersey, as elsewhere, is essentially a political one, and the only qualifications prescribed by law in 1966, and now, is that the person chosen by the freeholders shall be a licensed doctor of medicine who resides in the county and is a person of "recognized ability and good standing in his community." The "recognized ability" need have no connection with the ability to perform the medical examiner's primary function of determining the cause of death in unusual cases. Any respectable psychiatrist, ophthalmolgist, or allergist would meet the criteria, and the fact that none of them would have the necessary training or experience that a pathologist could provide is not legally material.

In fairness to New Jersey, it should be reiterated that in the great majority of jurisdictions throughout the nation the coroner need not even be a physician.

In 1966, the Bergen County chief medical examiner was Dr. Raphael D. Gilady, a seventy-three-year-old native of Palestine who had been named chief medical officer of the county back in 1929. Gilady had been practicing medicine for forty years and learned about hospital pathology when he established the first pathology laboratory at Hackensack Hospital after completing his internship there. By 1966, because of his age, Gilady left most of the work of the medical examiner's office to his chief assistant, Dr. Lawrence J. Denson.

But Dr. Denson, who had been a member of the county medical examiner's staff since 1952, was not even a hospital pathologist. Denson was chief of cardiopulmonary services at Hackensack Hospital and an expert in cystic fibrosis, who maintained a general practice of medicine in Hackensack.

According to the local newspapers, Dr. Denson is known as an outgoing man whom many people in Bergen County consider to be a bit of a character, given to philosophizing about life. Denson perhaps derives some qualification from the fact that his father was an attorney who once served as a part-time assistant county prosecutor.

It was Dr. Denson whom Prosecutor Guy Calissi called in on the Riverdell case that night in November of 1966 when he began his investigation. In light of the availability of knowledge that did exist, there were two obvious questions about Prosecutor Calissi's

1966 investigation: What efforts were actually made to determine the presence of curare in any of the dead, and what other scientific facilities were utilized? The answer to both questions appears to be practically nothing.

It was Denson who ten years after the incident said, "I remember thinking at the time that it was very unlikely that curare could be found in bodies because of our lack of technology at that time."

It was Denson who had also made the amazing comment to the press, "It was my feeling that I was quite peripheral to the whole thing. I was assistant medical examiner, and I was only involved for the first five hours of the investigation. . . . I was not contacted after that." Yet he was the only representative of the medical examiner's office ever to be involved in the case.

Calissi, on the other hand, has explained that the experts told him that there was no hope of detecting curare in the victims through exhumation of their bodies, and he relied heavily on that opinion when he closed his investigation, even before he reviewed Dr. Umberger's final report.

Regarding the search for evidence of curare in the bodies of any of the deceased, it appears that the only thing that was done was the single effort to examine the sliver of Shaw tissue, which was done by Dr. Helpern's office at the time of my intrusion into the matter. Dr. Denson and the Bergen County medical examiner's office made no apparent effort. This is borne out by Denson's more recent statement about the level of his own involvement. The fact that the county medical examiner took no independent action remains a glaring deficiency—unfortunately typical of the system that prevailed nationwide.

Calissi had received a report from the consulting laboratory that examined the needles taken from Jascalevich's locker, which did confirm that there was dog hair and dog blood present in at least one of the needles.

When Dr. Gilady resigned in July of 1968, it was Dr. Denson whom the county freeholders named as chief medical examiner. While Denson's stewardship of that office has been marked by very few controversies, there was one incident that sheds some light on the problems of administering this function.

In 1976 the body was found of a little eleven-year-old girl who had been missing since 1970. Initially, Dr. Denson announced that his examination revealed that she had been dead for only six months and the body appeared to be of a girl in her late teens. Joseph Woodcock, the county prosecutor, protested that the body had obviously been dead for six years, because the little girl was still wearing the same clothes as when she was reported missing. This forced Denson to look again, and after bone tests by the state medical examiner's facility confirmed that he had been mistaken, he revised his analysis and admitted that indeed the body had been dead for about six years.

Clearly, it was the competence of the medical examiner's office that was critical to the investigation of the Riverdell affair, and, when combined with the prosecutor's failure to pursue other avenues of assistance, became the decisive factor in terminating the 1966 investigation. The responsibility for the inconclusive nature of that investigation belongs primarily to the Bergen County medical examiner.

As the spring turned into summer in 1967, I felt like a character in a story without an ending: neither guilt nor innocence had been established, and the official and unofficial efforts to resolve the question had amounted to nothing. My own nature is such that despite my having no official responsibility, I could not accept the nonresolution of such a serious matter, so I assumed that some day something more must come of it all.

Whenever I saw Allan after a gap of more than a few weeks, our conversation would always open with the same question: "Have you heard anything about Jascalevich?" But the answer was always, "No."

PART IV

CHAPTER XVIII

A Decade Later

It was late in August of 1975 on peaceful Martha's Vineyard. The sun on Lucy Vincent Beach was brilliant, and it combined with a warm sea breeze which twisted the thin pages to make any careful reading of my *New York Times* too complicated a task, no matter how artfully I folded it. I was limiting my effort to a page-by-page check of the headlines, when one of them suddenly brought ten-year-old memories into sharp focus. It became the only article I would read in detail that day.

The headline that caught my attention on Sunday, August 31, 1975, on page 30, read, "Two More Patients Die at VA Hospital in Michigan," and the subheading, "Murder Hinted in the Death of a Retired Landscaper Who Had Been in a Coma." The three-column account told of a special office of the FBI being established in the Ann Arbor Veterans Administration Hospital, where 10 patients had died in an outbreak of respiratory failures which were being investigated as possible murder cases. Hospital officials had confirmed that the latest victim appeared to have been murdered by a deliberate injection of Pavulon, a paralyzing drug of the curare family, which is also used to suppress breathing during surgery.

Instantly I thought that someone from Riverdell Hospital had made his way to Michigan. Until that moment, a long time had passed since I had given the case much consideration. At the close of the 1966 investigation, Allan Lans and I were both convinced that if our suspicions about what had happened at Riverdell were true, it would occur elsewhere, and that some day, somewhere, it would have to come to light. Then our old suspicions would be vindicated. Was this that moment?

I watched the papers carefully for a few days, expecting the imminent announcement of the arrest of somebody whose name I would find familiar; but there was no follow-up story.

When I returned to New York the following week, I called FBI headquarters in New York to tell them about the Riverdell Hospital affair in 1966. As I dialed, I considered how such a call would be received. I was reluctant to become either an informer or a crank, but felt compelled by a haunting sense of obligation to facilitate justice.

The bureau has a system for handling such matters. It works this way. An information-intake clerk—not an agent—writes down whatever the caller tells her. She is unhurried and clearly trained to pin down names, places, and dates. I gave her an earful. In response, she would only say that the information would be passed to an appropriate person for review, and if they wanted anything else from me, they would call. An understandable position for the bureau, but most frustrating for the conscientious informer.

Nothing happened.

Three weeks passed. It was 7 P.M., and toward the end of a business meeting with some clients in my law office conference room, my secretary, Helen Guelpa, came in to say that a reporter from the *New York Times* was on the phone and had asked her to interrupt me. His name was unfamiliar, not one of the business or political reporters I knew. Curiosity compelled me to take the call.

"This is Myron Farber of the *New York Times.* Are you the same Matthew Lifflander that had some correspondence with the Bergen County prosecutor in 1966?"

I connected this call with the *New York Times* story on the Ann Arbor Hospital and my recent call to the FBI. I assumed that he must be covering the Michigan case.

"Yes," I answered, probing cautiously. "Did you know that I called the FBI?" Without hesitation, the voice said: "I assumed you did."

"Are you working on that story?"

"Not exactly. I'm working on the Bergen County story and I'm trying to figure out what you had to do with it. Will you talk to me about it?"

My spirits lifted—a decade of frustration might be coming to an end. Did this mean new hope that there was a chance to solve the mystery of the Riverdell deaths? I had always believed that the most likely way for the case ever to be reexamined would be if a

Reporter Myron Farber

good newspaperman, backed by all the resources of an important paper, would commit the time necessary to follow every lead and develop every clue. Suddenly, that possibility seemed to be momentarily at hand.

"I've been waiting for you for ten years," I said. "When can we get together?"

Farber was available and invited himself to meet me for dinner in half an hour.

My enthusiasm compelled me to explain the phone call in an

abbreviated form to my clients, who had been patiently awaiting my attention while listening to my end of the conversation. As our conference broke up, they were intrigued, but obviously incredulous. From the very few times that I had ever told the story I had learned that listeners found it impossible to believe.

Farber showed up at 7:45; he looked like he had been typecast to play the role of an ace investigative reporter. Very short and bearded, with dashing bright eyes in an intelligent face, he was in appropriate costume—a fully buttoned-up trenchcoat. He seemed to be enjoying his job immensely.

We completed amenities in the office and went around the corner to a local pub before getting down to cases. Upon my opening prod, Farber confessed that he did not know about my call to the FBI, but he was aware of the Ann Arbor story, and that others who knew the Riverdell story had also called the bureau. He told me that he had been working on the Riverdell story since mid-July, and that he had gained access to all the old files of the Bergen County prosecutor. In those files he found one of my letters to Calissi or one of his to me, and he couldn't understand what a vice president of Hertz Rent-A-Car could possibly have to do with such a matter.

I explained to Farber how my friend Allan Lans had come to me for help, and I summarized some of the things we had done back in 1966 and 1967. While Farber listened attentatively, he also seemed eager to get to his next question as I finished my brief summary by saying, ". . . Essentially we failed—despite an intensive effort and the hundreds of hours of time that I put into it, there was no result."

Then came Farber's next question: "Why did you get so involved?"

After all those years, he made me realize that I had never asked myself that question, let alone answered it. The fact was that it had just happened. I had been intrigued by the situation, and it had seemed so important at the time that I never examined my own motivation. But the question was a fair one, and I replied slowly: "Understand that Allan Lans was my closest friend. He is a very responsible person and our relationship was such that helping each other with any problem was something we both did.

"Besides, I must admit that there is a certain excitement about the challenge in this case. There was a chance to help correct an injustice. If that takes my time, it's worth it."

I asked Farber how he had come upon this story. According to his account, a woman had come to the *Times* a few months before and told them about the strange series of deaths at an unnamed hospital in New Jersey. Her apparent motive was to get the *Times* people interested in helping her investigate this affair, and in exchange for their doing so, she was offering them the inside track on the news story and credit in a book that she wanted to write on the subject. Farber told me she refused to reveal the precise details about names and places until she had some commitment for mutual cooperation. He said that no agreement was made with this woman because it would not be appropriate for the *Times* to do so. As a result of her tip, he had called some contacts he had at the New York City medical examiner's office, where he found that the story rang a familiar bell, and someone was able either to recall the Riverdell case or to find a file on it. Farber and the *New York Times* thus identified the pertinent facts without relying on their original informer or having to make any deal with her, enabling them subsequently to cut her out of the picture.

Ironically, the reason that Farber had been able to get the information he needed from the medical examiner's office was that he had established communications there when he wrote a series of articles about that office a year or so before. That series was highly critical of Dr. Milton Helpern's administration of the medical examiner's office, and made a number of charges about carelessness in the disposal of cadavers and some rather bizarre accusations about the use and disposal of some human bones. One of his stories even had Dr. Helpern using a skull for an ash tray. The series had the effect of casting a dark shadow on Dr. Helpern personally at the very twilight of his illustrious career. It affected Helpern deeply, as he considered it to be the result of a deliberate "hatchet job" by some of his ambitious would-be successors, and he detested Farber for his role.

Once Farber identified the fact that the 1966 deaths had happened at Riverdell Hospital in Bergen County, he somehow made another contact through which he obtained access to the entire file from Calissi's original investigation, all of which had been sent to a warehouse.

Farber was now spending almost all of his time on this case, and he admitted that he and his editor considered the effort to be worthwhile. By the time he got to me, he said, he had already satisfied himself through conversations with experts that there really was a possibility curare could be detected in exhumed bodies, even after a number of years had passed.

Farber revealed that he had also talked with Joseph Woodcock, who was then the Bergen County prosecutor, and had concluded that Woodcock could be persuaded to reopen the matter.

Farber had also reached some of the people who were involved with Calissi's original investigation, probably somebody in the prosecutor's office. It was also clear that evening in early September when we first met that Farber had not yet talked with Calissi, or Galda, or any physician at Riverdell.

There was comfort in the knowledge that an apparently competent newspaperman, supported by the resources of the *New York Times,* was now putting so much effort into a case I had long presumed a dead issue. This seemed to be an opportunity to salvage justice, and I was glad to help.

As Farber told me about his effort, he also revealed some key elements of his technique. What I saw was the quiet exuberance of a man who took the opportunity his work afforded him to play all the roles in life that he wanted to play. He came across as a working Walter Mitty. He knew when to lower his voice for dramatic effect, when to look furtive, and when to say nothing in order to imply something.

I think it was to impress me with his thoroughness that Farber told me that the next morning he was going to pick up a wire recorder, of a type no longer available, so that he could hear an old recording that he had obtained of Jascalevich's original testimony in the prosecutor's office. He had been frustrated by the fact that the transcript of that testimony was missing from the prosecutor's otherwise complete 1966 files. It was then that I made my first contribution to Mr. Farber's effort.

"I have that transcript," I told him, when he stopped talking for the first time.

"No, I'm talking about the transcript of the five hours of testimony that Jascalevich gave when he was called in by Calissi. I understand it contains his alibi," said Farber. "It's missing from the files."

Apparently, he had missed the significance of my words. "Yes, I know," I said. "Calissi gave me that transcript ten years ago. I had no idea it was his only copy; he didn't ask that it be returned. I showed it to Dr. Helpern with Calissi's consent for Helpern's opinion, and it's been in my basement file at home for all these years. As a matter of fact, I can recall the way I filed it—under the label 'Dr. X'—I didn't even want to have the man's name on my file jacket."

Farber could not contain his excitement. "Can I see it? Can I see it?"

"Of course," I said, "I'll make you a copy during the week."

"No, I need to see it tomorrow! I have an appointment in New Jersey in the morning, and having the chance to review it first is critical," said Farber, demonstrating his persistent singleness of purpose.

Sometimes I felt that he needed to be a better listener, because he would never get off the direction his thought was pursuing until he had absorbed every detail that he could think of. I had a hard time suggesting elements that I thought important. I explained to Farber all I could recall of the case and told him that I also had some correspondence and hospital records in my files which I would make available to him. I anticipated that reviewing them might trigger some additional recollections for me.

"How can I get these from you tomorrow?" he asked, eager to see the file before his 10 A.M. appointment in New Jersey. For mutual convenience, we agreed to meet at 9:00 the next morning at the western end of 125th Street on the Hudson River, under the West Side Highway. Farber also agreed to call me again the next afternoon to give me his reaction to the papers that I had agreed to deliver.

Before we broke up, we exchanged home and office phone numbers. As I wrote down his, Farber uttered the perfect line to end Act One: "You can call me at any hour of the night."

Obviously, the most effective investigator never sleeps.

At precisely 9:30 the next morning, I found Myron Farber behind the wheel of his Audi Fox, trenchcoat collar turned up and

Irish tweed fedora turned down, parked in that out-of-the-way corner of Manhattan Island that we had selected. I pulled alongside so that our cars faced opposite directions, and without getting out of my car, handed him my fat red file labeled "Dr. X." He promised that he would copy what he needed and return it all before the end of the week, and drove off.

During the next few months, Myron Farber became an important part of my life. Hardly a day went by when we didn't talk, sometimes three or four times and at all hours of the night. He didn't sleep very much and neither did I.

My role was to answer his questions to the extent that I could, to be a sounding board for ideas and reactions to new information as he developed it, and occasionally to make suggestions. Farber proceeded in a thoroughly professional manner and deserves both credit and responsibility for causing the prosecutor's office to reopen their investigation. Fortunately, the law in New Jersey provides no statute of limitations in murder cases.

The little man from the *Times* was one of the most expert users of other people that I had ever had the pleasure of observing. He did so relentlessly and efficiently, never failing to follow up to make sure that his bidding was done. He was ingenious at getting what he wanted, and the fact was that he could not be deterred from his objectives.

These qualities of Farber's were illustrated by one silly incident which is otherwise irrelevant to the case itself, but which illustrates the investigative reporter's techniques.

Farber had left his favorite pipe and tobacco pouch on my desk one afternoon along with an envelope of documents I had found for him, and by nightfall he drove by our Madison Avenue office building and asked the night guard if he would let him into my office to pick up his pipe. The guard, an extremely reliable man, refused. Whereupon Farber began a forty-minute effort at persuasion, which included showing his identification papers, using the prestige of the *Times* itself, establishing his relationship with me and his familiarity with my office, and mustering every ounce of persistence and persuasion necessary to wear the man down, eventually gaining supervised entry. He even promised that he wouldn't mention to me how he had recovered the pipe and envelope.

Late the next afternoon, a phone call came from Farber, gloating over his accomplishment and suggesting that the night man should be fired for giving in. Fortunately, the guard had come to work early to tell me about the incident and how he had been pressured.

Farber's effectiveness as an investigator comes not only from his own diligence, but from the fact that newspapers enjoy some unusual special relationship to the rest of society, which gives them and their representatives tremendous power. Such power hits not only their readers, but people they interview and write about, as well as public officials—especially elected ones, whose very political survival can depend upon what the papers tell their constituents. People who are interviewed by reporters respond out of either hope or fear of getting their names in the paper, which can be a most seductive force in light of its effect on people's careers and egos.

Once he had the opportunity to read the transcript of Jascalevich's 1966 testimony carefully, Farber began to check out the alibi by contacting Sal Riggi, who had been in charge of the animal quarters at Seton Hall College Medical School when Jascalevich said he was obtaining dying dogs there for his curare experiments.

Farber had brought the transcript with him, and he asked Riggi to review the pertinent portions. Apparently, the prosecutor's detectives in 1966 had neglected to show Riggi the transcript. Riggi looked it over, and according to Farber he said, "We just didn't have any dying dogs or any research in the quarters, and I'll swear to that in court or on my father's grave. The dogs were stored here and sent out to laboratories." (I wondered how to reconcile this statement with Dr. Boccabella's original confirmation that Jascalevich had done dog experiments for the American Cancer Society there—but Boccabella, who had apparently not been told of Jascalevich's statement, was probably referring to an earlier period of time.)

Farber had Riggi identify the attendants who had worked for him in 1965 and 1966, and he named Dewey Mincey and Lee Henderson. These were among the "colored fellows" that Dr. Jascalevich had described to Calissi as the sweepers who, in exchange for a two dollar tip, had provided him with access to the dogs that were dying and strapped to a table after being used by other experimenters.

Farber also interviewed Dewey Mincey, who he said corroborated Riggi's statements. Mincey said that this was the first time anyone had asked him about the matter. Nobody from the prosecutor's office had interviewed him in 1966.

Farber then began to search for Lee Henderson, the other sweeper at the animal quarters during the time Jascalevich had described, who was apparently the man that Jascalevich had told Calissi was named "Lee." The detectives had tried to find Lee at the time, but when they heard that he had left his family in Jersey City and moved south, they never followed up this lead. Farber did.

With the help of County Welfare Department records, Farber traced Lee to the little South Carolina town of Whitmire, where Farber went to visit him. When Henderson was told about Jascalevich's story, Farber reported that he said, "I don't know what the man is talking about." Farber told me he obtained a sworn statement that said Henderson never received a tip from anyone in return for providing dogs in any condition, dying or otherwise; that the former sweeper never saw any experiments conducted in the animal quarters; and that he never saw a dog strapped to a table there either.

As he proceeded to reconstruct the old investigation and fill in its gaps, Farber kept Prosecutor Woodcock's office informed of his progress. His conversations with Woodcock combined new information with questions about the investigation and why it should be reopened.

While all this was going on, Woodcock had provided Dr. Michael Baden, then the deputy chief medical examiner of New York City, with copies of the original autopsy reports, which Baden was reviewing while he also gathered information on the latest methods of the detection of curare in cadavers.

One week had passed since I had first met Myron Farber. One long telephone call after another, at all hours of day or the night, had made it seem as though we had already spent a month of activity, when he asked if I thought that my old friend Dr. Lans, would be willing to talk with him about the matter. Farber had still not contacted any of the Riverdell doctors.

Having to tell Allan that the Jascalevich affair was about to be aired in public was not a pleasant prospect, but the need to pursue this matter to a conclusion motivated me to invite him to meet with my new colleague.

When I told Allan the particulars that had occasioned the call, there was a long silence and then a resigned reply: "I'm not surprised—I always knew it wasn't over, that some day the subject would somehow come up again. . . . Matt, you know this won't be easy."

It was 7:30 in the evening in early October, the day after my call, when Allan came to meet with Farber in my office. There we spent two hours before remembering to go out to dinner.

At first, Allan appeared to be somewhat reticent in response to Farber's questions. Obviously, he was already beginning to feel the weight of the burden which was now in the process of descending upon him fully after the long respite. He was, as he later confided to me, rather suspicious of Farber himself because the impact of the potential publicity would be so pervasive, and after his earlier experience with the clumsy process of law, it wasn't quite apparent to Allan that Farber's efforts could really lead to more effective action by the authorities. Nevertheless, Allan responded fully and deliberately to each of Farber's questions, none of which came as any surprise to him.

Farber, whose style is such that he first gives each person he interviews the feeling that he doesn't believe him, was treating my old friend very suspiciously. Farber was really trying to ascertain how Alan felt about the matter and just how protective he would be about his hospital.

The fencing, for which I was not prepared, went on at peak intensity for the first hour, then gradually wore down as the evening proceded. Eventually they communicated well, especially after Farber had the opportunity to compare Allan's openness and helpfulness with the attitudes of his colleagues at Riverdell Hospital.

Allan confirmed everything that I had already related to Farber and added a number of details that had long ago slipped my mind. Farber asked Allan, "After Jascalevich left the hospital, and the investigation was over, what did you think in retrospect?"

"I was sure that something terrible had happened to at least some of those patients, if not all of them. Remember, to me they were people I knew or had probably seen when they were alive. It's a small community and a small hospital, and I would constantly run across these people or their families."

Farber was beginning to realize that he was dealing with a sensitive person. Toward the end of the two-hour interview, one of Farber's questions exacted a response from Allan that summarized so much: "How long has it been since you've had any occasion to think about this?" he asked Allan. The reply came promptly, but very softly:

"I've thought about this every day for the last nine years."

During the next few weeks, whenever Farber needed information about the hospital or the people there, he would ask me to ask Allan, but gradually they began to talk directly. Allan agreed to provide whatever else might be helpful to the *Times* reporter, and fell into stride with the new investigation. Soon he too was spending long hours on the phone answering Farber's questions, and we would find ourselves comparing notes about Farber's phone hours, and the point of his questions.

Allan refused Farber's request to introduce him to the other doctors at Riverdell, since he felt that to do so might be interpreted as a project he was sponsoring.

Except for Stanley Harris, Farber's initial effort to interview the doctors at Riverdell resulted in various forms of rejection.

The first to be called by Farber was one of the other physician-directors of Riverdell. Farber told me that he introduced himself as a *Times* reporter who would like to ask him a few questions about a matter which occurred at Riverdell Hospital in 1966 involving the use of the drug curare. The doctor hesitated momentarily, then said, "I don't have any idea what you are referring to. There is nothing for us to talk about." Farber, as usual, persisted: "It involved the deaths of a number of patients." Whereupon the director replied, "I've never heard anything about it; you must have the wrong man," and then hung up.

Apparently, others got the word. A second director called by Farber answered and then hung up as soon as he heard who was calling. A third simply refused to take Farber's call.

Of the four directors besides Lans, only Dr. Frieman was forthright with Farber at the time of these initial calls. He didn't deny the existence of the matter; he just told him that he would not discuss it.

The reporter was absolutely shocked by the reaction of Dr. Robert Briski, the earliest surgeon at Riverdell who had left there shaken to his core, after his patients started dying mysteriously in 1965 and 1966. Briski was now practicing in Traverse City, Michigan, where Farber located him. The reporter told me that when he came to the phone and heard Farber mention the name of Jascalevich, "The man started screaming at me; the more I went on, the more he screamed. He said something about never wanting anything more to do with that again. 'Leave me alone!' Briski must have been deeply affected by Jascalevich—that's all I could get out of him, but it was clear that he knew what I was talking about."

When Farber called Dr. Stanley Harris, he found a different reception. Harris seemed willing to talk and told him that he would get back to him shortly, and he called Allan Lans promptly to tell him that he had heard from the reporter. Lans allowed that he was not surprised and told Harris about his meeting with Farber in my office. Harris asked Lans to find out if I would set up the meeting and accompany him. He too was a little leery of the situation.

I decided against it, because there was no purpose. Instinct told me that another meeting with Harris would be repetitious.

So Stanley Harris got back to Myron Farber through his own attorney. While his interviews were never discussed with me in any real detail, it appears from subsequent newspaper accounts that Harris was not reticent about portraying his own role in uncovering the matter. From reading Farber's stories, one can also conclude that as Harris recalled the events of nine years before, he seems to have forgotten how closely Allan Lans participated in that effort.

Farber also tried to interview Calissi, who was now a New Jersey Superior Court judge, but was unable to get an appointment.

Fred Galda was willing to talk to Farber. He too had achieved the pinnacle of his political horizon, a seat on the Superior Court bench. When he went to see Judge Galda, Farber learned one significant new fact—that it was Galda, not I, who had the original file copy of the transcript of Jascalevich's testimony from the prosecutor's office. He showed it to Farber and said that he took it with him when he left the prosecutor's office because the story so fascinated him that he was considering writing a book about it one day.

News of the developing mystery of the VA Hospital in Ann Arbor acted as a reminder to a number of the people who had been aware of the Riverdell Hospital story in 1966. The FBI received several calls like mine, although I had no reason to be aware of it at the time. As a matter of fact, the deeper we got into the revival of the investigation, the more curious I became about whether or not there could be any possible link, especially because throughout the fall and early winter of 1976, the newspaper accounts of the lack of progress in the Michigan case kept revealing facts that were sounding more and more familiar. I finally satisfied myself on this point by a direct call to the FBI agent in charge of the Ann Arbor case, from whom I learned that they had already heard from the Bergen County prosecutor's office with sufficient details to be sure that none of the Riverdell players had access to the VA Hospital in Ann Arbor.

But Michigan did play a different and more practical role in this tale, because it was the appearance of that story that made people in Mr. Woodcock's office start reviewing their file again in order to provide information to the FBI. It was fortuitous too, because by the time the Midwest story made the news, Farber was already into his review of Calissi's files and had talked with Woodcock about it, so the two events had a separate but similar inpact on Mr. Woodcock and caused him to consider what more there was for his office to do.

After Myron Farber found Lee Henderson in South Carolina and told Woodcock about the deposition he had obtained from him which apparently refuted Jascalevich's testimony, and how he corroborated this with Dewey Mincey and Sal Riggi's statements, Woodcock realized the value of this information. The significance of the failure of Calissi's office to contact either Mincey or Henderson became clear. Their testimony could be critical, and Woodcock knew that he had to do something.

The key was to be provided by Dr. Michael Baden, a protege of Dr. Helpern, and extremely well qualified in his own right. He had become one of the nation's leading forensic pathologists. A forty-three-year-old, board-certified anatomic, clinical, and forensic pathologist, he teaches forensic medicine at the medical schools of both New York University and Albert Einstein, two prestigious institutions in this field. Mike Baden is a straightforward person with a finely honed sense of public responsibility, an articulate man who knows his business.

Farber had little trouble kindling Dr. Baden's interest in the Riverdell affair and getting Woodcock to ask him to review the old files.

Dr. Baden came to the same conclusion that Helpern had before him. Based on the autopsy reports and hospital records, a number of the patients described in these reports did not die of the causes attributed on the death certificates that were issued at the time.

Of the thirteen cases that Baden reviewed, he concluded that four of the deaths appeared to have been caused by the patients' illnesses, nine were at least "suspicious," and six of these could be classified as "highly suspicious." Dr. Baden told Woodcock that respiratory arrests do not usually occur in people without either heart or lung disease. His determinations were supported, he said, by the circumstances surrounding the deaths.

As a result of the VA Hospital case and Farber's intervention, Woodcock had his staff review the complete 1966 file, including the transcript of Jascalevich's testimony to Calissi. When Woodcock heard Dr. Baden's conclusions about the erroneous attribution of certain of the causes of death, concurrently with the discovery through Farber's effort that there were witnesses who refuted Jascalevich's testimony, he was ready to reopen the investigation.

The question that had not been answered in 1966 was whether or not curare could be detected in the remains of corpses which had been embalmed and buried ten years before.

Baden was ready to provide the necessary answer to that one as well. He knew of new techniques that did not exist in 1966 and that could now be used; moreover, he was convinced that curare is such a stable compound chemically that it could still exist in the bodies of alleged victims.

Woodcock's response to this news was that it might be worthwhile to exhume bodies even if he needed a court order and the permission of relatives to do so.

Woodcock assigned one of his least experienced assistant prosecutors to go to work on the case, an attorney named Sybil Moses, who had recently graduated from law school. Utilizing the knowledge imparted by Dr. Baden, she prepared an affidavit which was designed to convince a Superior Court judge to sign the necessary order of exhumation.

In this key affidavit, Dr. Baden explained that at the county prosecutor's request, he had reviewed the medical records of thirteen patients who died at Riverdell Hospital between December 13, 1965, and October 23, 1966. He had reviewed chemical findings, hospital course, and autopsies in those cases where they were performed. Baden's conclusion was:

> . . . it is my professional opinion that the majority of the cases reviewed are not explainable on the basis of natural causes and are consistent with having been caused by a respiratory-depressant.

Dr. Baden's affidavit spelled out the other key information:

> The ability to identify d-tubocurarine, often referred to as curare, in human tissue, was limited at the time of the initial investigation.
>
> It is my professional opinion that recent technological advances now permit the detecting of very minute amounts of d-tubocurarine in tissue removed from dead bodies. This is because d-tubocurarine is a chemically stable compound that can exist embalmed for many years.
>
> Therefore, the aforementioned new techniques to detect curare-like compounds can be applied to tissue removed from bodies that have been interred for long periods of time.

Baden concluded that, in his professional opinion, exhumation, autopsy, and reexamination were warranted to determine the validity of the causes of death originally attributed at the time and in order to attempt to detect curare with the techniques now available.

The prosecutor's course was now set. On the first working day of the new year, January 2, 1976, Mrs. Moses filed her papers in court to request a hearing on a motion to exhume bodies and initiate the autopsies.

CHAPTER XIX

Headlines

Nearly a decade had passed since the curare was discovered in Dr. Jascalevich's Riverdell Hospital locker.

The day was January 6, 1976, and Assistant County Prosecutor Sybil Moses had prepared her arguments for exhumation very carefully. Buttressed by Dr. Baden's expert analysis of the past and his opinion of the prospects for examination of exhumed bodies, the attorney's application for an order of exhumation anticipated each of the judge's concerns.

Included were consents of surviving relatives, along with the prosecutor's explanation of why they had decided to reopen this long-stale investigation. Mrs. Moses attributed the reopening of the investigation to two factors; "(1) newspaper articles indicating a series of similar deaths at the VA Hospital in Michigan during the Summer of 1975; and (2) questions and investigation by a reporter for the *New York Times.*"

Until this particular day, not one word of the entire affair had been disclosed in the *New York Times* or any other newspaper. Farber had held the matter in confidence, and in this regard, he and his editors had acted with a degree of responsibility not always found in the news media. The prosecutor gave the *Times* the credit it richly deserved. There can be no question that had the *Times* not permitted its resources to be utilized for the extensive work that Farber carried out over a period of five months, the case would never have been reopened. In these days when the economics of the newspaper business so rarely permit a reporter to work for so long on a single story, this was unusual. The fact that all of this could be accomplished without the paper having the advantage of even a single story to print during that time made the situation even more remarkable.

The prosecutor's office requested permission to exhume the five bodies which, based on Dr. Baden's study of thirteen of the cases, appeared to be the ones that might prove most fruitful for further investigation. The alleged victims whose cases the prosecutor proposed to review were Nancy Savino, Margaret Henderson, Emma Arzt, Carl Rohrbeck, and Frank Biggs. Orders were applied for on the first three of these during the initial session. The prosecutor had not yet obtained the necessary permission from next of kin in the Rohrbeck and Biggs cases, but these followed the next day and were filed with similar motions in New York, where their bodies had been buried.

Four other cases were also considered by prosecutor Woodcock as still "under investigation": Edith Post, Ira Holster, Mary Muetener, and Eileen Shaw.

Judge Theodore W. Trautwein signed the order in the Superior Court on the same day it was requested. It required the Bergen County medical examiner to supervise the removal of each body from the cemetery. Each was to be transferred to Dr. Baden's office in New York City for autopsy and examination to determine the cause of death and the presence of curare in the tissue. Then the body was to be reinterred.

The judge also placed responsibility for the actual disinterrment, transfer, and reinterrment on the county mortician, and he required the county sheriff's Identification Bureau to photograph the activities, with a representative of the prosecutor's office in attendance at all times.

The court imposed the cost of the entire procedure on the county prosecutor's budget.

The judge added a final condition—secrecy. He required that the entire record be sealed and that all persons to whom the order was directed refrain from disclosing anything about it.

The next day, the *New York Times* broke the story. It was page one material, and covered nearly a full page of copy inside. Rarely does any crime story get that much space in the *Times*. The next day, a second front-page article appeared on the case and received just about the same amount of space.

In these two articles, Farber related the details of what had happened in 1966, including the circumstances surrounding each of the questioned deaths and many of the details of Calissi's investigation. Jascalevich's name was withheld, the *Times* said, because he was still in practice and had not been charged with any crime. Just as he had been identified by me on the yellowing label of the file I had loaned to Farber, the doctor was introduced publicly by the *New York Times* as "Dr. X."

Except for the families of the deceased whose exhumations were under way (and who had been contacted by the prosecutor's office for their consent), this was the first time that any of the survivors heard of the Riverdell affair.

The *Times* stories of January 7 and 8, 1976, had the anticipated effect of generating major accounts in a number of other newspapers and all of the television stations that cover the metropolitan New York area. At first, the other stories were merely rewrites of the *Times* account. The *Record,* Bergen County's leading newspaper, began its own independent efforts as well, but they were able to come up with little more than what the *Times* already had.

The early editions of the *New York Times* reach the Hackensack, New Jersey offices of the *Record* sometime before midnight. The night people who work upstairs in the *Record*'s modern building routinely review the big city's paper to follow up on stories that should be of prime interest in their suburban area. This time they discovered that they had been scooped.

At five in the morning of January 7, one of the *Record*'s reporters was awakened by a call from his city desk, and Myron Farber's page one story was read to him over the phone.

An hour later, when the reporter arrived at the *Record*'s office, he was dispatched to find Mario Jascalevich to question him about the *Times* story. The desk man had already learned Jascalevich's name from hospital sources. All the reporter had to go on was Jascalevich's office address in seedy West New York, New Jersey. The reporter described his morning's work.

When he got to Jascalevich's office on the ground floor of a two-story building that was once residential, next door to the Hispanic Medical Clinic, it was 7:10 A.M. There was nobody around, and there was no answer when he pushed each of the several door bells.

He crossed the street to the West New York police headquarters to ask if anyone there knew Dr. Jascalevich. At first, there was nobody who knew his name. The cops asked the reporter why he wanted to know, and he showed them the *Times* article which he had carried with him. Then, one cop spoke up. He related that the doctor ". . . does a hell of a business. Sometimes there's a line twenty people long in the office, out the door, on the small stoop, and down the steps to the sidewalk."

By 8:00 A.M., the reporter was at Christ Hospital in Jersey City. He asked if Dr. Jascalevich was in and was informed that the doctor was already in surgery, with four procedures scheduled that morning. The reporter decided to wait in the hospital's main waiting room, and left a message for the surgeon to call him during any break.

While awaiting the surgeon's call, the *Record*'s man found Garrard P. Kramer, associate administrator of the hospital. He showed him the *New York Times* story, and after Kramer read about one-third of the story, the reporter asked him about Dr. Jascalevich. Kramer confirmed that Jascalevich was on staff with full attending privileges, had a good reputation, without any hints of trouble. He also said all Jascalevich's hospital peer reviews were within acceptable parameters.

The reporter continued his long wait. At ten minutes past one, he accosted Jascalevich between the hospital's emergency room entrance and the surgeon's 1973 Cadillac Coupe. The reporter introduced himself and asked for a word with the busy surgeon. Although Jascalevich never stopped walking, the reporter recalled that he responded effusively. He shook hands and placed his arm on the newspaperman's shoulder as they walked toward the parked Cadillac. The reporter showed Jascalevich the morning *Times* story. Jascalevich read the first paragraph and hurriedly handed the paper back, as though he was holding something terribly unpleasant. He said, "This is the first I know about this. . . . I've been in surgery all morning, I know nothing about this."

"You were on the staff of Riverdell at the time, doctor. Do you remember anything?"

"Please, I don't want to hurt you. . . . I respect your profession, I'm sure you respect mine; I really have nothing to say . . ."

"There have been some indications that you are the Dr. X in question."

"Please, I don't want to hurt you, but really, I have nothing to say about this."

"Did the *New York Times* try to reach you concerning this story?"

"I really have nothing to say, please, do not be offended, I just have nothing to say."

"You have my card, if you change your mind."

"Yes, yes, I have your card." Clasping the reporter's hand tightly, he said incongruously, "Let me wish you a Happy New Year."

Eventually, *Medical World News* and *Medical Economics* magazines, two of the leading national publications designed for physicians, did extensive stories, and later on, even *Newsweek* magazine gave the story almost a full page. It reached a point where almost everyone in the New York–New Jersey metropolitan area had heard about Dr. X., and thus pretrial publicity posed a potential legal problem for the prosecutors of the case should it ever come to trial. Sometimes, pretrial publicity can be held to prevent a jury from being able to render an impartial judgment, thus prohibiting a fair trial.

The impact of the publicity about such a bizarre series of alleged crimes was of far greater moment in human terms than the possible legal ramifications. Being a suburban community, Bergen County was hit especially hard, because people who live there prefer to think that the worst crimes are confined to the big city across the river. Besides, many of those who lived in the area served by Riverdell Hospital now had to consider whether they or their own friends or relatives were ever jeopardized by exposure to the newly disclosed menace.

The newspapers originally revealed very little about the suspected surgeon, except to say he was no longer at Riverdell, that he still practiced privately in New Jersey, and that he was affiliated with at least two other institutions. Such terse details caused people beyond the Riverdell area to wonder whether or not Dr. X was working at their own local hospital—or on them.

Everywhere, people were asking the question—Who is he? Worried callers telephoned their nearest hospital or their county medical society, demanding assurances that Dr. X wasn't their own physician.

The executive secretary of the Bergen County Medical Society reported that he had managed to calm down one hysterical caller who screamed at him, "What do you mean, letting that lunatic run around loose? If you don't put him behind bars immediately, I'm coming down there with a gun and shoot all of you."

There was a report that at one hospital, two doctors went separately to the administrator and told him that they were concerned that the other was Dr. X. Neither was.

At Riverdell Hospital itself, the atmosphere was tense and the directors were apprehensive about how the publicity would affect their future. Fortunately, the thrust of the initial stories was about the details of the alleged murders, and no real blame was attached to the hospital administration by the newspapers. As a matter of fact, the directors were credited with calling in the prosecutor and thus doing everything that could reasonably be expected. It would take some time before the impact of the story on Riverdell Hospital could be measured. On the advice of counsel and out of fear of being responsible for naming Dr. X publicly, the Riverdell people said very little.

Meanwhile, the local press had begun to seek out some of the relatives of the alleged victims in order to get their reactions. For this sensitive task, the *Record* selected two female reporters. They succeeded in finding relatives of five of the long-dead patients. The reactions of most of them were rather similar, and best summarized by the grandson of Emma Arzt, who told the reporters, "Her death seemed kind of strange, because she had been fine beforehand. But no one thought there was anything suspicious. When the doctor tells you something happened, you believe it."

CHAPTER XX

Reactions

Myron Farber told me he was in constant conversation with prosecutor Joseph Woodcock, and through Farber I learned that the prosecutor's office was awaiting the results of the pending autopsies before proceeding any further with its investigation. I was amazed when Farber told me that no effort had yet been made by Woodcock to speak with Jascalevich.

On Sunday, January 11, I happened to turn on a morning TV interview show, and caught a brief interview with Woodcock being queried about the case. At first sight, the man who now bore the entire responsibility for developing and prosecuting the case was singularly unimpressive. The former state senator appeared indefinite about his plans and looked as though he was being dragged into an uncomfortable situation. When Woodcock was asked if he planned to interview Dr. X, he replied: "Sometime in the coming weeks." The interviewer persisted: "Aren't you concerned about Dr. X leaving the jurisdiction?" Woodcock replied, "He will be available for questioning. He hasn't left in all this time, so I'm not very concerned that he would leave now."

The prosecutor's attitude was worrisome to me for a number of reasons, all of which were created by my disappointment with Calissi's first investigation.

I had studied Jascalevich's original testimony in Guy Calissi's office, and several experts confirmed that at least some aspects of his story did not hang together. Now there were witnesses from the animal laboratory ready to contradict the surgeon's story, and it struck me that Woodcock had an immediate obligation to himself and to Jascalevich to cross-examine him carefully about his original testimony. The dog story was, after all, his only alibi for having the curare, and even if the drug could not be found in the exhumed bodies, reviewing the alibi was certainly another avenue that needed exploration. Up until the moment of the TV interview, I had assumed that Woodcock had deliberately withheld information about his own interview of Jascalevich; but now it was clear that no such interview had taken place. This seemed a glaring deficiency at this late stage of the game. I thought it could constitute a major, and perhaps decisive, gap in any renewed investigation, and that it reflected poorly on Woodcock's thoroughness.

Woodcock's attitude in regard to his plans was further reflected in the comments attributed to him in the first *New York Times* story, to the effect that he had not decided what to do if curare was not found in the exhumed bodies, and that his chances of making a case depended heavily on finding the drug. I had long assumed that it would be impossible to get conclusive results from the new series of lab tests, and I could not understand why Woodcock had overlooked the significant potential of building his case with evidence contradicting what Jascalevich had said under oath when asked about the matter in the first place.

Furthermore, during the months when the new investigation was coming to a head, I had made some independent inquiries about the political structure of the Bergen County prosecutor's office and how Woodcock had earned his designation to the job by Republican Governor John Cahill.

From knowledgeable sources, I had learned of an interesting and unusual situation in Bergen County politics. Apparently, for many years there has been a bipartisan group of top-level political and business leaders in the county, called "The Executive Committee" by those sophisticated citizens who are aware of its existence. Reportedly, they get together from time to time to decide who shall be recommended as the major nominees for public office of either party. The same group existed at the time of Calissi's designation in the early 1950s, so there was cause for my concern about how willing Woodcock would be to open an investigation that might cause embarrassment to a predecessor with whom he shared common political support. This conflict of interest was compounded by the fact that Calissi and his former chief assistant were now both judges of the Superior Court—the same court where the prosecutor and all his assistants would be appearing in trials every day of the week!

There was another factor that concerned me about the extent of

Woodcock's enthusiasm for the case. It had always seemed to me that if the alleged activities at Riverdell Hospital were true, it was logical to assume that it was the work of a psychopath who might repeat such activities at any other hospital where he worked. Therefore, it seemed feasible to conduct a thorough study of records at the other hospitals to ascertain if anything unusual was happening, thus providing a fresher trail to be followed. I made that suggestion to Farber, and through his inquiry, we learned that Woodcock's office had neither the intention nor interest in pressing such an investigation.

Once the story broke, newspaper reporters quite naturally began seeking people to interview who could give them some singular newsworthy angle to call their own.

This created instant attention to the medical detectives and introduced another complication. Professional jealousies are flagrant among the elite fraternity of forensic medical experts. From the time I had first been exposed to Dr. Helpern, I learned that he never hesitated to criticize professional colleagues when he disagreed with them. He was most outspoken about his views of the incompetence he saw in others. Myron Farber had broken the story of Dr. X, but Farber had also previously written stories that were extremely critical of Helpern and his flamboyant methods. Furthermore, it was Helpern's former deputy, Mike Baden, and not Helpern himself, who had been responsible for the critical effort which permitted this case to be reopened. Thus, there was real concern about what Helpern, who was now retired, might say if interviewed.

To these circumstances must be added the fact that Woodcock had ignored both the Bergen County medical examiner (still Dr. Denson), and the New Jersey state medical examiner, Dr. Edwin Albano, whose office had been created in 1971.

Quite logically, depending upon the balance between their egos and their integrity, any of these experts might have been antagonized by the current investigation, and especially so because the law gave Dr. Albano's office responsibility and made no provision for the prosecutor to go outside of the state for help.

Woodcock made a sensible judgment: to get a more unbiased and competent review of the medical aspects of the case, it was certainly more effective to have Dr. Baden's office do it than the same Bergen County medical examiner's office that had failed to accomplish anything ten years before. Besides, apparently through Farber's initiative, Woodcock found Dr. Baden all ready, willing, and certainly more able than any existing resource.

Soon enough, on January 18, the *Bergen Record* story contained an interview with Dr. Helpern. According to the newspaper, he said that in 1966 the tests available could not unequivocally provide a positive finding for curare. Helpern did not indicate anything to the reporter about his own participation at that time, he just talked about the available tests: "The tests in 1966 were equivocal. You couldn't say this was curare."

When asked if newly available techniques would reveal the presence of curare after ten years, Helpern was somewhat evasive, but he certainly did not support the views already expressed by his former colleague, deputy, and protege, Dr. Baden. Helpern said, "It's not that simple, it's not like looking for a bullet. If you can't prove the presence of curare, you can't accuse anybody. I think Judge Calissi was right."

Both the *New York Times* and the *Bergen Record* had also located Dr. Charles J. Umberger, whose 1966 role was now revealed, if not clearly so. Umberger had retired from the New York medical examiner's office and was working in Dutchess County, New York, as a toxicologist for the county sheriff's office there.

Based on the chromatography tests that Dr. Umberger had done on the tissue of Eileen Shaw (which we had delivered to Dr. Helpern's office), it appeared that Umberger had filed a written report with Calissi on February 19, 1967, without being aware that Calissi had already given up his pursuit of the case. With respect to the Shaw tissue, that report said substantially what Umberger had told us in Dr. Helpern's office at the time: "The chemical findings should be considered suspicious without definite, positive or negative results."

Now Umberger told the press that Calissi's office had never contacted him about his report, that there certainly were techniques available to detect curare at that time, even if not so sophisticated as they are today.

According to Umberger, "The technology definitely existed."

He told a reporter for the *Bergen Record,* "Before it's over, this case will turn out to be the most bungled case ever to hit the eastern seaboard."

Watching Mr. Woodcock on television had reconfirmed my lack of confidence in the capacity of the Bergen County prosecutor's office to develop this difficult case properly. Remembrances of Calissi's efforts made me decide that every additional investigative resource should now be tapped.

During Senator Edmund Muskie's 1972 presidential campaign, I had worked in his national fund raising effort, and in that capacity had met a Trenton lawyer named William Hyland, who had subsequently become the attorney general of New Jersey. I presumed on that acquaintanceship to call Hyland on January 12, to see if he would be willing to discuss the Dr. X case with me.

The overriding consideration in my mind was that Woodcock's investigation appeared to be completely reliant on the prospective success of the newly employed methods of detecting curare. If that failed, he seemed all too ready to drop the case again.

The attorney general was most accommodating and keenly interested, and he had the chief of his criminal bureau, Robert DelTuffo, go over the details with me. DelTuffo (since nominated by President Carter to be the U.S. Attorney for New Jersey), was quick to grasp my concerns, and he asked me to provide him with a detailed memorandum preliminary to meeting with the attorney general the following week.

I outlined the several points which, insofar as I was aware, were not being pursued by the county prosecutor, any one of which might become critical in the event that the new tests turned up no positive evidence of curare in the exhumed bodies.

My plea to Hyland set forth these suggestions, with the disclaimer that I really had no basis to be certain they were not already being pursued.

1. A review of all post- and preoperative deaths of the surgical patients at the three other hospitals where Jascalevich practiced.

2. A check of all surgical supply houses and manufacturers to determine whether or not Jascalevich continued to purchase curare.

3. Some assurances that steps would be taken to to counter professional jealousies among forensic pathologists.

4. An expert cross-examination of Jascalevich based on his 1966 testimony to resolve open questions.

Allan Lans agreed to accompany me to see Hyland, and I picked him up at his home for the drive down to Trenton. The trip is memorable because of a story that Allan told me en route.

He became rather somber as we drove past the huge complex of oil refineries that clutter the edge of the turnpike just south of Newark airport. We had been discussing the approaching meeting, when he suddenly drifted into another subject. "I had quite an experience yesterday. Something happened that really made it all hurt more than ever."

"What was it?"

"I received a visit from Nancy Savino's little brother. He's only twelve years old—he's a beautiful person. He waited his turn in my waiting room, and I assumed that there was some medical problem. I hadn't seen him in about a year—you know I've continued to treat the Savino family.

"When he came in I asked him what was wrong, and he said 'nothing Doc—I just came by to see if you were okay. Ever since I read the story about Dr. X I've been worried about you—I've been feeling that you must feel very badly, and I remember how much you cared about my sister and how nice you've always been to all of us, so I just wanted to know if you're okay.' "

Allan told me that he reassured the boy, deeply moved by this child's sensitivity.

Then the boy, who was only three when his sister died, asked Allan, "Why would people do things like that to a little girl?"

Allan told me that he had never been so confounded by a question in all his life. He did his best. "There are some very sick people in this world, and they can do very terrible things that are difficult to explain."

The boy told Allan that he understood, and he just wanted to be sure that the doctor was okay.

Tears came to my eyes. I pressed a little harder on the accelerator.

Attorney General Hyland greeted us warmly when we arrived at his Trenton office, and I introduced Dr. Lans. Hyland ushered us into a conference room where Bob DelTuffo was waiting, along with Dr. Edwin Albano, the state's chief medical examiner. They had all studied my detailed memo.

They told us that while the attorney general now had the legal authority to supersede a county prosecutor in any particular case (which was not true in 1967), it was a power that could be utilized practically only where there was reason to believe that the prosecutor could not handle the case properly. If that power was used indiscriminately, it might appear that the attorney general was attempting to steal headlines. Because Woodcock seemed to be proceeding properly at the moment, there was no justification for immediate interference.

I understood the reasonableness of the attorney general's position, and then told him what I had heard about "The Executive Committee." DelTuffo and Hyland both said that they were unaware of that situation, and that while they really knew very little about Bergen County politics, nothing like that would surprise them. The attorney general told us that Woodcock had not discussed the case with him, but that he had announced to the press that if he was unable to establish a case he would turn over the facts of the previous investigation to the attorney general for whatever action he deemed appropriate. That did seem for the moment to alleviate my concern about the possible impact of the "Executive Committee" connection.

Dr. Albano said that he had been invited to participate in the autopsies along with Dr. Baden, and that his New Jersey laboratories would be conducting their own independent tests. He explained that a new radio-immuno assay (RIA) test had been developed since the original investigation which could detect curare, and was hopeful that it could prove effective in this case. He said his toxicologist was extremely able and his laboratories were well equipped to do the new tests, but they would take some time to complete. He admitted to being somewhat piqued about the fact that Woodcock had gone to New York City for help, but he had accepted this as a fact with which he had to live. He had only praise for the New York City medical examiner's office and its capacities. Later, when we had a few minutes alone, DelTuffo assured me that there would be no question of professional rivalry getting in Albano's way. He had a high respect for Albano, based on years of working with him.

DelTuffo was most interested in our concept of checking Jascalevich's record at other hospitals, and had a plan to carry this out, independent of Woodcock's investigation.

As the state's chief medical examiner, Dr. Albano was also the head of the State Board of Medical Examiners, which had responsibility for matters of physician licensing and discipline. The board had an assistant attorney general attached to it named Anthony LaBue, who, according to DelTuffo, was extremely competent. The plan was to have LaBue and Dr. Albano immediately subpoena and begin a close examination of all of the hospital records at the other hospitals where Jascalevich worked. We discussed the appropriate research design in order to determine from such records whether there had been any similar experience at the other hospitals during Jascalevich's tenure there.

This was about all they felt they could do at this time without seeming to interfere with the Woodcock investigation, except to assure us that DelTuffo would quietly monitor Woodcock's progress with the case. We left Trenton satisfied that something had been accomplished.

CHAPTER XXI

Exhuming Bodies

Grim witnesses shivered in the January wind when the grave diggers cracked the earth's frozen crust on January 13, 1977, to uncover the ten-year-old corpses. Uncertainty existed about the physical condition of their grisly goal or even whether the purpose of this odious task would be achieved. But the work was done, and one by one during the next couple of weeks, the remains of each of the five former Riverdell Hospital patients were delivered to Dr. Baden's facilities on First Avenue in Manhattan, the very same place we had delivered the tiny bits and pieces of some of the same bodies in parafin blocks and between glass slides exactly ten years before.

The smallest casket came first. It contained the body of Nancy Savino, Dr. Lans's four-year-old patient who had died so suddenly on March 21, 1966.

Only one week had passed since Judge Trautwein signed the order allowing Nancy's body to be dug out of Marycrest Cemetery in Mahwah, New Jersey, so that it could be brought to one of the eight stainless steel autopsy tables lined up on the tile floor of the basement of the New York City medical examiner's office.

The excellent condition of the small body he found within the coffin was a surprise to Dr. Baden. Good fortune had kept the casket unusually air-tight and prevented the seepage of water that would otherwise have facilitated decomposition.

According to Baden, the body was so well preserved that her facial features were still recognizable, and it was remarkable that even her funeral corsage was still intact. He said, "It was amazing how well preserved tissues can be after such a long time. This whole investigation points up the value of exhuming bodies when questions are raised. It shows that burial is not the end of it."

The unusual condition of this body permitted the experts to

perform a very thorough autopsy. Inside the dead child's abdomen, the pathologist found the evidence of her surgery precisely as it had been so carefully described in the hospital records. Even the original sutures were still in place.

It took about four hours for Dr. Baden to confirm that there was no natural cause of death by dissecting and examining each of the vital organs. He searched for any evidence of abnormality that might prove useful to forensic specialists working at one or another of the few facilities in America capable of such analysis. This team included Dr. Edwin Albano, New Jersey's chief medical examiner and the chief toxicologist of his office; people from the office of the medical examiner of Suffolk County, New York; Columbia University; commercial laboratories in California and Pennsylvania; as well as other members of Dr. Baden's own staff in New York City.

As Dr. Baden completed each of the autopsies, he distributed the samples of tissue among the experts working on the project. Some of the tissue samples to be worked on were picked up personally at the New York City medical examiner's office. In other cases they were carefully wrapped in styrofoam and shipped by air freight to the more distant locations.

The plan of the forensic specialists was to subject these tissue samples to each of the known tests for determining the presence of curare. Some of these tests had only become available subsequent to the original 1966 investigation. If curare could be found by different laboratories working independently and utilizing different tests, the cross-checking would provide the prosecutor with a quality of evidence that would be difficult, if not impossible, for a defense lawyer to impeach.

To conduct these tests, certain conditions were imposed in advance by the circumstances of the particular cases. First of all, none of the suspected victims had received curare as part of their hospital treatment. While curare is sometimes utilized by anesthesiologists during surgery, hospital records established that this was not the case with regard to any of these particular patients. So if curare was found, there would be no legitimate reason for its presence. Secondly, the scientists knew exactly what chemical compounds they were searching for—d-tubocurarine, of the same type that came in the empty vials found in Dr. Jascalevich's locker. This fact provided control solutions and eliminated what might otherwise be a time-consuming necessity, to search for a number of different drugs that could conceivably produce similar symptoms.

I learned the details of each of the laboratory tests available to discover curare during a long conversation with one of the expert toxicologists in the group that Dr. Baden assembled. Since he was working on actual tissue at the time and was scrupulous not to reveal anything about the specific case, we agreed that all of my questions would be of a general nature and would not specifically relate to the outcome of the tests he was doing for the prosecutor's office.

Because of his extensive experience, I asked him whether poisons seemed to be a desirable weapon of choice among doctors or other scientifically knowledgeable murderers. The forensic toxicologist smiled a grim smile:

"Yes, and it seems to be especially so today. The preferable substances are members of a group of chemicals we call 'quantanary compounds.' These include succinylcholine (used by Dr. Coppolino); Pavulon or pancuroneum, allegedly used by the nurses accused in Michigan in the VA Hospital case in Ann Arbor; and curare itself, under various names such as d-tubocurarine or curarine. What they all do is paralyze the muscle receptors in the respiratory system. This causes the patient to suffocate, because the chest and abdominal muscles he usually relies on for breathing won't work. The victim is trying to breathe and he can't. It is a helpless and horrifying experience. Laboratory doctors have tried it on themselves and have been resuscitated under test conditions in order to find out what it is like.

"Curare is so soluble that if you ate some, it would go right through your system and pass out of your body with no effort. It has to be injected directly into the blood stream to get to the area of the lung muscle and diaphragm. Remember, the South American Indians used it on the points of darts and spears in order to kill their prey; that was their primitive way of injecting it.

"What this means is that the drug acts only on very select targets within the body—that it doesn't act on the brain or the central nervous system. So in order to kill with curare there must be an overdosage, and it must get into the system fast and in concentrated form. If it entered only in a trickle it would begin to dissolve and it wouldn't kill—probably."

I asked the doctor to tell me what kind of poison detection techniques were generally available in 1966–67, when the events at Riverdell took place.

"Well, there were some pretty good techniques available. Paper chromatography (PC), which we still use, was available then. Thin-layer chromatography (TLC) was available then too. The radio-immuno assay (RIA) techniques were not available then, nor was the gas-chromatography (GC) test, all of which have been developed since. Nevertheless, without some hint that quantanary compounds were used, like the empty bottles found in Dr. Jascalevich's locker which provided the clue as to what to look for, the normal chemical assay—even as utilized today in the New York City medical examiner's office—would not find them, because they wouldn't be testing for them."

I asked the expert, "Then these are something close to ideal drugs with which to do someone in, and doctors have easy access to them?"

"Well, maybe," he replied. "But actually, massive overdoses of sodium or potassium would be even more difficult to detect. If you remember the recent movie *Hospital,* George C. Scott, the actor, played the part of a distraught physician who attempted suicide. It was potassium that he was going to inject into his arm when the beautiful Indian girl stopped him. Of the quantanary chemicals, however, succinylcholines are the best for this purpose. Of course, you have to have some reason to have sizable quantities in your possession. Normally, it's only anesthesiologists who use these drugs regularly.

"Let me tell you about the different tests and how they work. I believe that while mass spectrometry was in use in 1966, at least in the largest chemical labs, it was not in use in forensic toxicology. Even now, only a few laboratories have it available. This is a highly sophisticated technique of chemical identification. In a rather large machine, a vial with a test specimen is bombarded with a high-energy electron source. This causes the molecules present to 'explode.' Each molecule has a characteristic fragmentation pattern produced by the charged particles. The pattern exhibited by the sample identifies the chemical when that pattern is matched against a computer's memory bank of typical patterns for each of the chemicals that are in the program. What you really have, then, is a chemical fingerprint, and each of the 40,000 compounds in the memory bank has a different pattern. The identification is absolute. This technique has been utilized in forensic toxicology in only the last five years. The machinery and the computer memory packages are very expensive. I understand that the installation costs about $135,000. Even today, in the well-equipped New York City medical examiner's office, for example, mass spectrometry is available only for detecting the more common narcotic drugs. In the New Jersey State medical examiner's office they have a complete one available.

"The radio-immuno assay (RIA) test is the most recently developed one. It was first applied to curare in 1973. This is the preferred method for tubocurarine. The test sample is placed in a little vial that moves on a conveyor belt into a large piece of machinery. This contains a computerized memory, which recalls the predictable amount of antibodies produced for the particular amount of sample used. In the machine, the radio-labeled drugs are mixed with the sample, and the machine does the actual count of the antibody combinations produced by the sample. The printout will also say what the quantity of the competitive (poisoning) substance is in the sample."

This test was originally developed in the 1950s and used to detect insulin hormones in connection with the treatment of diabetes. Dr. Rosalyn Yalow, a nuclear physicist, won the Nobel Prize in 1977 for her role in this development.

"This radio-immuno assay technique is extremely sensitive, capable of detecting as little as a billionth of a gram. Very few laboratories have the capacity to do this test, but the experts feel that it can be used in this case.

"The most well-established test for curare is thin-layer chromatography (TLC). This technique is a good one for detecting curare. While it is not an absolute identifying test, it is fast, simple, and requires very little sample, most of which can be recovered and used again in other tests. The problem is that this test is subject to challenge, it's not absolute like the others. In this process the specimen to be tested is smeared along a base line drawn on a glass plate which has a coating of silica gel. The plate is suspended with its base in a chemical solution. The chemical solution travels up the plate by capillary action. Each chemical compound, including the compound tubocurarine, has a specific time that it takes before it precipitates and turns color in this solution. Therefore, the chemical detective watches to see how far up the plate a colored precipitate appears. This distance is a measure of time and solution, and both the color and the distance from the base line are measured to identify the particular compound present. This technique has been available for at least ten years, and is the one that Dr. Umberger attempted to use in 1967 until he was blocked by the formalin that the tissue had been preserved in.

"There is also gas chromatography. This method is very similar to thin-layer chromatography (TLC). In this method the difference is that the specimen is vaporized and the chemical identified by its color and its position in a tube through which the gas passes. This method has been around as long as TLC.

"There are a couple of other possibilities, but we are not likely to make use of them."

For those of us who are not scientifically oriented, or who otherwise had difficulty with their college chemistry courses, some of these explanations may be a little difficult to follow. But understanding them is important for understanding certain technicalities in the forthcoming trial.

CHAPTER XXII

Other Doctors

A suspicion that I had been harboring for some ten years was confirmed by my conversation with the toxicologist. With their peculiar knowledge and special access, physicians have a very special capacity literally to get away with murder. In everyday practice, they have convenient access to the most efficient weapons of death. I began to assemble some examples to prove the point, and for this it wasn't necessary to go back very far in history.

The Coppolino case really called the possibility of this sort of medical poisoning to public attention just before the events at Riverdell Hospital, and it was the notoriety of that case which prompted Dr. Harris to look into Dr. Jascalevich's locker for succinylcholine, only to find the d-tubocurarine form of curare instead.

Dr. Carl Coppolino was a successful anesthesiologist who also practiced in New Jersey until a heart condition forced him to retire. He lived in Middletown and was only thirty-three years old when he was arrested there in 1965 and charged with the murder of his next-door neighbor, a retired army officer, Lt. Col. William E. Farber, the husband of a woman with whom Coppolino was alleged to be having an affair. The doctor was indicted for suffocating the colonel with a pillow, but he was acquitted after a brilliant defense by F. Lee Bailey, who became famous himself as a result. Marge, the colonel's wife, testified that she was Dr. Coppolino's hypnotized love slave, and at her lover's direction had injected her husband with succinylcholine. Apparently, the dose was insufficient to achieve the intended effect, and so she had watched Dr. Coppolino finish the job by suffocating her husband with a pillow as he struggled for his last breath.

Four months after his acquittal in December 1966, the doctor was tried again. This time he was accused of murdering his own wife, Carmela, on August 28, 1965, in their home at Longboat Key, near Sarasota, Florida, by injecting her with a lethal overdose of succinylcholine.

Before his conviction, Dr. Coppolino had married another woman, Mary Gibson, a wealthy divorcee, and the state contended that the doctor killed Carmela in order to enable him to marry Mrs. Gibson. The jury in the Florida case found Dr. Coppolino guilty.

Dr. Milton Helpern and Dr. Charles Umberger were the key witnesses for the prosecution in the second Coppolino case. Their testimony about finding a needle mark in Carmela's left buttock and evidence of succinylcholine in her liver and brain tissue was decisive. The state had established that Coppolino had acquired six bottles of succinylcholine a month before his wife's death.

In addition to the type of drug and the involvement of Helpern and Umberger, there were other striking similarities in the Coppolino case with what might be the situation in the Riverdell affair. Dr. Helpern had done an autopsy on Carmela Coppolino's exhumed body some four months after her death, which had originally been attributed to a heart attack. He testified that, based on his thirty-six years of experience and some 18,000 autopsies, a heart attack could not have been the actual cause of her death. It was during Dr. Helpern's thorough autopsy that he discovered a needle mark in the left buttock of the corpse. The vital organs were turned over to Dr. Umberger, who isolated components of succinylcholine in Carmela's liver and brain tissue, which Umberger testified were in excess of the amounts of those compounds that would normally be found in the body. He said he was convinced of the presence of an overdose of succinylcholine. The case was a landmark, because it was the first time that this particular drug had been identified in a body after death, and Dr. Umberger had developed the tests to find it.

Dr. Coppolino was convicted despite the defense producing expert witnesses to refute Helpern's and Umberger's conclusions. One was Dr. Francis Foldes, who was the first person to introduce the drug into the United States and had written the definitive work on it—a book which Helpern admitted on cross-examination that he had not read. Another defense expert failed to sway the jury when he testified that Umberger and Helpern had neglected to test the site of the injection. Instead they relied on the vital organs as the eventual repository of the drug, claiming that it would not have stayed at the injection site long enough to be found there after so much time had passed.

Dr. Coppolino was sentenced to life imprisonment.

At the time of the trial, the New York *Daily News* reported another fascinating parallel case which had occurred in Italy in 1963. The headline on that story could only have been concocted by the ingenious headline writers of the *Daily News:* "I Love My Wife: An Italian Parallel." Reporter John Quinn told of the conviction in a Bologna court on February 15, 1965, of thirty-seven-year-old Dr. Carlo Nigrisoli, who had said he found his wife, Ombretta, dead of a heart attack on March 14, 1963. The prosecutors alleged Dr. Nigrisoli had purchased curarine just prior to her death, and that traces were found in her kidneys and urine after an autopsy which Ombretta's suspicious physician father had demanded. One parallel came from Dr. Nigrisoli's admissions that he had several mistresses. The doctor was convicted and sentenced to life imprisonment, after pathologists testifying for both sides clashed repeatedly over the chemical tests that had been performed.

There seemed to be obvious connecting threads among several of these reported cases. The most recent notorious case was the one at the Ann Arbor Veterans Hospital, referred to earlier as a factor triggering the second Riverdell investigation in Bergen County. In this case, multiple deaths from a curare-like drug in a hospital setting were alleged.

In July and August of 1975, the hospital's intensive-care unit experienced thirty-four respiratory failures among twenty-three patients, about five times the normal rate of such incidents in that particular unit. Twelve patients died as a result. The others were saved by quick action of the hospital staff. Originally, ten deaths were considered to be suspicious, but indictments were returned in only four cases. A number of the patients who had suffered respiratory failures survived, and some of the dead ones were deemed to have died as a result of natural causes. The FBI deployed more than thirty agents in an effort to solve the crime, when it was discovered that someone had injected the drug Pavulon, which is used in surgery similarly to d-tubocurarine and succinylcholine. It was further alleged in this case that the drug had been administered by injection in intravenous tubing at the coupling devices. The FBI isolated the persons who had access to the victims during the particular time periods when the deaths were occurring. The sharp increase in the incidence of the respiratory failures, plus an anesthesiologist's noticing symptoms consistent with those caused by an injection of Pavulon, led to the criminal investigation.

When the case was presented to a federal grand jury, two nurses, Filipina Narcisco and Leome Perez, both immigrants from the Philipines, were accused of murder, attempted murder, and conspiracy to commit murder. No apparent motive was disclosed until the trial, when the prosecutor tried to demonstrate that the two accused nurses were unhappy because of serious understaffing at the hospital, and he attributed to them a desire to call attention to this problem by creating medical emergencies. The prosecutor said that while murder was not their object, they intended to create a dangerous problem which they would then detect.

During the trial, the murder counts were further reduced to one count of murder and four of poisoning against Miss Narcisco and three of poisoning against Mrs. Perez. The conspiracy count survived against both of them, and after a three-month-long trial, both were convicted. Eventually, their convictions were reversed on appeal as a result of prosecutorial errors.

There are a number of other recent cases that demonstrate the relationship between medical killers and poison. Some of these cases are still awaiting legal action.

Succinylcholine figured recently in the detention of a doctor in New York City in March of 1977 as he was attempting to leave this country after the death of his wife only a month before. The doctor was detained as a material witness because an empty vial of succinylcholine was found in his Fort Lee, New Jersey, home, after his wife, who was also a physician (as was Carmela Coppolino) died just after her husband had admitted her to a New York City hospital. After the doctor had left the hospital, a nurse who had been in to check her intravenous feeding apparatus only fifteen minutes before found her dead. This case has not been finally resolved as of this writing, but the doctor was indicted and a trial resulted in a hung jury. According to newspaper accounts, the doctor was planning to marry an American woman so that he could stay in this country after his visa expired.

Another case still pending should be pointed out here because of its alleged motive. On June 14, 1977, the district attorney of Suffolk County, New York, announced the indictment of an anesthesiologist on charges of second-degree assault. While no patient died in this incident, the anesthesiologist was charged with improperly injecting Benadryl, an antihistamine, into intravenous tubing attached to a patient in a postoperative recovery room, which caused serious medical problems for the patient. Fortunately, the patient recovered completely. In addition to the use of intravenous tubing, an interesting aspect of this case is the alleged motive: competition between the accused physician and three nurse-anesthetists who were allegedly cutting into the doctor's business volume. The patient who was supposedly attacked was not this physician's patient. She had been served by one of the nurse-anesthetists.

One of the last cases in which Dr. Helpern was to testify for the prosecution as an expert witness, shortly before his death, also involved a doctor murderer. In that case, Dr. Charles Friedgood, who had been arrested at Kennedy Airport as he was about to emplane to Denmark with a satchel full of valuables to meet his Danish mistress, was found guilty of murdering his wife by injecting a massive overdose of Demerol into her buttock in June of 1975 at their Long Island home.

All of these incidents were recent, having come to my attention originally through newspaper accounts which I have collected since the 1966 affair at Riverdell Hospital. The number of them can only make us wonder how many others have gone undetected.

With the exception of Ann Arbor, all of these cases occurred in the greater New York area. Every one of the medical murders involved the use of some form of poisoning discoverable only through autopsy, and the victims in the physician murder cases are all wives or family.

It is not easy to accept the horrendous accusations against Dr. Jascalevich. People find it difficult to conceive of a respected surgeon possibly doing such a thing. The preceding tales of medical atrocities may give us another perspective on the events at Riverdell Hospital.

CHAPTER XXIII

Exhumation

The unpleasant task of exhumation seemed to be justified by the beginning of March. Confirmed reports of the presence of curare started to come in from the different laboratories that had been analyzing the tissue of Nancy Savino's body. At least that case could now be viewed in a new light.

At the same time, the initial tests in process on tissue from two of the other bodies were also indicating that curare was present, but final confirmation was still pending, while the medical detectives were just beginning their work on the other two cases.

The results of the initial forensic analyses convinced Prosecutor Joseph Woodcock to present his case to a grand jury and seek an indictment, and he began to do so on March 16, 1976.

James E. Anderson, the same lawyer who appeared with Dr. Jascalevich to represent him in former-prosecutor Calissi's office in 1966, did a very unusual thing on March 16: he called a motel press conference to discuss his still-anonymous client's position. Fortuitously, I caught this rather bizarre affair on the late-night television news. It seemed ludicrous for an attorney to try to keep his client's name out of the public eye by calling a press conference to discuss him.

Responding to a wild cacophony of questions by the assorted menagerie of newspaper and television reporters, Anderson attempted to convince them that they shouldn't use his client's name, already known by most reporters at that point anyway. Anderson told them,

"I am the attorney for the so-called Dr. X. There has been created in this investigation the appearance of a Roman circus spectacle instead of a calm, logical, and scientific approach by reason of the publication of details of scientific tests. This may well have created in the public mind an image leading to the belief that the results of scientific tests are always absolutely correct, valid, and reliable. This is simply not so. The results of such tests rely almost completely upon the knowledge, skill, and competence of those performing them, and the techniques used to guard against error. This is particularly so when the tests are as complex as, and in some cases apparently untried and unproved as, those involved in this investigation.

"Even the most skillful investigator is susceptible to error under these circumstances and many of them disagree completely with each other. Despite this, the public references to these tests have simplified, without saying so, that there is no question concerning their accuracy. Any man of science who is pure-minded, honest, and fair will admit what I have said concerning them.

"The premature publication of alleged results of the tests is grossly unfair, prejudicial, and unjust. It is partially for the foregoing reasons that I am making a statement.

"The question as to why the doctor has not disclosed his identity should be clearly apparent. There are always those who are anxious to believe the worst of a man in public life or a professional man. Further, referring to the practical side of this phase of the matter, should his name be disclosed, he would be overwhelmed, besieged, beset by the curious and the morbid to such an extent that he would be unable to function personally or professionally and would be obliged to go into seclusion. He has not been charged with any offense. This is an investigation. Another of the unfair aspects of this matter is the reference to curare. Because of its origins, it conjures up a bizarre, even perhaps sinister, atmosphere which is very prone to prejudice the public's attitude.

"The doctor was not the only man in the hospital who had access to curare. It was in common use in most hospitals, as well as in this hospital, as a muscle relaxant in surgery. All technically trained hospital personnel are aware of the nature of curare, its properties, and its potentialities. It follows, therefore, that if indeed any of these patients expired of curare poisoning, anyone could have done it. To date there have been veiled references to the results of the tests.

"The doctor is a highly intelligent man. It would therefore appear incredible that a man of his intellectual capacities, using any substance in a hospital for unlawful purposes, would have his own supply when there are ample supplies in the hospital's stock. Even more so, keeping it in his own locker would be amazingly stupid under such circumstances.

"Nor has there appeared any motive for anyone to have done anything wrong here, any more than there is any valid proof that anything wrong has been done.

"One of the patients whose death is under investigation was the doctor's, having been referred to him for surgery by another medical man. This patient was scheduled for surgery and interviewed and examined by the doctor. Based upon the interview and his examination, my client concluded that surgery was inadvisable and so informed the doctor. The autopsy disclosed that this patient had advanced heart disease and coronary occlusions. In fact the referring doctor was annoyed by my client's refusal to perform surgery on his patient. What motive would my client have had for doing anything wrong under such circumstances?

"Another patient was seen by my client on consultation. My client's advice was that surgery should not be performed. Surgery was nevertheless performed that same day and the patient expired. In 1966, my client voluntarily appeared before Mr. Calissi and his staff and testified from 10:30 in the morning until 3:30 in the afternoon, under oath. No constitutional right, privilege, or immunity was at any time raised by me as his attorney or by the doctor. During the current investigation, my client has spent approximately eight hours again being examined without any objection to any question or raising any rights, Mr. Woodcock having been permitted to ask any question he desired concerning the entire case. Common experience is that a man who has anything to hide will not cooperate with the authorities, will raise his constitutional privileges, and will insist on every right, privilege, and immunity available to him under our system of justice. The doctor has chosen, after having had all these rights explained to him by the prosecutor and myself, to continue testifying under oath. This course of conduct on the part of the doctor should make it abundantly clear to everyone that he has nothing to hide, has done nothing wrong, either legally or morally, and that he is utterly innocent of any wrongful act.

"It has been suggested that the doctor resigned quietly from Riverdell Hospital. Not at all. This resignation, which I prepared, was made in a formal meeting with the hospital directors, at which time I informed them that I considered them to have acted most unfairly to my client and that he was resigning at my suggestion because of this. Prior to this resignation, in mid-1965, the doctor had tendered his resignation from the hospital, which resignation was refused, and he was persuaded to remain.

"I must say that I refuse and will continue to refuse to believe the slightest intimation that the doctor has done anything wrong; and no matter what the outcome of this investigation, my faith is not based on emotion—he has not been a close friend, but I have adequate knowledge of his character, reliability, intellect, and morality to convince me that he has done no wrong."

All that Anderson's strange press conference had accomplished for his client was to stimulate the press to publicize the doctor's name, while increasing the degree of public attention to the affair, before any official announcement about it had ever been made.

The next day, the *New York Times* published Dr. Jascalevich's name for the first time, citing the grand jury presentation and legal documents publically available in connection therewith as justification.

At the same time, the *Times* also reported that Dr. Richard Coumbis had found evidence of curare in all four of the bodies that he had thus far examined in the New Jersey medical examiner's laboratory, and that Dr. David P. Beggs of the Hewlett-Packard Lab in Pennsylvania confirmed that he had detected curare in at least one organ in each body and in some cases more than one organ. Beggs told Farber, "The curare is there." At that point, only the tissues of Carl Rohrbeck's body remained to be analyzed.

When the *Times* reported Jascalevich's name in its March 17 story, along with the results of the curare tests and the commencement of grand jury proceedings, reporters began calling the doctor directly for his side of the story. Jascalevich refused to respond to any of them, so they called Anderson to ask if he was going to sue the *Times* for publishing Jascalevich's name.

He told them, "Someone has made a decision to publish the doctor's name. It was their decision; they will have to live with it and take the consequences of it."

Reporters and photographers waited outside of the home in beautiful Englewood Cliffs, into which the doctor had moved in

1973 with his wife and two children. (Until then the family had continued to live over his office in the run-down neighborhood in West New York.) They were unable to find him there. *Newsweek* magazine of March 22, 1976, published a pathetic photograph of the discomfited surgeon wearing a Halloween mask in order to avoid publicity. The masked photo left a grotesquely sinister impression.

Public identification of Jascalevich created a host of new problems for him, for the authorities, and for the medical profession.

When his name was revealed, the executive committee at Christ Hospital attempted to suspend his operating room privileges. Some people close to it described the announcement of Jascalevich's suspension as apologetic. The attorney for the hospital expressed the hospital's position that while it still had great respect for Jascalevich, they were afraid that the pressure of his legal difficulties could have a detrimental effect on his surgical skills and that the hospital had a responsibility to act. They emphasized that they were only suspending his operating room privileges and that otherwise, according to the hospital's lawyer, "He is still a member in good standing of the hospital staff. We are very proud to have him. No one has ever suggested that he is held in less esteem than any other surgeon in the hospital."

But Dr. Jascalevich took the hospital to court to enjoin the suspension, and Christ Hospital was forced to reverse itself after holding a hearing on whether or not to restore Jascalevich's privileges in full in order to avoid violating the doctor's rights. During that hearing, a urologist and a nurse were called as witnesses by Jascalevich to testify that they had observed the doctor perform surgery and that he had not been nervous during the procedure. The urologist said, "He showed no signs of hesitation, fatigue, or incompetence, and no signs of pressure." Jascalevich also had two of his patients testify that they had been willing to undergo surgery knowing that he had been accused of murder.

A body of law has developed making it difficult to suspend a physician's hospital privileges, no matter how serious the charge, until they can be irrefutably established. The situation with which Christ Hospital had to deal displayed no evidence of professional misconduct. If a hospital acts without affording a physician due process and without actual proof of misconduct, which is very difficult to establish, it can be sued for damages by the suspended physician for depriving him of a loss of his livelihood and for defamation, or it can be enjoined from suspending him. As a result, hospitals consider themselves helpless to act in such situations and are understandably reluctant to expose themselves to potential lawsuits. One of the basic problems in obtaining the necessary evidence of misconduct is the conspiracy of silence among physicians, who generally adopt a see-no-evil, speak-no-evil, hear-no-evil attitude concerning their colleagues. The usual method of handling such matters, therefore, is to try to get an offending physician to resign voluntarily in exchange for a promise of good references. Thus, problem physicians are frequently exported to unsuspecting hospitals in other communities.

At the time of the announcement in the press of the continuing investigation into the Riverdell deaths, the New Jersey State Board of Medical Examiners, headed by Dr. Albano, the chief medical examiner of New Jersey State, had commenced an investigation, which included a study of the hospital records at all of the institutions where Jascalevich worked; but at that time the board had not yet found any grounds to suspend the doctor's license.

CHAPTER XXIV

Awaiting Justice

The grand jury's responsibility is to determine if a person should be accused of a serious crime. The county prosecutor's role is to present competent evidence to a grand jury, and if that evidence convinces the jurors that there is reasonable cause to believe the accused did commit the crime, the legal procedure leading to a trial is commenced by the grand jury's indictment.

In Bergen County, the grand jury meets only one day each week, and so it took two months for Woodcock's office to complete its presentation in this complex case. Eleven witnesses were heard. On May 18, 1976, a sealed indictment was handed up, accusing Mario Jascalevich of murdering five patients at Riverdell Hospital some ten years earlier.

It was just before seven o'clock in the morning of the next day, May 19, 1976, when Dr. Jascalevich, wearing a tan trenchcoat and a blue suit, shut the front door of his elegant split-level home at 10 Priscilla Lane in Englewood Cliffs. He was on his way to the Jersey City Medical Center, where he had four operations scheduled, when the detectives who had been patiently waiting outside approached him to advise him of his indictment and tell him that he was under arrest. The usual Miranda warnings were recited on the sidewalk before the surgeon was placed in the detective's car to be taken to the courthouse in Hackensack.

The arraignment procedure, in which the court finally advises the accused of the charges and his rights and sets bail, took place before Judge Theodore W. Trautwein at 8:30 A.M. Witnesses described Jascalevich as calm and serene throughout.

Raymond A. Brown, a prominent criminal lawyer, was present. The attorney had been called into the case by Dr. Jascalevich, shortly after the ill-advised Anderson press conference. Brown enjoys a great reputation as a very smart and articulate criminal defense lawyer, with an excellent track record. The attorney entered a plea of not guilty on behalf of his client, who did not speak during the proceeding.

Assistant Prosecutor Sybil Moses requested the judge to set bail at $250,000, saying that "I don't think there is a more serious crime in the history of jurisprudence or in common law." Her words caused the only noted reaction from Jascalevich, who momentarily raised his eyebrows, and to some of those present he appeared visibly shaken by that remark.

Mr. Brown protested that such bail was excessive and pointed out that the surgeon had deep roots in the community, that he had not left it despite the pretrial notoriety. Brown added that the purpose of bail was not to punish but to assure the defendant's attendance at trial.

Judge Trautwein agreed and set bail at $150,000, with $15,000 to be provided in cash and the balance through a surety bond and pledges against the doctor's real estate.

The details of bail were arranged for by 1:55 P.M., and the doctor, who meanwhile had cancelled his waiting surgery, was released from custody. He left the courtroom hurriedly with his attorney and two other men, who whisked him away in a waiting car without answering the questions of the covey of reporters.

A few days later he was back at work, with a full schedule of surgery. Reporters began to inquire at his hospitals about possible suspension. The chairman of the department of surgery at Jersey City Medical Center told one of them that Jascalevich would continue on staff provided his license was not revoked, and that he would, of course, continue to operate.

Some went by his office a few days later to see if the usual line of patients would still be waiting on the stoop. They were. His patients' loyalty was impressive. A woman told one reporter indignantly, "He doesn't take lives, he saves them."

The continued loyalty of Jascalevich's patients was later confirmed to me by a curious female reporter who, in an attempt to find out as much as she could about Jascalevich, made an appointment to see him as a patient complaining of some purported female difficulty. She was impressed by the fact that she had to wait over an hour to see the busy doctor, and by how swiftly he conducted her examination. She described him to me later as cold, correct, calm, and efficient; and when his thorough examination was completed, he told her that he could find nothing wrong.

The New Jersey State Board of Medical Examiners had been busy working on the Jascalevich affair ever since the reopened investigation had first come to public attention.

Following the meeting that Dr. Lans and I attended in the attorney general's office, Assistant Attorney General Anthony LaBue subpoenaed a great number of hospital records from each of the three institutions where Jascalevich had practiced since leaving Riverdell in 1967. He had privileges at North Hudson Hospital in Weehauken and Jersey City Medical Center, but most of his surgery was performed at Christ Hospital in Jersey City. At each hospital he enjoyed an excellent reputation, and colleagues described him with such phrases as "an excellent surgeon," "tops in his field." He was also known to be extremely busy. Nobody among his colleagues or neighbors was found to know him well personally, and the general view was that of a cold, aloof professional without ordinary social attachments.

LaBue's panel reviewed all of the subpoenaed records in order to determine if there were clusters of unusual postoperative deaths at any of these hospitals. Nothing unusual was found, and so there was no basis for attributing any other patients' deaths to Dr. Jascalevich.

Although Prosecutor Woodcock had called his investigation to the State Medical Board's attention in January, there was no basis for their acting on the alleged murder cases prior to indictment.

Eventually, the close examination of the array of hospital records did uncover some other matters which gave the Medical Board some justification to prepare charges against Jascalevich. These could lead to revocation of his license.

On May 21, three days after his indictment, the board charged that, based on its investigation of hospital records and testimony from certain physicians, Jascalevich had injured and endangered the life of a patient at Christ Hospital in 1975 by performing unnecessary surgery, and then had falsified medical records in order to justify the operation. In the detailed charge signed by Dr. Edwin Albano, in his capacity as president of the State Medical Board, it was alleged that Jascalevich knowingly misdiagnosed J.E., as the patient was identified, and then sent tissue from another patient to a laboratory in J.E.'s name in order to justify his misdiagnosis of cancer. The surgery he then performed treated the patient for a condition he knew was not his. Fortunately, this patient survived, although Jascalevich had allegedly failed to treat for the true ailment.

The Medical Board decided to utilize this charge in a summary proceeding which would allow them temporarily to suspend the accused physician before holding a full hearing on the matter.

Jascalevich's new attorney, Ray Brown, was served by the Medical Board with a copy of their final charge, to which were added additional charges of misconduct stemming from the five murder counts of the indictment. The hearing was scheduled for May 25. The board accused Jascalevich of fraud in the practice of medicine, professional incompetence, and gross neglect that endangered the life or health of a patient, all of which are grounds for revocation of a license under the New Jersey statutes.

On May 25, just prior to the meeting of the State Medical Board, Dr. Jascalevich entered into an agreement with the board that he would voluntarily surrender his license to practice temporarily, pending the outcome of the criminal proceedings and without prejudice to whatever rights he had regarding the revocation procedure.

While the board had effectively achieved its goal, they continued with their effort to obtain a permanent revocation, and on September 1, 1976, began final hearings to decide whether or not Jascalevich's license should be suspended.

By that time they had come up with another charge against Jascalevich. In this one, the board accused the beleaguered surgeon of altering the operative records of a patient identified as T.R. in 1973.

While the hearings on all these charges began in September of 1976, they were eventually suspended until after the trial. These proceedings are rightly confidential. Assumedly, Jascalevich's attorney has argued successfully that because Jascalevich has surrendered his license voluntarily, there is no reason to proceed until after his trial, and that the testimony elicited in any such hearing could unfairly prejudice the trial on the criminal charges.

With his license temporarily and voluntarily suspended, Dr. Jascalevich was free to concentrate his time and resources on the preparation of his defense.

A number of legal motions were made during the pretrial period, and this activity, while essentially turning out to be futile, has certainly been consistent with a proper and well-financed defense.

An educated guess at Dr. Jascalevich's personal income during the past ten years would place him in the category of easily earning no less than $100,000 a year, and possibly much more. This estimate is based upon the figures brought to our attention at the time of the Riverdell incident, the fact that he was also working at three other hospitals, the number of surgical procedures he was performing daily (three at one hospital the day of his indictment, four the day the story broke), and the long line of patients almost constantly awaiting his attention during office hours. These figures are also in line with general information available on surgical income. Jascalevich was a busy and prosperous surgeon. His prior professional facility and acuity provided him the means for the most expert legal defense.

Defense counsel Ray Brown first made a motion to dismiss the case against Jascalevich on the grounds that too much time had elapsed since the alleged murders and the indictment. While there is no statute of limitations on murder cases under New Jersey law, the defense argued that the defendant was unconstitutionally deprived of an opportunity to prepare an adequate defense as a result of the long time which had elapsed since the events in question and the pending trial. Judge Trautwein denied the defense motion on the ground that the New Jersey statute of limitations was the governing law.

The judge also denied defense motions to move the site of the trial from Bergen County to Mercer County in the southern part of the state. This effort was founded on the argument that pervasive adverse pretrial publicity in Bergen County made it impossible for the surgeon to enjoy a fair trial in Bergen County. The judge held that the newspaper and other media coverage "has been neither so vitriolic nor so adverse as to have created an overly inflammatory or inherently prejudicial atmosphere" in Bergen County. He added, "The news media, although not always as circumspect as it might have been, has not convicted this defendant in the court of public opinion."

Other motions made by the defense had to do with the rights of pretrial discovery. The judge granted the defense request for access to the sixty-two-page handwritten report on the Riverdell deaths which had been prepared by the detectives in Calissi's office. His decision in this matter, which Mrs. Moses opposed on behalf of the people, was based on the legal determination that even though working papers of an attorney (the prosecutor) were confidential, that confidentiality was lost when the papers fell into the hands of the press, where they had already been extensively disclosed by the *Record.*

Brown also moved unsuccessfully for an opportunity to have the five bodies reexhumed in order to allow his own defense experts to examine them.

Finally, in the months preceding the trial, the worst fears of the Riverdell directors were realized. Civil lawsuits by relatives of the victims began.

The first one was filed in July, 1976, by Eileen Shaw's husband and their four children. The defendants named in that case were Riverdell Hospital, its five directors, its ex-administrator, and all the members of the hospital mortality and tissue review committee at the time of Mrs. Shaw's death. The theory set forth in the plaintiffs' papers was that Mrs. Shaw, while a patient at the hospital, was a victim of assault and battery which resulted in her death. The attorney for the plaintiffs argued that the defendants were negligent in caring for Mrs. Shaw because they had failed to investigate the cluster of deaths prior to hers or to follow proper procedures, and had fraudulently concealed their unexplained nature. Nowhere in the plaintiffs' papers was Dr. Jascalevich named, nor is he a defendant in the lawsuit.

In November, a second civil action was filed against Riverdell Hospital, but in this case Dr. Jascalevich was also made a defendant. This case was brought by the son of Frank Biggs and charges Dr. Jascalevich directly with intentionally causing his father's death.

During 1977 Riverdell Hospital filed for permission of the bankruptcy court to reorganize under Chapter Eleven of the bankruptcy laws. This occured in anticipation of the publicity expected to attend the forthcoming trial, difficulties with Blue Cross reimbursements, and partially as a result of a serious decline in admissions. It is reasonable to assume that the attitude of prospective patients was affected by the publicity.

Motion after motion by Jascalevich's defense attorney attempted to delay, transfer, or avoid the trial. On February 16, 1978, Judge Trautwein denied the defense's last effort to move the site of the trial, and he ordered it to proceed.

PART V

CHAPTER XXV

Preparation for Trial

People involved in a murder trial find the experience to be unlike anything else they will ever encounter. It is likely to affect them forever. Even the professionals for whom it is a regular part of life will not forget it, especially when the case encompasses an accusation of five killings instead of just one.

There is no other drama in which so many otherwise unrelated players assemble to play such different roles, any one of which might be critical to the outcome. Judge, jurors, lawyers, and witnesses, all have the opportunity to fulfill one of these decisive functions, and each of them can make a life or death difference to someone with whom they may be only momentarily acquainted. For most, it will probably be the only time in their lives when they will have to bear such a heavy burden, and each will face this responsibility from a different perspective, based on his own talent, temperament, and experience.

No single case in memory had ever been filled with such a complexity of unprecedented elements. Twelve years had gone by since the supposed victims had died, and since there were no eye witnesses to the crimes charged, the people's case would be entirely circumstantial. The motive ascribed to Dr. Jascalevich was obscure at best, and because he was a respected surgeon, the terrible accusation was more difficult to believe.

When the Bergen County prosecutor's office first decided to take another look at its nine-year-old file, nobody there perceived that it would someday develop into a triable case, so it was natural for Mr. Woodcock to ask a very junior member of his staff to review the matter.

Although she was thirty-five years old, Sybil Moses was only one year out of law school when she received the assignment. She had spent her postcollege years as a suburban housewife, part-time college instructor, and youth worker before she was able to undertake her legal training. Because her husband is a practicing lawyer, she knew what to expect of the legal profession. Mrs. Moses had demonstrated a capacity for self-discipline in the excellent academic record she acquired for her first two degrees. However, when the biggest and most complex criminal case in the history of Bergen County was assigned to her, she was still very much a novice prosecutor who had never tried a murder case.

Like everyone else who had ever been involved with the case, Mrs. Moses found the facts fascinating as she marshalled the evidence for presentation to Bergen County's part-time, one-day-a-week grand jury, a process which took two months before Dr. Jascalevich was actually indicted. Until the trial began, Mrs. Moses also prepared responses for one motion after another that her more experienced opponent was devising on a regular basis. Mrs. Moses had also handled the critical effort to get court permission to exhume bodies.

Contrary to the impression conveyed to most people by television programs about prosecutors, the resources available to the suburban prosecutor are sparse. Only one full-time investigator was available to help Mrs. Moses gather the necessary information; and with no other lawyers to assist her, the inexperienced prosecutor did all of her own research and prepared briefs and memoranda while still responsible for prosecuting other cases in the office until September of 1977.

Sybil Moses came to my office on October 17, 1977, to discuss the history of my involvement in the case. A nice-looking, dark woman, dressed in a conservative tweed suit, she wore her thick black hair in a rather old-fashioned pageboy, the bangs of which accentuated her large and attractive brown eyes. She impressed me as a cautious and not overconfident person, with a deliberate thoroughness that I found almost plodding, because I was unable to lead her to the facts that seemed most salient to me until she had fully grasped the minor ones that came first. Clearly, Sybil Moses would not be obstructed by the sort of self-importance that frequently gets in the way of young lawyers who are bearing important responsibilities for government. Her maturity and intelligence might help to compensate for the legal experience she was lacking. Throughout our first discussion, and others to ensue, she was thoughtful about acknowledging my long-standing interest in the case, and seemed attentive to my suggestions. I had been apprehensive that she would treat me otherwise because of the unofficial nature of my interest, but that was not the case once she understood the matter well enough to know that I had no ulterior motive.

I told her about some of my concerns and of the meeting I had had with Attorney General William Hyland in January.

"Why didn't you come to us?" she asked with just a trace of indignation.

"Well, Myron Farber led me to believe that he was in touch with your boss regularly and had told him of my involvement, and considering the previous handling of this case by your office, as well as the fact that Woodcock never called me, I was very skeptical. Do you really blame me? Besides," I pointed out, "I heard that there may be a common political heritage between Woodcock and Calissi, and so there may be some desire to protect Calissi because he is now a judge."

Mrs. Moses acknowledged that from my perspective, my action was understandable to her; but she took pains to assure me that she had explored every aspect of the case and that when there appeared to be sufficient evidence, she had been free to present it to the grand jury. She also explained how the county prosecutor's office had been improved since Calissi's day, that there were more assistant prosecutors, that they were not selected on a political basis alone, and that as a matter of fact, although she was a good Democrat, she had been appointed to her job by a Republican incumbent who was a good friend of her husband. This did not dispel my concern about the possibility of a prosecutor protecting his predecessor.

Without disclosing that the attorney general's office had already undertaken to do so, I pressed her about whether or not they were going to do a thorough search of patients' records at the other hospitals where Jascalevich worked to see if there were any similar patterns of postsurgical deaths.

"No," she answered, obviously having considered the matter. "We have a problem about our jurisdiction to issue subpoenas outside of the county, but I do not think the situation is comparable at the other hospitals, because Jascalevich was not the chief of surgery anywhere else, and so the same motive would not exist."

I was not convinced, but expressed the hope that she was right on this point. Eventually, I came to believe that she was, because it seemed that the results of the attorney general's survey supported her theory.

Mrs. Moses asked me to find out from Dr. Helpern what had become of the physical evidence that was delivered to him so many years ago. When I called Helpern, whom I had not been in touch with since 1967, he greeted me warmly and said that he felt sure that he had kept everything intact and would call me as soon as he found it. He said it was either still at the medical examiner's office or among the items stored at his private office at home, where he had been working since his retirement. As before, he was extremely cooperative, and we had a long telephone conversation during which he denounced Myron Farber emphatically, blaming him for the "terribly unfair stories" about the medical examiner's office which had appeared just before Helpern's retirement. He also attributed Farber's source of information to the ". . . ambitions of some of my own staff, people I had trained and trusted."

Only two or three days passed before Dr. Helpern called to tell me that he was sure he had the material until recently, but that he was unable to find it, although he had searched everywhere. He was conferring with his wife in the background as he told me it had been in a big red envelope in his office for a long time, and while it was possible that it had been thrown out, they did not think that was the case. He was genuinely distressed about his inability to come up with the material and apologized profusely, promising he would continue to search for it; but the following week he called again and said that it was nowhere to be found.

Some weeks later I suggested to Mrs. Moses that she might want to meet with Dr. Helpern. He had made statements to newspaper reporters when the story first broke which could be construed as somewhat inconsistent with the views he had expressed to me at the time of the original investigation. Because I had become aware of Helpern's negative feelings about Dr. Baden, who had been credited in news accounts with the theory that the deaths were not attributable to their officially ascribed causes (which had also been Helpern's original theory), as well as the expectation that curare could be discovered on exhumation (which Helpern had never mentioned), I was concerned that Helpern's perspective on the case might be affected by the fact that he was no longer the central forensic medical expert. Besides, I had already seen enough evidence of ego getting in the way of medical objectivity, that it seemed important to me that Helpern should not be allowed to feel left out now that the matter was coming to a head after all these years.

I arranged a meeting in my office for Dr. Helpern and Sybil Moses. Dr. Helpern was again apologetic about the missing material, but his recollections about his reactions to the transcript he had reviewed and the slides he had examined were now too imprecise to be of much value. Mrs. Moses felt that he was being less than fully candid, and afterwards she expressed her concern to me that perhaps someone on the defense side of this case had already approached him. I did not share this concern, because Helpern did confirm to us that his recollection of Dr. Umberger's test on the Shaw tissue was the same as my own.

On April 22, 1977, Dr. Helpern died after suffering a stroke while he was on a speaking trip in San Diego. The unique contribution he made to the development of forensic medicine during his lifetime was without parallel.

During the period prior to the trial, I had several other opportunities to talk with Sybil Moses, since she had decided to list me as a prosecution witness in the event that certain material with which I was familiar could not be introduced in some more first-hand manner. As it turned out, my presence was not required by the prosecutor.

One thing that impressed me was the awesome respect that Moses had for the defense counsel, Ray Brown. During our pretrial preparatory meeting she said, "Now remember, Brown's a very tough cross-examiner, and you have to be prepared for anything he may come up with."

"Sybil, I'm not worried about that; there is nothing that I will say that he can use to his advantage. Frankly, I'd like very much to have him try."

"But," she persisted, "he's very tough and will try anything. You had better be on your guard."

"Sybil, I think you're afraid of him." I risked the consequences of such a charge because I wanted to test her reaction, and because I was worried that she might already be intimidated by Brown's experience and reputation.

She was not visibly ruffled by my attack, and she responded logically by pointing out the imbalance between the resources of the prosecutor and the defense in a case where the defendant had sufficient financial resources. She said that Brown had several younger lawyers working for him, while she was working on her own, so she had a lot to be worried about. This turned out to be prophetic.

Dr. Jascalevich's selection of Ray Brown was one of the smartest moves that anyone in his position could possibly have made, and Sybil Moses had every reason to respect her opponent. Raymond A. Brown is something special.

Everyone I have come across who ever knew Brown believes that he is the best criminal defense lawyer in New Jersey, and perhaps in the nation. He is considered to be a superb courtroom fighter.

The highlight of sixty-two-year-old Ray Brown's courtroom reputation is his skill at cross-examination, where he is known to pursue hostile witnesses ferociously, a trait designed to intimidate prosecutors and witnesses alike.

Ray Brown has built a legend about himself, frequently citing his humble beginnings as the son of an illiterate manual laborer. A black man who looks white, he has long been an advocate in the civil rights battle in his home town of Jersey City. Brown worked his way through Fordham Law School after a stint in the Civilian Conservation Corps of the New Deal era, preceded by four years in an all-black college in Florida.

Neither Dr. Jascalevich nor the other Riverdell Hospital doctors who would be witnesses were unacquainted with the county courthouse in Hackensack. It also houses the prosecutor's office, with which all of them had become familiar twelve years earlier. As an institutional building, it is a musty, conventional sort of place; as a courthouse, it is somewhat better than most, although the paneled chamber scheduled for this trial did not hold as many spectators as would have liked to attend at first.

On Monday morning, February 27, 1978, eleven years after Dr. Jascalevich resigned from the Riverdell Hospital staff, the process of selecting the jury that would try him began. The list of over 200 prospective scheduled witnesses was unusually long, so it was assumed that the trial might last as long as three months.

Sixty-four-year-old Justice William J. Arnold, whose retirement was imminent, had reportedly asked for the assignment to try the case. Courthouse observers assumed that this would be his final trial. Judge Arnold had once been the second assistant to former County Prosecutor Guy Calissi, but he had left the prosecutor's office in 1960, long before the Riverdell investigation, and he had been appointed to his first judicial post later that same year, following a typical career path of active Democratic party lawyers of his day.

After eighteen years on the bench, Justice Arnold's record as a jurist remained undistinguished. "Ordinary" was the closest thing to a superlative that one of his judicial colleagues whom I spoke with could think of to describe Arnold, although he assured me that the judge was "a good fellow."

It took four days to select eleven men and seven women as jurors from among a panel of 140 prospects. Under New Jersey law, eighteen panelists are chosen to hear the entire proceeding, and at the end of the trial, six of the eighteen are severed by the selection of lots, thus reducing the panel to the traditional twelve. In other jurisdictions, only twelve are selected along with additional alternates, but the New Jersey approach is designed to assure that the panelists, all of whom are unaware until the end if they will have the actual responsibility, all pay equal attention throughout the trial. This system is especially useful for a long trial.

For the most part, the jurors ultimately selected were not college educated; half were married, and they represented a realistic cross-section of middle-class Bergen County. Among them were a registered nurse, two accountants, two housewives, and a student, as well as a plant manager, a phone company splicer, a secretary, a cosmetic chemist, a stock clerk, a payroll clerk, a bank teller, a salesman, an engineer, a copywriter, and a retired postal employee. They were generally young or middle aged.

Because of the anticipated length of the trial, Judge Arnold did not sequester the jury. They were free to go home each night, but when they took their oath as jurors, the judge admonished them against discussing the case, or reading or listening to media accounts of it. The judge did say that they might be sequestered when it came time for their deliberations at the end of the trial.

Judge Arnold ordered that prospective witnesses be excluded from the trial until after they testify, a customary procedure intended to make certain that witnesses will not be influenced by the testimony of others.

This order created a problem for the *New York Times,* which had assigned Myron Farber to cover the trial. Farber was listed as a witness by the defense and was therefore subject to the court's sequestration order. Judge Arnold offered Farber the opportunity to testify in chambers in advance to enable him to cover the trial, but the reporter declined, and did not cover the trial. The *Times* decided that a basic freedom-of-the-press issue was at stake. Its attorney argued unsuccessfully before Judge Arnold that Farber should not be asked to testify at all, since he enjoyed a privilege as a reporter. This was only the first of a number of major legal issues involving the rights of the press to arise out of the Jascalevich case.

On Monday, March 6, 1978, each side presented its opening arguments, outlining its theories in public for the first time. Sybil Moses's half-hour opening was relatively brief.

She began by pointing out how Jascalevich had been the hospital's only general surgeon until 1965 and 1966, when several new surgeons joined the staff, and she alluded to the impact of this on Jascalevich's practice. The prosecutor pointed out that curare had been discovered in Jascalevich's locker and that Jascalevich had been seen near the various patients just before they died, but she acknowledged that there were no eye witnesses to the administration of curare. According to Mrs. Moses, the state would establish the presence of curare in the bodies of the dead patients, and she would prove that the victims died as a result of an injection of curare. "There was no reason, save one, to have that curare in that locker, and that reason resulted in those deaths." Glaring directly at Dr. Jascalevich, Mrs. Moses concluded by saying, "In every single case, one name, one person was there before and after the deaths of these people. He's there. This defendant."

When the prosecutor finished, tall, lanky, and balding Ray

Brown rose to his feet to deliver his opening statement. Impressive despite the threadbare baggy grey suit that he was going to wear for weeks at a time, Brown was eloquent when compared to the inexperienced prosecutor. The defense counsel started by saying, "This entire case is based on speculations and concepts that have no factual basis."

His defense would be that this was simply a case of a frame-up engineered by Jascalevich's inept former colleagues, who were desperately trying to cover their own mistakes. Brown said that because Dr. Jascalevich was concerned about the way medicine was practiced at Riverdell, he had been attempting to prevent unnecessary surgery and had called for a meeting of the hospital's directors in order to raise questions about the high mortality rate among other surgeons' patients. Brown asked the jury, "Why should Jascalevich pay this horrible price because Harris and others knew he was too well trained to allow the horrors of excessive mortality by other doctors?" He specified Dr. Stanley Harris and Dr. Allan Lans, saying that they were the ones who had "conspired in the night" to gain access to Jascalevich's locker. Demeaning the importance of the fact that the curare was found in Jascalevich's locker, a fact which he never denied, the defense counsel said, "The writing was on the wall, Dr. Jascalevich was not satisfied with the way surgery was going in the hospital, ergo, go into his locker, find the curare, the poison. Ladies and gentlemen, curare is no more a poison than aspirin, unless it is misused." He told the jury that there are legitimate uses for curare in the hospital and that it was found in other places in the hospital besides Jascalevich's locker.

Waiving a handful of notes in one hand and his eye glasses in the other, the attorney concluded his sometimes stirring fifty-minute opening to the jury by saying, "This case will prove once and for all the fact that prosecutors, newspapers, and politicians can use their freedoms to risk the lives of others for the sake of their careers. . . . The entire case is based upon speculation. It has no factual basis."

CHAPTER XXVI

The Prosecution Case

The state called Allan Lans as the trial's first witness. In his capacity as secretary of the hospital's board of directors, Mrs. Moses had him review a 1964 memorandum from the hospital records which categorized Riverdell's various surgeons into three groups, A, B, and C. The A category was to have unlimited surgical privileges, while the B category could do only limited major surgery on their own and the C group, only minor surgery. Only three surgeons were listed in the A category, Jascaelvich and two others who were then in the process of leaving the hospital, which meant that only Jascalevich had unlimited privileges. The B category had two names, but both doctors had already left the hospital dissatisfied over the limitations on their practices; and twelve others, including Lans himself, were in the C category. The memorandum was a policy proposal by Dr. Jascalevich as chief of the surgery department, and Lans testified that the board rejected it as too restrictive, because it did not provide for elevating someone from one category to another. Lans told the jury that this policy was in part responsible for the board's dissatisfaction with Jascalevich, especially because it was sometimes difficult to find him when an emergency arose.

Throughout the State's opening testimony, Ray Brown interrupted with one objection after the other. Rarely would he let the prosecutor finish a question, or the witness finish an answer, without rising to protest on one ground or another. Sometimes he shouted his objections, and, although most were overruled, a deliberate and disruptive process of generating confusion and making everyone uncomfortable had begun. Within days, Brown's tactics would degenerate into name calling of the witnesses and ridicule of the prosecutor.

Prosecutor Sybil Moses and Defense Counsel Raymond A. Brown Arguing before Judge William J. Arnold

Whenever the prosecutor attempted to introduce any document into the record, Brown would be on his feet openly deriding her competence or her personality and denigrating the value of the document. Each time he did this, Brown took the opportunity to testify about his own views on a variety of matters, and the judge allowed him to do so despite the prosecutor's objections.

Soon Brown's tactics, and not the testimony itself, began to grab the jury's and the press's attention. Typical headlines during the first two weeks of the trial were, "DR. X LAWYER OBJECTS A MILE A MINUTE"; "LAWYERS CLASH OVER EVIDENCE IN DR. X TRIAL"; "JOUSTING CONTINUES BETWEEN LAWYERS IN DR. X TRIAL"; "DISPUTE ON RECORD SNAGS TRIAL OF DR. X."

These distractions grew in intensity, and each day Mrs. Moses and Mr. Brown would become more sarcastic to one another as Brown hacked away at minutiae and the acrimony of his personal assaults on Sybil Moses intensified. Judge Arnold did little to improve the situation—his rulings were slow in coming, and he soon seemed to be losing control.

For the most part, Allan Lans kept his cool, and according to people who watched, the jury could not help but be impressed with the sincerity that came through his soft voice as he told them the story which I had heard so many years before.

The media highlight of the first week of the already bizarre trial was the scene of a banner-carrying crowd of some thirty white-uniformed nurses and former patients of Dr. Jascalevich, surrounding him outside the courthouse with their fingers raised in a "V for victory" sign for the benefit of the news photographers and TV cameras as the accused multiple-murderer warmly beamed his gratification. At the same time, Jascalevich also broke his long public silence and began talking to reporters, telling them how his patients were wishing him luck and waiting for his office to reopen. Inside the courthouse, he had been personally thanking people for coming to his trial.

That was Jascalevich's mood on the same day that Dr. Lans broke down in tears as he described the death of four-year-old Nancy Savino.

As the trial entered its second week on March 13, Mrs. Moses was still examining Allan Lans. Alan recalled for the prosecutor how he had once asked Jascalevich why Dr. Robert Briski was having so many postoperative deaths among his patients. Lans testified, "He said that perhaps Dr. Briski was jinxed."

Later that morning, in response to Mrs. Moses's request for his opinion about what had happened at Riverdell, Allan Lans said,

"My opinion was that, in fact, these patients had been tampered with, and, in fact, they had been murdered."

"Did you form any further opinions?"

"Yes, my opinion was also that Dr. Jascalevich was responsible for these deaths."

The response brought Ray Brown to his feet rightfully demanding a mistrial, but Judge Arnold ruled that the trial should continue. He instructed the jury to disregard Dr. Lans's opinions, telling them that forming opinions was their job, not the witness's.

Ray Brown's cross-examination of Allan Lans began on Tuesday, March 14. Brown started by quoting a part of Allan's sworn statement to Calissi in 1966, when Allan had said of Jascalevich, "He's operated on my wife. He did a marvelous job. I would trust him, you know, surgically. His surgical technique is marvelous." Using this statement, Brown brought out the fact that Jascalevich had stayed on as chief surgeon and had actually performed thirty-six more operations after the 1966 investigation was closed. Brown even got Allan Lans to admit that he had assisted Jascalevich in some of those cases.

Brown found an occasion to tell the jury that there were sixty-seven vials of curare in the hospital in 1966 in stock in three different places. He also attempted to use Allan to demonstrate that the presence of curare in the hospital was not so unusual. As he strode back and forth in front of the witness, Brown asked, "It's perfectly legal to have curare in your locker, or your pocket, in your home. So, why does he need to explain it to you?"

Allan replied cooly, "It's legal, but mighty unusual."

Then Brown initiated his effort to discredit the quality of medical practice at Riverdell. He examined Allan Lans about one of the hospital's anesthesiologists, Dr. Robert Baba, who Brown said had sometimes left the operating room while his patients were under anesthesia, and that Lans had been so concerned about Baba's practice that he had once admonished him about it. Brown tried to establish that on the occasion of Margaret Henderson's operation, Baba had left the patient with a high-school student to monitor the anesthesia. (Baba had died in a fire in his home on July 19, 1976, and the origin of the fire was never determined.)

During the cross-examination, Brown elicited from Lans that the hospital had at one time used unlicensed doctors as house staff.

He also used the case of Margaret Henderson to discredit Lans by pointing out that Jascalevich had cautioned against the surgery she underwent and that Lans, although only a consultant on the case, had recommended that she be operated on. Under Brown's questioning Lans was also forced to relate that when Mrs. Henderson came out of surgery she was returned to her room because there was no recovery-room staff available in the hospital. To emphasize his point, Brown asked Lans, "Didn't she die in the hallway?" (Actually she had not.) Driving his point home, Brown pointed out to the jury that in 1965 Jascalevich had threatened to resign unless the hospital did something to improve its recovery-room facilities.

On the third day of cross-examination, Ray Brown shifted his effort from discrediting Riverdell Hospital to embarrassing Dr. Lans. His questions became nastier. Referring to the break-in of Jascalevich's locker, he asked, "Why didn't you tell him face to face, man to man?"

Lans answered, "Because it was a matter for the prosecutor, and in the locker was the very thing that substantiated all my fears."

Brown accused, "Because you and Harris knew all along you had found your pigeon, isn't that so? You knew the answers?"

"I know the truth," Lans replied.

Referring to Allan Lans's stock interest in the hospital, Brown asked, "Your 18 percent was above any sense of justice, wasn't it?" But without giving Allan time to answer the question, Brown went on, "That motivated your life from that day to this, didn't it? You have been on this one track, haven't you?" Finally, Allan was allowed to respond, "I have not spent my life in the pursuit of Dr. Jascalevich. When the story came out and the prosecutor reopened the case I was ready, willing, and able to tell my version."

Both the lawyer and the witness became hotter, and Judge Arnold ignored Sybil Moses's objections to the line of accusatory questioning. When Brown wheeled toward the witness and asked, "Did you see Dr. Jascalevich do anything to these patients?" Allan replied softly, "I hadn't seen that."

Brown continued to take every opportunity to testify himself through his questions, asking Allan Lans at one point, "You knew you had to defend your poorly run hospital against suits because of its excessive mortality rate?" Sybil Moses objected strenuously, and Brown, now the accuser, outshouted her to the judge, "He is an 18 percent owner of the hospital. He faces high mortalities and he had to find a sacrificial lamb."

In response to Mr. Brown, Allan Lans reaffirmed his view of Jascalevich as cold and aloof, a man who "just went about his business."

Brown asked, "Was he kind to people?"

"Most people," Lans answered.

"Who was he unkind to, you?"

"No."

"Whom was he unkind to?" Brown probed, thinking he was scoring a point until, after a long silence, Lans responded,

"Nancy Savino and Margaret Henderson."

By the end of the third week of testimony, the cross-examination had already taken twice as long as Dr. Lans's direct examination. Allan Lans was on the witness stand for the eleventh and final day. The prosecutor was concluding her redirect examination, her second round of questioning after the defense had conducted its cross-examination. She had Allan Lans introduce the hospital's mortality statistics for surgical deaths: in 1963 they accounted for 2.4 percent of the total; in 1964, 1.9 percent; in 1965, the year Jascalevich arrived, the figure went up to 7.5 percent; in 1966, it rose to a peak of 20 percent; and in 1967, the year that Jascalevich left the hospital, it was 12.5 percent.

Brown used the same mortality statistics to attempt to show that the surgical deaths were primarily responsibilities of Dr. Harris, who had lost 10 of the 15 deceased surgical patients in 1966 and 11 of the 14 surgical patients who had died at Riverdell in 1967, after Jascalevich had left the hospital.

Lans's testimony had been interrupted frequently by bitter outbursts between the prosecutor and the defense counsel, outbursts which continued to be very personal in nature. The defense objected to just about everything the prosecutor did and to most of what the prosecution witness said. The defense objected to the blown-up hospital charts that the prosecutor wanted to utilize to show evidence to the jury, claiming they were prejudicial. He objected to the qualifications of the witness to testify on certain matters; but while doing so, Brown himself testified on matters of which he could have only second-hand knowledge. Motions were made about the lack of availability of evidence or documents to the defense, and arguments were heard about the relevancy of such material.

All of these legal issues were being determined in the midst of a rather circuslike atmosphere created by the presence in the courtroom of TV and news reporters, as many as seven different artists busily sketching the scene for various media outlets, and Dr. Jascalevich's former patients filling the courtroom each day to demonstrate their support. The slow pace and general disorder were enhanced by a judge who frequently started the day's activities late, usually took a luncheon recess of not less than one and a half hours and sometimes two, and ended each day's "work" by 4 P.M. or earlier.

From the prosecutor's perspective, all of this was bound to create terrible frustration, while the defense found the delays, disruptions, and distractions advantageous. In a criminal trial it can be a legitimate tactic for the defense attorney, acting within certain boundaries of professional conduct, to do whatever he can to distract the jury from the real issues when they are not helpful to his client and, more importantly, to create as many different reasons possible to demand a mistrial or to develop a basis for an appeal of a verdict of guilty.

Keeping these distractions under control and keeping the trial moving is the judge's responsibility, and if he fails, chaos can result which usually benefits the defendant.

Lans was followed by the state's second witness, Miriam Oshust, the hospital's current administrator, who was brought in to authenticate the hospital's records, and her testimony took all day on Tuesday, March 21. Dr. Jay Sklar was then on the stand for two days, during which Brown ridiculed his competency as a physician by demonstrating the osteopath's lack of familiarity with certain medical terms which Brown read to him from a textbook that he claimed should have been common knowledge for any physician.

On Thursday, March 23, with the trial nearing the end of its third week of testimony, while Dr. Jay Sklar was on the witness stand testifying about the death of his patient Carl Rohrbeck, Dr. Jascalevich gave his second interview to the courtroom reporters.

He told them, "I am absolutely sure that we will disprove the charges. The truth will emerge, and I shall return to my dear profession. Two years waiting for a trial. It's terrible." Then, he smiled and said, "I'm here to celebrate justice."

Meanwhile, numbers of his loyal Spanish-speaking patients had been continuing to attend the trial, greeting him warmly and ostentatiously each day in full view of the jury.

Dr. Jascalevich's second interview session with the press made all of the television station news broadcasts that night, just as the demonstration of his former patients carrying signs of support had the week before. Sybil Moses was incensed and felt that the entire production had been programmed by the defense to influence the unsequestered jury. As a result, she asked Judge Arnold to issue a "gag order" requiring all of the participants in the trial—lawyers, witnesses, and the defendant—to remain silent outside the courtroom. Defense counsel Brown objected, saying that for two years all of the publicity had been against this defendant, but he told the judge that he had cautioned his client and all the defense witnesses to refrain from making any more comments. Judge Arnold denied Mrs. Moses's request.

(During the arguments over the prosecutor's motion, it was revealed that it was Prosecutor Joseph Woodcock himself who gave Myron Farber access to the case file in August of 1975.)

The gag-order motion had been made during a one-day recess in the trial occasioned by the illness of one of the jurors. When the trial reconvened on Tuesday, March 27, the prosecutor presented a surprise witness to back up Dr. Sklar's testimony of the previous week, describing Carl Rohrbeck's death. The witness was Annette O'Brien, who had been the floor nurse on the day Rohrbeck died.

Mrs. O'Brien testified that she was with Jascalevich when he examined Mr. Rohrbeck and that Jascalevich had told her he observed a distended neck vein on the patient which could indicate a heart problem. But Mrs. O'Brien said that she was standing only a few feet away from Mr. Rohrbeck and had not seen any such distension. She explained that Dr. Jascalevich had requested that she bring him an intravenous apparatus and feeding of dextrose and water, which she did, and that she gave the equipment to Jascalevich to set up himself before she left the room. According to the nurse, it was unusual for Jascalevich to set up an I.V. himself, and she had never seen him do so before—that task was usually performed by the staff physician.

Mrs. O'Brien described Carl Rohrbeck as talkative, alert, and appearing well when she left the room, after which Jascalevich had remained for five minutes, setting up the intravenous feeding. She had seen Jascalevich leave the room and walk briskly down the corridor. A few minutes later, he returned and said to her, "Mrs. O'Brien, your patient is dead."

When his time came to cross-examine Mrs. O'Brien, Brown attacked the witness's ability to remember so clearly by demonstrating a number of things which she was unable to recall, such as what Jasclaevich was wearing and the name of the nurse assigned to Mr. Rohrbeck that day. In his cross-examination, Brown accused her of reflecting the *New York Times*'s account of Rohrbeck's death, which she had admitted reading, rather than relying on her own memory.

Mrs. O'Brien was followed on the witness stand by Dr. Arthur F. DeMarco, who was the chief anesthesiologist at Riverdell in 1965 and 1966. He testified that although he had used other muscle relaxants routinely during surgery at Riverdell, he did not use curare, which was used only rarely by others. He added that whatever ampules of the drug were found in the operating room at Riverdell had been ordered by one of his predecessors.

Dr. DeMarco also testified that in two cases in which he was involved, Emma Arzt and Frank Biggs, Dr. Jascalevich had been present at the bedside and had assisted in emergency efforts to resuscitate each of those patients by administering heart massage and artificial respiration as each patient stopped breathing. In Mrs. Arzt's case, Dr. DeMarco also recalled the blue pallor associated with cyanosis.

During the effort to resuscitate Mrs. Arzt, a breathing tube had been inserted in her throat by Dr. Harris, and in his cross-examination of Dr. DeMarco, Ray Brown tried to show how the insertion of the tube could have caused heart failure which, according to Brown, was the real cause of death.

Brown did get Dr. DeMarco to testify that the Arzt chart did not show Jascalevich as being present in the patient's room during the four hours preceding her death, and that a lethal dose of curare would have had a paralyzing effect on the patient for one hour at most in situations like this where the patient's breathing had been taken over by a mechanical respirator. Without such a respirator, DeMarco said, death from curare would occur in minutes.

The testimonies of Nurse O'Brien and Dr. DeMarco each took up about one day of the trial, and so the month of March ended with only five witnesses having been heard in full.

On the 30th day of March, all of the frustrations engendered by the tension of the trial's first three weeks culminated in Judge Arnold's citing Sybil Moses for contempt of court. Longtime courtroom observers in Hackensack had never before seen that happen to a prosecutor. The citation came as a result of Mrs. Moses's demanding that she be allowed time to respond to a forty-five-minute argument by Brown during which he charged that, "there is a prevasive air of chicanery, fraud, and at the very least, negligence on the part of the authorities of this county." Brown was complaining that some of the physical evidence was missing from the inventory of Jascalevich's locker, including some of the curare vials, syringes, and needles, and Brown claimed that the prosecutor had deliberately thrown the evidence away, along with a tape recording and some of the slides of tissue. Brown, protesting that "the chain of evidence had been tampered with," was trying to make it more difficult for Mrs. Moses to introduce into evidence those curare vials that were still in her possession.

Sybil Moses contended that following her nine-minute argument in support of the evidence she wanted to introduce, the judge had afforded Brown forty-five minutes to object, so she was entitled to have some time to reply to his extensive allegations. Judge Arnold said he had heard enough and ordered her to sit down and be quiet. When she stayed on her feet and continued to talk, Arnold again ordered her to sit down and be quiet, but she did not comply. Arnold warned her twice that she could be held in contempt, but the prosecutor persisted loudly until the judge raised his own voice and once more told her to sit down: "Are you refusing to obey my order?"

"I will obey your order if you will allow me to respond. Don't yell at me, Judge."

"I'm yelling at you," the judge replied, and then cited her for contempt.

Moses demanded to be tried immediately on the contempt charge, but the judge refused to do so, ruling that he would deal with the contempt citation at the end of the trial, as is customary in such cases.

After a brief recess, the judge eventually ruled in Mrs. Moses's favor on the evidentiary point, allowing her to introduce the locker's contents into evidence just as she had wanted to.

Everyone involved in the trial, including Sybil Moses, was well aware that this was her first murder trial and that she was a beginner pitted against an attorney who was generally believed to be the best in the state. Unfortunately for her, Brown had not hesitated to exploit this fact openly, and to exacerbate her sensitivity about it by making frequent derogatory comments about her lack of experience, including such statements as, "Is school in session?" a reference to his earlier career as a schoolteacher.

Judge Arnold had played into Brown's hands by being far more critical of Mrs. Moses and at times harsh, once telling her publicly that she was not doing a good job. He let Brown say and do things that were completely out of the ordinary, allowed him to taunt Mrs. Moses, and ignored her frequent objections that Brown was abusing his rights as a cross-examiner by testifying for the witness he was examining. Frequently, the judge would appear to have difficulty remembering the prosecutor's name. Perhaps most frustrating was the fact that Judge Arnold's eyes were sometimes closed and he appeared to be napping during the testimony. The judge's frequent requests to have questions or testimony repeated contributed to the impression that if he was awake he was inattentive.

Shortly after the judge ruled on the admissibility of the evidence, Mrs. Moses asked for an adjournemnt, and she went to confer with her boss, Roger Breslin, Jr., the county prosecutor who had been appointed to succeed Joseph Woodcock when he resigned to run for governor in 1977. That night, Breslin issued a public statement in support of his assistant.

The next morning, Mr. Breslin himself appeared in the courtroom for the first time, and made an unprecedented motion before Judge Arnold. He asked the judge to disqualify himself from presiding over the balance of the trial.

Breslin stood up before Judge Arnold to tell him, "It has become more and more evident that your honor does not have the personality, the temperment, the intellectual intensity and stamina necessary to cope with the issues in this case and to control the attorneys in the case."

Prior to Breslin's motion, Sybil Moses had read into the record a five-page list of reasons why the judge should not allow himself to continue. Included in her list was the judge's failure to curb the defense counsel's provocative and insulting comments, an allegation that the judge appeared to be inattentive during parts of the trial, and that the additional threat to try her for contempt at the end of the trial would have a chilling effect on her ability to prosecute the case without fear. Mrs. Moses concluded by saying that she had only one purpose—to make certain that the state, as well as the defense, received a fair trial. (The prosecution cannot appeal from a verdict of not guilty.)

Of course, Ray Brown rose to the occasion and objected to the prosecutor's motion. He attributed it to frustration growing out of the realization that, "Their case has begun to fall apart because the substance isn't there." Looking at Judge Arnold, who would have to rule on this motion, Brown pointed at the American flag, and said, "If the day comes when the prosecutor can pick the judge it wants because its case isn't going well, then that flag to your right doesn't mean anything."

That comment generated applause among the spectators who packed the courtroom, and Judge Arnold made no attempt to restrain them; but he did adjourn the trial for the weekend to consider how he would rule on the pending motion.

On Monday, April 3, Judge Arnold rejected the prosecutor's effort. He called the attorneys before him and, speaking with a firmness of voice that had not been seen before, he said "The court favors no one." He said he had reviewed the record in light of all thirty-five alleged instances of shoddy treatment and judicial mistakes and found "nothing in the record to convince me that justice is not being done. . . . The State's motion to disqualify myself is denied."

A handclap started, but this time, Judge Arnold stopped it. The jury was brought back into the courtroom for the trial to continue.

Testimony during the first week of April revealed that the prosecutor's files had certainly been handled carelessly during the past ten years. The pictures taken by the Riverdell doctors the day before they went to see Calissi of Jascalevich's locker containing eighteen curare vials showed some discernable differences from the pictures taken by Calissi's own people eighteen hours later, the precise significance of which is unclear; but this did lend support to Brown's contention that his client was being framed. It also became apparent that the security methods of the property clerk who had custody of the locker's contents were not foolproof, and some items were apparently missing because the clerk had not compared the inventory list with the contents on all occasions when the evidence was taken to the prosecutor's office.

It was also discovered that ex-prosecutor, now judge, Fred Galda, had given Myron Farber of the *Times* a copy of the detectives' sixty-two-page hand-written summary of the investigation.

Brown, of course, found the explanation of time and carelessness unacceptable and seized on the missing materials to justify his claim of deliberate tampering with the evidence by the prosecution.

Lawrence J. Denson, M.D., Bergen County's chief medical examiner, testified for the prosecution in early April, and for the first time, the jury had to grapple with some of the extensive scientific evidence that might become decisive. As the county's medical examiner, Denson had to provide his opinions on a number of medical matters for the attorneys for both sides.

When he was an assistant medical examiner in 1965, Dr. Denson had done the autopsy on Carl Rohrbeck. Under Mrs. Moses's questioning, Denson admitted that although he had attributed Carl Rohrbeck's death to a coronary occlusion at the time of the autopsy, there was really no indication of any fresh heart damage to warrant his finding. (Apparently, Denson had based his diagnosis on the fact that the patient did have a history of earlier heart attacks.) He felt that Rohrbeck's death was "a little unusual," and because he had a suspicion that drugs of some kind might have been indicated, he had ordered a toxicologist's examination. Denson testified that the toxicologist's report found nothing; but they could not have found curare unless they were specifically looking for it, and they weren't.

Denson was examined outside the jury's presence about his view on whether or not an intravenous feeding of dextrose and water was appropriate in Mr. Rohrbeck's case. He said that had he been treating Rohrbeck, he would have removed, not added fluids (similar to Dr. Helpern's reaction when we discussed that case). Under cross-examination, however, Denson said, "it's a matter of choice," a concession that does not seem to make medical sense.

Dr. Denson also testified that when the entire affair was first presented to him by Calissi, his first reaction was to assume that the deaths were due to poor practice at Riverdell, and Mrs. Moses never asked him if he ever revised this view.

Brown was also able to get some statements out of Denson on cross-examination that tended to show Riverdell Hospital practices in a bad light, and thus buttressed Brown's contention that patients were dying because of the incompetence of the Riverdell staff.

Denson was further asked to review the findings of Dr. Raphael Gilady and Dr. Vincent Gillson, two of his former colleagues (both now dead), whose original autopsy report had attributed Margaret Henderson's death to a liver problem. Denson rejected their conclusion completely and based his view on a microscopic examination of Henderson's liver tissue. He said that in those days, when the county did not have the proper facilities they now have, autopsies were done at funeral homes and were frequently haphazard, with records being kept more informally.

During his testimony, Dr. Denson remarked that, "there are no absolutes in medicine."

A few days later, Mrs. Moses brought Dr. Donald B. Brown to the witness stand. He had done the microscopic exam on Mrs. Henderson's liver tissue when he was an assistant medical examiner to Dr. Gilady. Dr. Brown, an assistant medical examiner for the county, testified that there "was not a shread of evidence" to support the finding of hepatic necrosis of the liver which his former boss had attributed as the cause of Henderson's death.

Moses's next witness was Irene Nelson, the nurse who had attended at Nancy Savino's death, and her testimony placed Jascalevich near the child's room at the time of her death.

It became obvious by the first week in April that Sybil Moses was beginning to feel more at ease in the courtroom, and Ray Brown was finding it more difficult to provoke her with his insults. Until the prosecution had made the motion asking Judge Arnold to disqualify himself, it appeared to nearly everyone who followed the case that the battle between the attorneys was completely one-sided; but risky as it was, the very gutsiness of the prosecutor's effort had seemed to add a heavy weight on her side of the scale. On April 10, Ted Rohrlich, the *Bergen Record*'s reporter who had been following the case daily, wrote that Mrs. Moses is "... trying to mount a comeback. ..."

Nevertheless, the veteran Brown was still the dominant figure, his eloquence and years of experience enhanced by a briefcase full of trial lawyer's tactics all designed to keep the jury's attention on himself. Even his attire had a purpose: he wore old-fashioned suspenders under the baggy, threadbare suits which he usually changed only once a week. One experienced observer wondered whether the suits that Brown wore were so old that they just didn't fit well, or whether he had selected them deliberately to be ill-fitting.

The defense strategy had become clear. It was simple and calculated, and it has been employed over and over again in the history of American jurisprudence. Distract the jury's attention from anything that would remind them that the defendant has been charged with a crime and blame anyone else who happens on the scene for whatever you can. To whatever extent this tactic succeeds, it is helpful to the defense and it requires the prosecutor to assume the additional burden of clarifying the real issues.

Brown's client played his own role perfectly, always appearing to be a man who had nothing to fear. Frequently wearing a smile at times when a smile was inappropriate to a man whose freedom was in doubt, Jascalevich appeared practiced and disciplined. His appearance kept the role of a prominent surgeon, dressed impeccably in suits that bordered on flashy, with each accessory carefully color-keyed, every one of his long grey hairs flat and in place, and every gesture so measured that careful observers noticed him adjusting his hands and feet from time to time to look as intent or as relaxed as the circumstances required, while ostentatiously making notes on legal pads with a shiny gold pen. He appeared to be a vital source of corrective facts and information for his counsel, whom he frequently whispered to. Only the most sophisticated follower of the case would recall that Jascalevich's silver-grey hairs had been dark and wavy when he was indicted a year before.

As the trial entered its second month, Brown had succeeded in putting the hospital and the doctors who worked there on trial for incompetence. He was also beginning to put a certain amount of blame on the *New York Times* because of Myron Farber's involvement in the matter, and he was raising doubts about the motives of the prosecutor's office, because former Prosecutor Woodcock, the man who decided to reopen the case, had left his office to run for governor after getting a great deal of publicity because of Dr. Jascalevich's plight.

Rohrlich wrote on April 10, "at this juncture most of those in the press section are placing their bets on the defense."

Knowing that the jury was not sequestered, Brown made sure that some of each day was spent with the press, among whom he had become quite popular as an open, intelligent, and interesting story teller.

Another very significant legal motion in the case was made by the prosecutor on April 12, when she asked Judge Arnold to admit into evidence the 200-page transcript of the sworn statement that Prosecutor Calissi had taken from Jascalevich in 1966. (This is the one that Calissi had given to me.) In rebuttal, the defense took the position that it would not oppose the introduction of the statement, providing the prosecutor would also introduce into evidence a more informal taped interview that Jascalevich had given to Assistant Prosecutor Fred Galda eight days before he made the formal statement that Mrs. Moses wanted to introduce. The informal statement had been tape-recorded, and it came as no surprise to Brown when Mrs. Moses said that it could not be used because the four hours of recording were in such poor condition that much of it was unintelligible, and indeed one of the reels of tape was missing entirely. Brown argued that the evidence would be exculpatory of Jascalevich, that the missing tape and the poor condition were the prosecutor's responsibility, and that without all of this evidence available, the judge should not admit any of it. According to Brown, "the prosecutor's office has ruined them and now the defendant must suffer?"

With the jury excused, the debate on this motion went on for several days. The judge had the tapes played for himself in the presence of both attorneys and also heard testimony from retired Lieutenant Detective John J. Dunn of the prosecutor's office about the tape he had made while hiding in the closet in Eliot Weiner's home when the Riverdell directors first confronted Dr. Jascalevich. That tape was also missing, and Brown added the loss of that tape to the list of reasons why the transcript should not be admitted.

During the argument before Judge Arnold, Sybil Moses told the judge that Brown was trying to block admission of Jascalevich's statements because, "the State will show that these statements are lies, that these are the quotes of a man who calls a four year old child—a dead baby—a creature."

Brown had been waiting for that remark, and he jumped to his feet again: "She is as low as any prosecutor has ever sunk. The word creature is analogous to a word in Spanish that is not derogatory in any sense." Brown explained that Spanish was Jascalevich's native language and that he was relying on a literal translation of a Spanish word, *criatura,* which, according to Brown, is a creature, a baby, or a child.

As witnesses in the hearing, Brown called the former prosecutor and his former assistant, Superior Court Judges Calissi and Galda, and both supported Brown's position that the missing or garbled tapes were all part of a whole picture, along with the transcript. When Mrs. Moses attempted to cross-examine Judge Calissi, Brown objected, and Judge Arnold, ever protective of a colleague, smiled and said, "I am not allowing either one of you to cross-examine Judge Calissi."

Pleading with the judge, Mrs. Moses said that the statement she wanted to introduce would show that Jascalevich had tried "to explain away the smoking gun that was found in his locker" and that the surgeon had made a "deliberate effort to cover up his tracks."

After eight and a half days of hearings outside the presence of the jury, Judge Arnold decided that the muffled twelve-year-old recordings were so unintelligible that they could lead to erroneous impressions; but the prosecution could have the transcript read into the record, eliminating those portions that dealt with patients other than those whom the indictment had accused Jascalevich of murdering. The prosecution had won a significant victory. Ernest A. Frahm, formerly a detective at the county prosecutor's office, was called to read the transcript to the jurors, who clearly seemed to be dividing their attention between Frahm as he read and Dr. Jascalevich as he listened.

After the transcript was read, Frahm was questioned about another aspect of the investigation that he had participated in. He described his 1966 interview with the hospital pharmacist, who had seemed unaware that the hospital had any curare on hand, even though the detectives later found four vials in the hospital pharmacy and one in each of the two operating rooms. While this testimony was helpful to the defense case, it did not support the bare statement that Brown had made earlier in the trial that sixty-seven vials of curare were then in stock in the hospital. Earlier, during the cross-examination of the then chief anesthesiologist, Dr. Arthur DeMarco, Brown had uncovered the fact that one of DeMarco's predecessors had used curare from time to time, but Mrs. Moses told the court that all of the curare found in the pharmacy and operating rooms was manufactured before 1963.

The next phase of the prosecutor's case was to introduce witnesses who would belie the statements in the transcript that had just been read into the record. First came Joseph Salerno, the controller at the Seton Hall Medical School, where Jascalevich had said he had done his dog experiments. Reading from actual hospital records, Salerno verified Jascalevich's grant from the American Cancer Society to do research at the medical school between April 1, 1963, and February 29, 1964. Using actual purchase orders, Salerno told the jury that Jascalevich had been given nine dogs to experiment on between June 24 and August 26, 1963, but there was no record of Jascalevich getting any more dogs for research after that date. In rebuttal, the defense produced one of the articles from *Surgery,* the medical journal in which Jascalevich wrote that he had used twenty-five dogs in his experiments.

Then Dr. Anthony Boccabella took the stand. He was chairman of the anatomy department at the New Jersey College of Medicine and Dentistry, formerly known as Seton Hall. Boccabella said that on November 2, 1966 (the same day Jascalevich learned that curare had been discovered in his locker at Riverdell), he was in charge of the animal laboratory at Seton Hall, and was called out of a meeting to see Dr. Jascalevich rummaging around for the key to the cabinet that held research instruments. Boccabella described Jascalevich: "He was upset, more animated than I had seen him before, he was anxious. He asked me if I had a dog. I said I did not, period."

Boccabella, a witness most damaging to the defense, told the jury that dying animals were never left behind on the tables and that it would be a serious breach of ethics for a researcher to work on the dog of another researcher without asking permission to do so, because the results of the research could be severely affected if something were done to an animal without the original experimenter's knowledge. According to Boccabella, "one does not tamper with other people's experiments."

On cross-examination Brown dug deeply into Dr. Boccabella. He asked if it wasn't possible to obtain an animal by tipping the attendant, which Boccabella denied: "If you came in at 5 o'clock and asked a sweeper to get a dog, you couldn't do it . . . it would be tantamount to trying to steal." Brown probed, asking Boccabella if dogs were not left to die on the tables at the end of the day, and Dr. Boccabella explained that special efforts were made to treat the dogs humanely and to kill them quickly, because the hospital had been under attack by antivivisectionists in the past. At this point, Brown shouted at the witness, "you were under attack because you did leave animals on the tables."

Boccabella also testified that he had never heard of Jascalevich's curare experiments, although he had helped him get his 1963 grant from the Cancer Society, and that on one occasion, in 1965, Jascalevich had asked him about the possibility of acquiring a dog on which he could test his surgical stapling gun.

Boccabella was followed to the stand by Salvatore Riggi, who identified himself as the supervisor of animal care at the college laboratory and the last one to leave at night. Riggi proved to be another witness damaging to the defense, when he said that he never took any tips and that none of his subordinates were even on the premises after 5 P.M.

According to Riggi, the men left by 4:45. They changed their clothes, cleaned up, and went home. "I stayed until 5:30 and I was the last one to leave. I would lock up." Riggi told Mrs. Moses that there were never dying or dead dogs left on the tables, that he had the only key to the dog storage area, and that the cleaning employees were not supposed to come into it. He also testified that individual experimenters, and not caretakers, killed the dogs dying of experiments by giving them lethal doses of Nembutal.

Riggi also refuted Jascalevich's 1966 statement to Calissi that he had halted his experiments because "since February we did not have any more dogs at Seton Hall." According to Riggi, "we never ran out of dogs, we always had dogs." Salerno, the controller, had given identical evidence.

When Brown cross-examined Riggi, the only significant hole he could puncture in Riggi's evidence was that no record was kept of visitors to the lab, and therefore it was indeed possible that people entered at night, even though Riggi kept the laboratory locked.

Mrs. Moses never called Dewey Mincey or Lee Henderson to testify. They were the two clean-up men who Jascalevich had testified were the source of his dogs. It would remain to be seen whether Jascalevich would call them as witnesses.

More refutation of Jascalevich's explanation of his dog experiments came when the prosecution introduced as a witness Dr. Timothy Regan, head of the Cardiology Laboratory at the New Jersey College of Medicine and Dentistry (Pollack Hospital). He testified that Jascalevich came to him on November 2, 1966 (the day he had been confronted by his colleagues), and asked if he could have the use of a dog that might be left over after another experimenter was finished for the day. According to Regan, Jascalevich told him that his research funds had run out and he wanted to complete studies he was doing on a surgical stapling device.

Dr. Regan said he had never seen Jascalevich before and made a phone call to verify that he was a visiting lecturer to the college, after which he told Jascalevich he could use any dog left at the end of the day. Sybil Moses asked the witness if there was anything unusual about the surgeon's manner when he came to the laboratory. "He was just a little pushy. That is all, that's the adjective I would use." They said little to each other at the time, according to Regan, who later saw Jascalevich upstairs in a room with one of the dogs. Regan also testified that, besides passing him in the hall on one subsequent occasion, he knew of no other time when Jascalevich was at the college laboratory at Pollack Hospital.

Under cross-examination, Raymond Brown got Regan to admit that there was nothing unusual in Jascalevich's request for an animal. Regan also told Brown that he would not necessarily have seen Jascalevich if he was doing an experiment on the sixteenth floor of the adjacent building.

As April ended, Judge Arnold gave the jury "some very unpleasant news." He told them that the trial was certain to go beyond the original estimate of eight to ten weeks.

When the trial entered the month of May, the prosecution began to introduce a number of witnesses to describe Jascalevich's relationship with and attitudes toward his colleagues. First came a hospital technician, Herman Fuhr, who described a dispute between Jascalevich and Dr. Briski which he had observed while assisting at surgery during the operation on Frank Biggs. Fuhr said the argument took place as the two doctors were working feverishly to find the source of Mr. Biggs's internal bleeding which, according to Fuhr, Jascalevich found and corrected after Briski had said to him, "Stop, you are ruining the whole thing."

Dr. Frank A. Grosso described the morning of Emma Arzt's death, when he came upon Jascalevich attempting to revive a blue and motionless Mrs. Arzt by pressing lightly on the patient's chest with the tip of his fingers. Dr. Grosso, who described himself as a resuscitation expert, said that what Jascalevich was doing was all wrong and quite unusual. He said that he arrived at the patient's bedside and watched Jascalevich for two minutes and, "I was embarrassed. I told him, 'Let me do it.' "

"Did he respond?" Mrs. Moses asked.

"He just walked away. He left the room and never came back. I can't forget that patient, because the method of resuscitation was so unusual and unacceptable."

Dr. Grosso had succeeded in reviving Mrs. Arzt that morning, but in the afternoon she died suddenly.

Ray Brown tried very hard to attack the accuracy of Dr. Grosso's recollections and finally, responding to Brown's repetitive questioning, Grosso said, "You asked me three times. How many times are you going to ask me? I says 'Can I help' and he walked away."

Dr. Hubert M. Stavrand also testified about the operation on Frank Biggs. Dr. Stavrand had been Mr. Biggs's family physician and had assisted Drs. Briski and Jascalevich at the surgery. According to Stavrand's recollection of the incident, Briski had become very excited when he could not find the bleeding vessel because Jascalevich's hands were in the way. He said that after the bleeder had been clamped off, "Dr. Jascalevich left the operating room in a very upset manner." Stavrand testified that Dr. Jascalevich turned away from the table, very forcefully took his gloves off, threw them to the floor, and walked out of the room, leaving

Stavrand to assist Briski in completing the operation.

Stavrand also said that Mr. Biggs, who had told the nurses he was feeling well only one and a half hours before his death, had suddenly turned blue and had difficulty breathing, according to the notations on the medical record, which also showed that Jascalevich and the house staff physician, Dr. Jorge Ortega, had tried unsuccessfully to revive him with heart massage and adrenalin injections. Mr. Biggs had died by the time Dr. Stavrand arrived at the hospital, where he met Dr. Jascalevich, who was on his way out the door. Stavrand testified, "He looked at me very quickly and said, 'too bad about your patient.' "

Stavrand said that he never agreed with the autopsy report that Mr. Biggs had died from a distended bladder which had caused heart failure. He also testified about another incident in 1966, after Jascalevich had given his statement in the prosecutor's office explaining his use of the curare for dog experiments. Stavrand had already heard about the statement when Jascalevich stopped him in the hospital one day "and told me he hoped I didn't believe what they were saying about his locker and the curare. He told me he had no knowledge of the curare and that he was being framed. . . . I knew the conversation with Dr. Jascalevich directly conflicted with what I had heard." But Stavrand said that he had never confronted Dr. Jascalevich with that fact.

Dr. Robert J. Briski also came to testify for the prosecution about the operation on Frank Biggs. He said Jascalevich's hand in Mr. Biggs's abdomen had been in the way, making it impossible to locate the source of the bleeding, and he had asked Jascalevich to remove it. He also confirmed that "shortly after that he abruptly left without a comment." Briski said that Jascalevich had restricted his surgical operating privileges and criticized his competence. Briski actually made a terrible witness, speaking haltingly, groping for words, having difficulty breathing, and staring at the floor—he gave the appearance of an extremely nervous man under terrible stress.

Mrs. Moses's next witness, Dr. Robert M. Livingston, had other problems. Since the 1966 affair at Riverdell, Dr. Livingston had become famous as Bergen County's leading abortion specialist. In 1972 he had successfully challenged the state's abortion law, but his problem as a witness against Jascalevich was that he was under indictment himself, having been charged as an unlawful intermediary in arranging an adoption over the objections of a fourteen-year-old mother who had delivered a child at the clinic that Livingston ran.

The gynecologist was there to testify about how vividly he remembered his first operation at Riverdell Hospital, because his patient, Margaret Henderson, had died so suddenly and unexpectedly.

Dr. Livingston confirmed that Jascalevich had advised against surgery in the Henderson case when he was first called in as a consultant. Livingston testified, however, that he had decided to operate after doing some of the tests that Jascalevich had recommended. After doing the tests and consulting with others, he consulted with Jascalevich a second time, and Jascalevich agreed that there was no alternative to the exploratory surgery.

Livingston also challenged the appropriateness of Jascalevich starting an intravenous feeding on Mrs. Henderson, and said that he had never known a chief of surgery to start an I.V. on a patient. According to Livingston, Jascalevich had told him he started the I.V. because the patient was dehydrated, but Livingston was firmly convinced that she was not.

Like the other prosecution witnesses, Livingston also disagreed with the autopsy report which stated that the patient's death was due to an "acute hepatic necrosis," or liver failure.

Livingston's testimony was interrupted when Ray Brown shouted, "He is a liar. First he is for sale and now he wants to distort." Brown asserted that Livingston was extending himself for the prosecutor in order to buy favorable treatment in his pending illegal adoption indictment.

But despite the rough time he gave Livingston, Brown was unable to get him to change any of his testimony. When his chance came to cross-examine the gynecologist, Brown tried to shake his testimony about the negative consultation with Jascalevich. He charged, "The fact is he told you not to operate?" Livingston replied, "That is a lie. No question that he gave permission, recommended the operation."

Brown tried again, pointing out that while the first consultation was on the hospital record, there was no record that Livingston went back to Jascalevich a second time, to which Livingston answered, "It is not in the history, but it certainly occurred." He reiterated that Jascalevich had "absolutely and positively approved going ahead with the surgery."

If he disagreed with the pathology report on the reason for Mrs. Henderson's death, Brown asked, why had he signed the death certificate? Livingston's response was that he did not want to get into a hassle with the county medical examiner, indicating he had already had an argument about it, and, "I said if that is the way he wanted it, that is the way I'd do it." Livingston's position was that he was "ordered" to indicate liver failure as the cause of death.

If anyone was to be considered a star witness for the state, in the eyes of the press it was Dr. Stanley Harris. On the afternoon of May 16, his chance came to testify. One of the habitues of the Hackensack courthouse told me that as he took the stand, wiry Stanley Harris reminded him of a bantom-weight boxing champion entering the ring. It was obvious, said one sensitive observer, that Harris felt a "long-awaited moment had arrived, and he was going to enjoy it." The newspaper reporters played up Dr. Harris in their accounts; here, after all, was the man they considered to be Jascalevich's chief accuser.

As the pugnacious surgeon presented his credentials for the prosecutor, he enhanced his own reputation by repeatedly describing himself as both a scholarship student and an honors graduate at the different schools he had attended. He also managed to give the impression that he was going out of his way to say how concerned he had been for his patients' well-being. In doing this, he played into the defense's hands, as Brown repeatedly interrupted him with objections. At one point Brown, himself the leading courtroom actor, pointed his finger at Dr. Harris and accused him of "trying to win an Oscar."

Dr. Jascalevich's reaction to his chief accuser was not what one would have expected. He had moved his chair so that he would face Dr. Harris directly, and throughout Harris's testimony, Jascalevich wore a smile of self-content and confidence. His posture also changed; he leaned far forward and seemed to be confronting Harris with his grin.

At points during Harris's testimony, Jascalevich's conduct visi-

Dr. Stanley Harris Testifying at the Trial
(left to right: Brown, Harris, Arnold, Jascalevich)

bly distracted the jury to the point where half of them were watching Jascalevich and smiling along with him.

Harris testified, "those deaths ran a pattern, all had smooth uncomplicated operations, all were recovering smoothly." According to Stanley Harris, all the patients who died had I.V.'s running, and in those cases where I.V.'s were not already running, Dr. Jascalevich had started them himself. He pointed out that Jascalevich was always around the hospital when the deaths occurred and that all the patients who had been observed in their death throes had turned blue.

Harris went on to explain that because of these factors, he had "felt compelled" to open Jascalevich's locker. He then described what he had found and related that he had "told Dr. Lans this was the curare Dr. Jascalevich used to kill all those patients."

Harris testified about a conversation he had had with Jascalevich concerning Dr. Briski's mortality rate, in which Jascalevich said to Harris, "everything Briski touches turns to death."

Harris also said that he had been present at the autopsy of Margaret Henderson and had noted nothing wrong with her liver.

Defense counsel Ray Brown used the Henderson autopsy as the take-off point for his cross-examination, because Harris had told the grand jury two years earlier that he did not recall being at the autopsy. Waiving a copy of Harris' grand jury testimony in Harris's face, Brown challenged, "Why did you lie to the grand jury or here?" But he did not phase the surgeon, who responded, "all I can say to that, Mr. Brown, is that I was at the post mortem, even if I did not recall it at that time. I didn't lie."

Harris, who had succeeded Jascalevich as chief of surgery in Riverdell, testified he had done some 400 operations at Riverdell in 1967, the year after Jascalevich left, and experienced no sudden deaths among his patients.

In his cross-examination of Harris, Brown was exceedingly rough. He attempted to disparage the surgeon's competence, raising questions about why he had been unable to diagnose Nancy Savino's cysts before the operation.

Brown raised the point of possible partnership between Jascalevich and Harris. Harris then told how Jascalevich had had a brief conversation with him about the possibility, and the next thing he knew there was a memo out to the staff announcing the partnership, which Harris rescinded four days later.

Brown tried also to show that Harris had a motive for hurting Jascalevich. He asked him how much surgery he performed in 1966 when Jascalevich was there and how much in 1967 after he became chief of surgery. Harris responded that he had done 100 operations in 1966, as compared to 400 in 1967.

Brown attempted to discredit Harris by challenging his assertion that he had no surgical deaths in 1967. With hospital records in his hand, Brown paced up and down in front of the jury, reading off the names of eleven Riverdell patients who had died in 1967 following surgery by Dr. Harris.

Mrs. Moses got a chance to salvage Harris on her redirect examination, when she elicited from the surgeon that of the eleven patients, either Harris had only been the assistant at surgery or the patients had died from their illnesses, frequently cancer, and not from the surgery. But Brown was not going to let this one go so easily.

On recross, he tore into Harris again and specifically mentioned two operations Harris had done on a seventy-year-old cancer patient. He accused Harris of earning extra income by performing unnecessary operations on aging patients who were going to die anyway.

Dr. Harris denied Brown's accusations. In three of the eleven cases, Harris said there had not been any operation at all, only rectal examinations, which were recorded in the operating room log because the examination had been performed there. In one case, Harris had only been the assistant at surgery done by another surgeon, and in another, the patient had died of peritonitis, not of any surgical error or mishap. In one case, the patient died a month after the operation as a result of gangrene that had set in in an amputation. Five, he said, were cancer cases where the cancer killed the patients, not the surgery.

The jury was excused again on May 23 to enable Judge Arnold to hear arguments on another defense motion. This time Mr. Brown's motion was to exclude as evidence the statements that Dr. Jascalevich made to the county prosecutor in 1976. Mrs. Moses wanted to use this material to show that it conflicted in parts with the sworn statements that Jascalevich made to former Prosecutor Calissi in 1966, which had already been put into the record. Joseph Woodcock, the 1976 prosecutor, was called as the hearing's first witness.

Woodcock had made two of the most critical decisions in this case: first, to reopen the investigation, and then to ask the grand jury for an indictment. He was potentially the hero or the goat, depending upon matters that were no longer in his control; but in any event, the case had already gained him far more publicity than anything else in his public career.

Several months after the Jascalevich indictment, Woodcock retired as the Bergen County prosecutor in order to seek the Republican nomination for governor, a pursuit which ended in failure. In this post-Watergate era, the motivations of anyone who seeks public office are suspect, and Raymond Brown capitalized on that by raising the argument that Joseph Woodcock had exploited the Jascalevich situation by "conspiring" with *New York Times* reporter Myron Farber, leaking information to Farber, and otherwise encouraging him to write the Dr. X stories, thus making Woodcock himself more famous.

Before Judge Arnold, Raymond Brown branded Woodcock as an "absolute liar" who "played with the press and lied to the defendant." He offered Woodcock's unsuccessful efforts to gain the gubernatorial nomination and then a nomination to congress as evidence of the prosecutor's real motivation, and claimed that this proved that Woodcock had worked with Farber for his own political purposes.

Until the day Woodcock testified, I had no idea that the transcript of Jascalevich's 1966 testimony that I had loaned to Myron Farber was so important to Woodcock's decision to reopen the case. Woodcock testified that it was the decisive factor, that the transcript had been missing from his own office files until Farber provided it to him in late 1975, but he had no idea where Farber got it. I was amazed to learn this, because Farber had never revealed to me that it was Woodcock who had given him access to his files. Farber had told me that he was in constant touch with the prosecutor, and I had specifically told him that he was free to tell Woodcock about my involvement and my willingness to be helpful. Though Farber had never said so, he let me believe that he had discussed my role with Mr. Woodcock. For that reason, I was surprised that Woodcock had never called me. I erroneously interpreted Woodcock's silence to mean that he was protecting his predecessor, Calissi; that Woodcock had neither the desire nor the intention of reopening the case; and that Woodcock was probably just humoring the *New York Times* reporter. Had I known that my involvement was kept secret from Woodcock, my conclusions about Woodcock's interest at the time would have been very different.

As these facts developed during the trial, the more complete perspective demonstrated to me that Myron Farber had done whatever he could to exclude me. The pains that I learned Farber had taken to do so appear a bit diabolical in retrospect, especially so since I had not asked him to keep my name from Woodcock.

Furthermore, when Farber broke his extremely detailed Dr. X series early in 1976, I anticipated that he would include something about the efforts that Allan Lans and I had undertaken in 1966, as it would have been appropriate in the context of the other things he was writing; but he did not do so.

At the hearing it emerged that Farber had actually refused to tell Woodcock where and how he got the transcript of the Jascalevich testimony. To Ray Brown's question about the transcript, "Did you ask him where he got the statement?" Mr. Woodcock had responded, "We asked the question, but he invoked the reporter's privilege and we did not go any further than that." Woodcock also admitted on the witness stand that he had given Myron Farber access to his files when Farber came in and asked for it. He had not offered that access to any other reporter.

Brown's argument in favor of excluding the 1976 statements was that Dr. Jascalevich had been tricked into making the statements, because when the first of the two interrogation sessions took place, Woodcock had not told the surgeon that he was the target of an investigation, something that legal propriety would have required, even though prosecutors have been known to get indictments in cases where they fail to inform the target of his status. Brown's argument was doubly impressive because Farber's original Dr. X articles had appeared in January of 1976, and Woodcock did not interview Jascalevich until February of 1976. Despite the articles, Woodcock told Jascalevich that he was not the target of the investigation and that there was no evidence that any crime had been committed. The only warning Woodcock gave the surgeon during his first interview was that anything he said could be used in a court of law. Judge Arnold quite properly ruled that this was insufficient. The February interview took place at the request of Jascalevich's then attorney, James Anderson, because of the publicity from the *Times* articles. Anderson's posture was that Jascalevich had cooperated ten years before and he wanted to continue to do so. Woodcock also revealed that after he had received reports that curare had been found in the exhumed bodies of patients, he asked Jascalevich to come in to give him another statement in March of 1976, when he did tell him that he had become the target of a criminal investigation.

Sybil Moses tried to overcome the mistakes that had been made by the man who appointed her. She claimed that all of Jascalevich's statements were made in his lawyer's presence and, for that reason, could be introduced at the trial.

Trying to defeat Brown's motion, Moses made it very clear that her reason for needing to introduce the 1976 statement was that when compared to the 1966 statement it would show that the defendant had lied to the prosecutor on at least one of the occasions. She pointed out significant inconsistencies between Jascalevich's 1966 and 1976 statements and pleaded that their introduction was essential to the prosecution. For one thing, Jascalevich had changed the location of his dog experiments.

In the 1966 statement, Jascalevich said his experiments were done on the sixteenth floor of the Seton Hall College of Medicine in Jersey City. Ten years later, he switched the site of his experiments to the third floor Cardiology Laboratory of Pollack Hospital, which is adjacent to the Seton Hall College building. (The Pollack Hospital laboratory is the place where Jascalevich found himself a dog to work on the day he discovered his locker had been opened.)

In the 1976 statements, Jascalevich had also admitted that he had himself started the intravenous feedings in the cases of Carl Rohrbeck and Margaret Henderson.

Another discrepancy between the two Jascalevich statements was that Jascalevich had attributed Mrs. Henderson's death to a liver failure when he talked to Calissi in 1966, but took issue with that statement ten years later when he talked to Woodcock.

After Woodcock's testimony on this issue, Ray Brown called Myron Farber to testify at the hearing. Farber confirmed that Woodcock had obtained the 1966 transcript from him, but declined to answer when Brown asked him where he had obtained the transcript.

While questioning Farber, Brown showed him a memorandum which he had obtained from the prosecution during pretrial discovery identifying me as Farber's source for the 1966 transcript; but still, Farber continued to refuse to confirm that I was his source.

The only information that Farber gave to Brown when he was examined was that he had not given anything but the 200-page transcript to Woodcock.

Farber, who was accompanied to the hearing by three *New York Times* lawyers, based his refusal to answer Brown's questions on a newsman's privilege not to disclose his sources of information, which privilege he said came from the American Constitution and the New Jersey Shield Law.

After Farber testified, Judge Arnold ruled that the 1976 statements to Woodcock could not be introduced into evidence before the jury. He based his ruling on Woodcock's testimony that he had told Jascalevich he was not the target of the investigation when in reality he was, and regardless of Woodcock's intention, the totality of his treatment of Jascalevich during his 1976 interviews, Arnold felt, constituted a ruse.

Judge Arnold also said that even if there were inconsistencies between the two statements, they would only affect the defendant's credibility and would not, in Arnold's opinion, indicate whether he was guilty or innocent. The judge did indicate that the defense might itself be allowed to introduce the 1976 Jascalevich statement when it came time to present the defense case.

Flushed with the success of excluding the 1976 statement, Mr. Brown made another motion on the last day of May, in anticipation of the prosecution's next scheduled witness, Dr. Michael M. Baden. In the papers filed with Judge Arnold to support this motion, Brown said the court should determine outside the jury's presence if curare could survive ten years in embalmed bodies and whether the tests made by the scientific witnesses would be admissible in a court of law. The four-month-old trial was about to begin dealing with the complexities of scientific evidence. Brown buttressed his eighteen-page motion with a report from Dr. Frederic Reiders, a toxicologist who said "it is my scientifically, reasonably certain opinion that any curare which may have been found . . . was in fact not present until the time of exhumation but got into the specimens either during or after exhumation."

Pleading with the judge to bar the scientific evidence, Brown argued that Dr. Reiders's report established that the presence of curare could be explained only by outright fraud or gross negligence. Dr. Reiders's report further asserted that embalming fluid used in preparing the bodies would have destroyed any curare present.

This time Brown failed to impress Judge Arnold sufficiently and the motion was taken under advisement, while Michael Baden was allowed to begin his testimony.

At the beginning of June, 1978, Baden was the acting chief medical examiner of the City of New York and was scheduled to be officially confirmed as chief. Baden had by then already achieved a nationwide reputation and as head of the New York City office; his medical examiner's credentials were tops in the country. In addition to his other qualifications, Dr. Baden had also become a member of a congressionally appointed commission to investigate President John F. Kennedy's assassination. (I had come to know Baden personally during 1977, when he agreed to serve as one of the members of the advisory council to the Medical Practice Task Force investigations I was directing for the New York State Assembly.)

Dr. Baden, who projects tremendous sincerity, has the capacity to exude confidence without losing his humility. He was an experienced witness.

His testimony confirmed that he had told the prosecutor that after reviewing the deceased patients' hospital records, he found either no reason or an incorrect reason attributed to the causes of death. He told the court that Mr. Woodcock had approached him late in 1975 to ask him to look at those charts and to describe the drug curare and its action in the human body. Dr. Baden said that he had done this consultation as an unpaid courtesy, and by the time he did so, he understood that Woodcock's investigation had already been reopened.

Baden was interrupted by Raymond Brown's objection to his specific reference to the drug curare, because, Brown argued, there had been no proof in the case that curare was the cause of any death.

Having set the scene, Mrs. Moses then had Dr. Baden review the death of each of the alleged victims. Baden's opinion was emphatic that Mr. Biggs could not have died from a bladder overloaded with urine which made his heart work too hard (the cause attributed in the 1966 autopsy). Baden said that in all of his experience, he had never known of anyone in reasonably good health to die of a distended bladder.

He testified that the 1966 autopsy report on Margaret Henderson was also obviously wrong in attributing her death to liver failure. According to Baden, liver failure is a gradual process which involves jaundice, and there was no evidence of jaundice in her case. Furthermore, he testified, the laboratory report on the examination of liver tissue after autopsy indicated no liver problems.

Dr. Baden pointed out that the 1966 autopsy of Nancy Savino, which attributed her death to an undetermined physiological catastrophe, was the only one that was obviously valid, because there was no adequate cause of death present at the autopsy to explain how the child had died.

Emma Arzt had not had the benefit of an autopsy and all Dr. Baden could say was that, in his opinion, the symptoms of death were not compatible with the heart failure attributed in her case; while heart failure was possible, it had not been demonstrated. In addition, the doctor pointed out, an electrocardiogram taken just before death showed a normal heart.

In his analysis of the Rohrbeck case Baden was equivocal, saying that while it was possible that Mr. Rohrbeck could have died of a heart attack because he had a preexisting history of heart disease, it was also possible that another cause of death intervened.

Dr. Baden gave detailed descriptions of the autopsies that he had performed on the exhumed bodies in 1976. He reported that the bodies of four-year-old Nancy Savino and seventy-year-old Emma Arzt were in an excellent state of preservation. Margaret Henderson's corpse had begun to show evidence of decomposition, and the body of Frank Biggs was less well preserved, with some skeletonization. The body of the fifth patient, Carl Rohrbeck, was not at all in a good state of preservation.

In spite of the differences in condition in the exhumed bodies, Baden related, he was able to make certain examinations, comparing his findings with the results of earlier autopsies and with hospital records. In none of the cases did he find anything that pointed directly to the cause of death.

When Sybil Moses asked Baden, "Did you form an opinion at the time as to the cause of death?" he replied, "Yes, I did." Raymond Brown immediately leaped to his feet again and objected, asking to have the jury excused so that he could make an argument before Judge Arnold, which the judge promptly agreed to hear.

After the jurors filed out, Brown told the judge that he assumed Dr. Baden was about to say that curare was the cause of death. Yet no toxicologist had yet testified to finding curare in the tissue, and Judge Arnold had not yet ruled on Brown's motion to prevent the toxicologists from testifying at all, on the ground that the scientific tests for finding the curare may not be valid.

However, the moment of truth was postponed when Dr. Baden, a witness with a lot of experience in such matters, spoke up and told the judge that he was only going to say that after his examination of the bodies, the cause of death was still unknown, and further tests on the tissue were required.

The seventeen remaining jurors were called back into the courtroom to hear Baden testify that he had given samples of the tissue to toxicologists at the New Jersey State Laboratory and in Suffolk County, New York, to conduct independent tests to discover what was in these tissues.

In 1966 Jascalevich had told Woodcock that he had noticed a distended bladder on Mr. Biggs after the patient had died. Jascalevich said that he inserted a catheter into Mr. Biggs's bladder and drew off some of the fluid. Dr. Baden described the procedure as improper. He said that in the thousands of deaths that he had autopsied, he never heard of a physician inserting a catheter into a patient after the patient died. He called the procedure illegal without permission of the next of kin, and pointed out that it would interfere with a pathologist's ability to discover the cause of death, because the procedure distorts the body for the person performing the autopsy.

When his time came for cross-examination, Ray Brown attempted to dissect Dr. Baden's testimony. He questioned Baden's analysis of the Rohrbeck case by eliciting from Baden that the heart was missing from Rohrbeck's exhumed body. Baden said that he did not know what had become of Rohrbeck's heart, which might have been removed at the time of the 1966 autopsy or by the mortician who had embalmed the dead patient.

Although Brown zeroed in on Baden's capacity to do an autopsy on bodies that were partially decomposed or had organs missing, he was unable to elicit any change or diminution of the salient facts that the medical examiner had previously testified to.

On June 2, while Baden was testifying in Hackensack, a New York State Supreme Court justice made a ruling that led to a legal battle ancillary to the trial itself, which eventually received as much, if not more, attention than the fate of Dr. Jascalevich.

New York Supreme Court justice Harold Rothwax, acting on a motion submitted on behalf of Dr. Jascalevich by attorney Brown, decided that Myron Farber should turn over to the trial court all of his notes from interviews with witnesses during the lengthy investigation. Justice Rothwax ruled that Judge Arnold should determine whether Farber's notes should be made available to the defendant's lawyer so that he could properly prepare Jascalevich's defense. The New York court rejected the argument by the *Times* and its reporter that Farber had a constitutional and statutory right to have the New York court protect his sources. Justice Rothwax said this would have to be decided in the New Jersey court.

The New York court had become involved because of an interstate compact which allows the courts in one state to request the courts in another to issue a subpoena for a witness required to appear in a criminal trial in the sister state. Brown had used this statute to begin the legal process necessary to obtain Farber's testimony and notes to discover the facts of his involvement with the prosecutor and his role, if any, in initiating the case against Dr. Jascalevich.

When Michael Baden stepped down, defense counsel Brown asked Judge Arnold to hold a formal hearing outside the jury's presence before deciding on the pending defense motion to exclude the state's scientific evidence of the tests for curare. Brown produced letters from six toxicologists and medical examiners attacking the validity of the prosecution's tests. Judge Arnold decided to listen to some of the arguments.

Brown protested that the radio-immuno assay (RIA), the newest of the tests to be utilized by the prosecution, was not specific enough to distinguish between curare and other chemicals with a similar pattern. He claimed that the mass spectometry (MS) test was a more accurate chemical fingerprint and what appears to be curare under RIA might turn out to be something else under mass spectometry.

In making this argument outside the jury's presence, Brown

revealed to the court that even the defense had found curare in one of the bodies through the mass spectometry test, but the defense experts had concluded that the curare they found was so pure that it must have been added to the bodies after they were exhumed in 1976.

Sybil Moses argued vigorously in her effort to contest Brown's motion. She explained to the judge that the methodology that the prosecution used was well recognized and the fact that it was never done before to test for curare in tissues did not mean that it was not reliable. She asserted that if the court were going to bar admission of new scientific evidence every time someone found a new way to commit murder, many murderers would go free.

Mrs. Moses brought pharmacologist Sidney Spector as her first witness to inform the judge how RIA works. He explained how specific antibodies he had developed to match the curare they were testing for were added to the material to be tested, and these antibodies "would act like a pair of hands" to grab on to the tested material. The scientists knew how much of the antibody to expect because they added it, but if additional amounts of the drug being tested for are revealed in the test patterns, that is evidence of their presence. But, Dr. Spector admitted under cross-examination, the tests were not foolproof, and other substances could throw off the test.

The separate hearing on the quality of scientific evidence took several days, and the Hackensack courtroom took on the air of a chemistry class as a parade of scientists came to explain their work.

Dr. Richard J. Coumbis, New Jersey's chief toxicologist, described RIA as a routine approach that he was using every day and verified that he checked each of his findings with another test, high pressure liquid chromatography (HPLC), because he was unable to develop adequate controls to make certain that his RIA test had confirmed curare.

When Brown cross-examined him, Dr. Coumbis said that RIA alone was not sufficient for identification, but that it would constitute scientific proof when backed up with HPLC. Coumbis also said that to his knowledge, this was the first time RIA was being used to detect curare.

Dr. Leo A. DalCortivo, the chief forensic toxicologist at the Suffolk County medical examiner's office, explained how he performed the HPLC test there on the same tissue that Dr. Coumbis had tested with RIA in Jersey.

In summary, it appeared that while the prosecutor's witnesses agreed that each of their tests would create a presumptive evidence, it was only when two were taken together that a "reasonable scientific certainty" of the evidence of curare could be given. Under Ray Brown's cross-examination, Dr. Coumbis admitted that "there is no such thing as an absolute in toxicology." The scientists described the various controls they established for each of their tests, but admitted that no one knew all of the factors present in the case of tissue buried for ten years. As Dr. Coumbis put it, "Here we have an unique situation and this uniqueness cannot be duplicated."

Under cross-examination by Brown, Dr. DalCortivo admitted that in one of the reports of tests that he had published, the RIA procedure had given false results ten times in an attempt to find morphine. This had happened because there were other compounds reacting with the RIA in a manner similar to morphine.

Raymond Brown also attempted to discredit the tests by producing affidavits from other toxicologists calling it "unwarranted speculation" to say that curare might remain detectable in dead bodies buried for a decade. Using these affidavits for his cross-examination of Dr. DalCortivo, Brown was unable to shake the scientist's confidence. DalCortivo insisted that curare can remain stable. "I found it," he affirmed. Brown then tried to get DalCortivo to say whether or not he could determine that the curare had been in the patient for ten years, and DalCortivo admitted that his HPLC test could not do that. Although he could test for the presence of curare, Dr. DalCortivo admitted he could not test for its age.

DalCortivo did reveal during the hearings that according to his tests, he had definitely found curare in the exhumed tissues of Carl Rohrbeck, Nancy Savino, and Frank Biggs.

Judge Arnold took an active part in the questioning of the scientists, and it was obvious that he was troubled by the decision he had to make.

When Brown's turn came, the defense brought in Dr. Frederic Reiders as its own expert. Confirming the written report that Brown had produced earlier, the former chief toxicologist for the City of Philadelphia said it was his opinion that no curare could have survived in the bodies for ten years. To make his point, he cited older literature and experiments with which he was familiar in order to make analogies, but the prosecution found these analogies questionable.

During his testimony, however, Dr. Reiders did admit that he found a substantial amount of curare in the body tissue of Nancy Savino, but because he was so sure that curare could not have lasted in a buried body for a decade, he felt the drug could not have been there at the time she died.

On Tuesday, June 20, after five days of hearing arguments and testimony, Judge Arnold made his ruling.

"There is no doubt in my mind that these tests are not absolute," the Judge declared. "There is a very sharp difference of opinion among the experts as to the reliability of these tests. . . . I am not commenting on the value . . . all I am saying is that under the law the evidence is admissible. . . . The ultimate decision must be made by the jury."

Raymond Brown indicated that he wanted to appeal the ruling, but Judge Arnold would not delay the trial while he did so.

The long line of scientific experts who gave evidence at the Jascalevich trial was headed by Dr. Richard J. Coumbis, who came to testify for the prosecution on June 20. He had been present when Nancy Savino's little body was brought to Dr. Baden's mortuary after exhumation and had watched the second autopsy being performed. In response to Sybil Moses's inquiry, Dr. Coumbis remarked that the child's body "looked in perfect condition" even though it had been buried for ten years. He described obtaining samples of various organs, which he then submitted to RIA to determine if curare were present, and the toxicologist said that he had found curare in the liver, lung, muscle tissue, and urine of the four-year-old child. He also explained that to control his tests he had taken samples of earth and water from around the coffin and, using the identical test as he had for the tissue, he found that curare was not present in these elements. Dr. Coumbis told the court that he had also used RIA to check the results of ten numbered experiments which had been forwarded to him after being tested for curare under the HPLC system in another laboratory, explaining that he did not know which of the numbered solutions had been found to contain curare in the other tests.

Throughout the questioning of Dr. Coumbis, Ray Brown rarely allowed Sybil Moses to finish a question, nor Dr. Coumbis to finish an answer. He made one procedural objection after another, but Mrs. Moses's hide had obviously thickened over the earlier weeks of the trial, and the confidence she demonstrated since asking the judge to step down was such that Brown was not able to distract her with his legal heckling. It is not clear if he succeded in destracting the jury.

In preparation for this testimony, the prosecution scientists attempted to be extremely careful. Dr. Coumbis had established a triple-check procedure. Separate pieces of tissue from the same organ had been tested by RIA and the HPLC method at different laboratories, and then as a further cross-check, a portion of the tissue that remained after the HPLC test was then retested with RIA.

With respect to the Arzt, Biggs, and Savino cases, where both tests were positive for curare, Coumbis had another tissue sample from the same body checked at another laboratory using the MS method.

Because Margaret Henderson's body was the most badly decomposed of those exhumed, Dr. Coumbis indicated that while he had found presumptive evidence of curare in that body, he was unable to confirm it through a different test. This statement brought Ray Brown to his feet again, objecting to the testimony indicating that there was curare in Mrs. Henderson's body since it had not been confirmed by another test. Brown's argument impressed Judge Arnold, who instructed the jury that the testimony regarding Mrs. Henderson was not scientifically reliable.

As to the fifth alleged victim, Emma Arzt, Dr. Coumbis said that the test he had made on her liver tissue did not show curare, and his negative finding was also confirmed by HPLC.

Mr. Brown started another legal argument by objecting to Mrs. Moses's effort to have Dr. Coumbis testify to a positive finding of curare in the case since that report was based on a mass spectrometry test. Brown's position was that during the preliminary hearing on the scientific tests for curare, Mrs. Moses had not made mention of evidence based on the MS procedure, to which she responded that in his own motion papers, Brown had contended that the MS test was the only one the defense considered valid. Upon hearing that, Judge Arnold ruled that the mass spectrometry evidence could be used.

The defense counsel was eager to cross-examine Dr. Coumbis. Even before the trial began, it was obvious to everyone in the courtroom that this cross-examination would be critical to the defense's case.

Brown had armed himself with a sheaf of scientific papers, most of which had been published more than twenty years before. As Brown interpreted it, all of the published accounts supported his view that curare is rapidly absorbed and deactivated by human tissue and was thus destroyed so that it could not be discovered again years afterwards. Dr. Coumbis stood his ground as Brown pummeled him with questions. He explained to the lawyer that the fact that curare was inactive or absorbed did not mean it was undetectable, and whether its muscle relaxant qualities were destroyed was immaterial to the scientists searching for the drug.

Judge Arnold attempted to follow all this as best he could. He asked Dr. Coumbis if he disagreed with one of the authors whose paper the defense had read from. The doctor replied, "Your Honor, they disagree with themselves."

At the conclusion of his cross-examination Dr. Coumbis pointed out, "there is no publication that can tell us what happens to curare in bodies buried ten years."

It was clear from Dr. Coumbis's testimony that the work he and the other prosecution scientists had done was an unprecedented achievement.

Coumbis was cross-examined for the better part of six days as Brown tried every way he could do to demean the toxicologist's report and otherwise make the scientist look silly. But he could not shake Coumbis's confidence in the RIA system.

Dr. David P. Beggs was the next witness for the prosecution, a chemist from the Hewlett-Packard Company, the manufacturer of the mass spectrometry (MS) machines sold to laboratories for between $50,000 and $200,000, depending on the model. Dr. Beggs described his company's machine as "one of the most sensitive and specific analytical machines available," and said that it was "used very often to identify complete unknowns." The chemist said that Dr. Coumbis had brought him the tissue samples to be tested for curare because his company had recently sold one of its machines to the New Jersey State Laboratory. Dr. Beggs's MS tests had found conclusive evidence of curare in the liver tissue that came from the exhumed body of Nancy Savino. He testified that evidence of the presence of curare was also found in the tissue given to him from the bodies of Frank Biggs and Emma Arzt. In the Arzt case, Dr. Beggs reported "a good indication that it is there," but in the Biggs case, he said he found only a "possibility" of curare. (Dr. Coumbis had found evidence of curare with RIA in all of the bodies except that of Mrs. Arzt.)

Hearing Dr. Beggs characterize his findings equivocally, Judge Arnold commented, "as far as I am concerned, 'possibility' is negative evidence . . . nobody could ever be convicted beyond a reasonable doubt on a possibility." The judge said this in the presence of the jury, whereupon Raymond Brown requested that Dr. Beggs's testimony be barred because it was speculative. While Judge Arnold refused to bar the testimony, he ruled that the jurors could hear it subject to his instruction that Beggs's testimony would not be sufficient for them to convict Dr. Jascalevich in the Arzt and Biggs cases.

When Brown's opportunity to cross-examine Dr. Beggs came, he succeeded in suggesting to the jury that the various tissue samples might have been mixed up because Dr. Coumbis had identified them by number, except for the Savino tissue, which were labeled with the child's name.

The wiley defense attorney also questioned whether Beggs could be certain that the tubocurarine which had been provided as a standard to him by Dr. Coumbis was really tubocurarine. Brown challenged the chemist, "You cannot personally vouch for the accuracy of the standard?"

Dr. Beggs answered, "Dr. Coumbis provided me with the standard labeled tubocurarine."

When Brown wanted to know if he was sure he had actually received tubocurarine, the chemist replied, "Sir, tubocurarine is tubocurarine."

"Are you saying a scientist cannot have an inaccurate standard?" asserted Brown, confusing the issue some more.

"It is conceivable," replied Dr. Beggs.

After the fourth of July recess, the prosecutor introduced her third expert witness, Dr. Sidney Spector, chief pharmacist at the

Roche Institute of Molecular Biology in Nutley, New Jersey, and the scientist who had developed the specific antibody used for finding curare in the RIA procedure. According to Dr. Spector, this antibody had been used for determining the curare content in body fluid, but the case at hand was the first time it had been used to detect the presence of the drug in body tissues. Spector was certain that this could be done "with reasonable scientific certainty" and described how he had compared his curare test with that of a dozen other drugs that were close in composition to it; the antibody had not worked in the same way that it had with curare. However, under cross-examination, Mr. Brown was able to get Dr. Spector to admit that he could only speculate that his antibody would detect curare in body tissue, because he had never done it before. The "speculative" quality of his testimony convinced Judge Arnold to rule that Spector's opinion on the validity of the test in question was not admissible. Dr. Spector had said, "I cannot answer definitely whether or not curare could be synthesized by something else in the body . . . all you can say is it looks like it is there. Let me know: prove it is there by using another procedure." He suggested that the MS test would be appropriate as the other procedure.

The fourth expert to test for curare for the state was Dr. Leo A. DalCortivo, the chief toxicologist for the Suffolk County, New York, medical examiner. Dr. DalCortivo had done the HPLC tests on tissue samples provided to him in numbered vials by Dr. Coumbis. DalCortivo testified he found curare was present in the liver tissue of Nancy Savino and Frank Biggs, and in the kidney tissue of Carl Rohrbeck, but he had not found evidence of curare in the Arzt case. He characterized his own findings as only "presumptive evidence," but when considered along with Dr. Coumbis's tests in the New Jersey laboratory, he felt his findings were "reasonable scientific evidence."

Dr. DalCortivo had also tested the fluids found in the vials taken from Dr. Jascalevich's locker in 1966 and confirmed that they had indeed contained curare. When he testified, Dr. DalCortivo had sixteen of the vials with him, but he said that only eight of them had enough material present to be tested, and all contained curare. Brown attempted to denigrate the toxicologist's method for testing the fluid in the vials that came from the locker, but DalCortivo revealed that he had used another test, thin-layer chromotography, as a control and that the second test confirmed the first.

Brown pressed him as to whether or not there was any chance that the contents of the vials he was testifying about could possibly have contained anything else, to which DalCortivo responded, "There are no absolutes in science, but in my opinion, the probability of this being anything else other than curare is reasonably remote."

The last of the prosecution's curare experts took the stand during the second week in July. He was Dr. Francis F. Foldes, a seventy-year-old retired professor of anesthesiology at the Albert Einstein College of Medicine in New York. Dr. Foldes is probably the most prominent curare expert in the country, and he was not without experience in such trials, having testified for the defense in the Coppolino case.

Dr. Foldes said that it was his opinion "with reasonable medical certainty" that Frank Biggs had been poisoned with curare. He based his opinion on an examination of Mr. Biggs's hospital chart, on his review of the 1966 and 1976 autopsy reports, and on the reports of the other prosecution scientists who had found curare in Mr. Biggs's liver tissue with reasonable scientific certainty. Sybil Moses asked her expert, "Based on Mr. Biggs's chart, how do you think the curare was administered?"

"I think it was administered intravenously," Dr. Foldes responded.

"And, could it have been self-administered?"

"Well, I doubt it, because I don't think the patient would have had a vial of d-tubocurarine under his pillow and a ten-cc syringe."

Dr. Foldes was also asked by the prosecutor whether or not he agreed with the cause of Biggs's death attributed in the first autopsy, that of heart failure caused by a distended bladder. Dr. Foldes's opinion emphatically agreed with the earlier one given by Dr. Baden: "I think it is ridiculous, there is no connection. . . . I don't think a distension of the bladder can cause cardiac arrest."

The Hungarian-born physician also described his own experiments with curare to explain how curare paralyzed its victims' breathing mechanism. He had had curare administered to himself by colleagues who stood by with a respirator, and he described the dramatic experience: "My eyelids drooped, I couldn't focus, I couldn't swallow my saliva, my grip strength fell to almost zero. It took about 30 minutes for my muscle strength to return." These effects, he said, came from a diluted dose of the drug, which was not strong enough to paralyze his respiratory muscles. Dr. Foldes explained that if a patient received 15 to 20 miligrams, a normal dose for a 150-pound man undergoing surgery, and if nothing were done to maintain his breathing, the patient would die in three to eight minutes.

All of this testimony was heard at first by Judge Arnold outside the jury's presence, because Mr. Brown had argued that his responses would not be based on facts, but merely speculation. The next day, Judge Arnold allowed Dr. Foldes to testify in front of the jury with certain limitations.

The retired anesthesiologist told the jury that three of the alleged murder victims had died of curare poisoning: Nancy Savino, Carl Rohrbeck, and Frank Biggs. He also said that he could not give an opinion in the Arzt case with any degree of medical certainty. Judge Arnold had refused to allow the physician to give an opinion in the Henderson case.

Mrs. Moses attempted to elicit Dr. Foldes's comments about Dr. Jascalevich's dog experiments, and she got as far as introducing Foldes's testimony that he had been doing experiments with anesthetized dogs since 1929; but Raymond Brown jumped to his feet again and convinced Judge Arnold to rule out any such testimony by the witness.

Waiving his half-glasses in front of him, Brown paced up and down before the prominent anesthesiologist and began his cross-examination. Clearly, he wanted to portray the retired professor as a quack. Brown had done his homework. On the defense counsel's table was a long list of medical articles Dr. Foldes had published over the years, including some fifty on the subject of curare and its effects. Brown picked out one written in 1934, when Dr. Foldes was only twenty-six years old. In that article, Dr. Foldes had written that a water massage was an appropriate cure for hemorrhoids and a number of other problems, and was also useful for treating hysterical people. Brown wanted to know if Dr. Foldes still stood by his article, to which the physician responded that he had given up on water massage in 1938, commenting, "You have to look at it with the perspective of the times."

Reviewing the basis for Dr. Foldes's opinion on the hospital charts, the autopsy reports, and scientific tests used to detect curare in ten-year-old tissue, Brown questioned the expert's competence: "You would do anything in the medical field and say it is alright; would you do neurosurgery?"

"I do not do neurosurgery," Foldes responded.

"How about pathology?"

"I don't have the competence to do it, but I have the competence to evaluate the results."

Later, Brown required the doctor to give his opinion about the observations of previous witnesses regarding the fact that Frank Biggs's body was entirely blue when he died. Dr. Foldes said that he would not accept that observation because only selected portions of the body would turn blue as a result of the lack of oxygen.

Brown questioned him about the testimony of a nurse who said that Mr. Biggs had continued breathing shallowly for twenty minutes before he died, but under cross-examination, Dr. Foldes refuted that observation, saying that he could not accept the fact that a patient dying from an overdose of curare could continue breathing for twenty minutes unless only a very small dose had been given.

Returning to the issue of whether or not curare victims turn blue, Brown was able to get the prosecution's expert to equivocate. Dr. Foldes said that if a patient were conscious when the drug was administered, it was possible that instead of a bluing, there might be a pallor resulting from to the body's shock reaction to the drug.

When Brown finished his five days of cross-examination, Mrs. Moses was given another opportunity to reexamine her witness. Referring to Carl Rohrbeck's death, when according to the previous testimony, Dr. Jascalevich had told the nurse on hand that the patient was dead and had left the room only five minutes after starting an intravenous feeding, Mrs. Moses asked if such conduct would be considered good medical practice. Dr. Foldes asserted, "I consider it bad medical practice."

"Why?" probed Mrs. Moses, to Brown's objection, which was overruled.

"There was no indication that any effort was made with respect to cardiopulmonary resuscitation."

According to Dr. Foldes, good medical practice requires that a physician attempt resuscitation for twenty minutes before giving up.

Mrs. Moses then asked the doctor how long it would take for a skilled person to inject curare into intravenous tubing. Before the doctor could respond, Raymond Brown objected strenuously on the ground that there was no testimony from anyone seeing Dr. Jascalevich do that. Judge Arnold sustained the objection.

On Friday, July 21, nearly five months after the trial began, the state called Dr. Michael Baden again as its last witness, because Dr. Baden had not previously been allowed to give his opinion about the cause of the alleged victims' deaths until after the curare tests were admitted.

Because Judge Arnold had already ruled that the evidence of curare in the bodies Emma Arzt and Margaret Henderson was speculative at best, Dr. Baden was barred from giving an opinion about those cases. However, Mrs. Moses asked him about the Rohrbeck, Biggs, and Savino cases. The final portion of Dr. Baden's testimony was clouded by one defense objection after another. Dr. Baden was allowed to attribute the Rohrbeck, Biggs, and Savino deaths to curare poisoning, but after a brief recess with the jury excused, and a vigorous argument by Mr. Brown, Judge Arnold instructed the jury to disregard Dr. Baden's opinion.

During the second recess, Dr. Baden told Judge Arnold that he could give a medical opinion with reasonable certainty that Mrs. Henderson had died of acute curare poisoning, if he were allowed to take into consideration the presumptive finding of curare in her body. But before Baden could even tell the judge what he was going to say about Mrs. Arzt's death, Raymond Brown interrupted again, shouting, "There is a fraud being perpetrated on this court. They are trying to shift scientific testimony from negative to positive."

Judge Arnold accepted Brown's position once more, saying of the Arzt and Henderson cases, "There is no valid scientific testimony, no evidence to a reasonable scientific certainty to this court that curare was present in these two bodies." This time, Mrs. Moses objected and demanded that the judge reconsider. His face reddening, the judge snapped at her, "You cannot use presumptive evidence in a murder trial, dear."

On Monday, July 24, following Brown's brief cross-examination of Dr. Baden, the state rested its case.

Brown immediately requested that the trial be delayed until the resolution of legal issues involving material that he was unsuccessfully trying to obtain from *New York Times* reporter Myron Farber. Brown argued that he needed this material to present the defense case properly, but Judge Arnold told him that he would not provide for such delay and Brown must proceed promptly with the appropriate motions.

CHAPTER XXVII

The Defense Case

It is customary at the end of the people's case in a criminal trial for the defense to ask the judge to direct a verdict of acquittal based on the state's failure to present a *prima facia* case. In this case, the motion was also made on the grounds that because twelve years had passed since the alleged crimes, because much evidence had been lost and witnesses had died, it was impossible, according to the defense, for Jascalevich to present an effective case on his own behalf.

Raymond Brown claimed that the prosecution failed to link the defendant to the deaths and did not demonstrate with certainty that curare was found in the bodies.

Supporting his motion, Mr. Brown attacked the validity of the state's tests and the adequacy of the evidence as to whether or not, even if there was curare in the tissue of the dead, it was there in sufficient quantity to cause death. Brown summed up, saying, "Nobody saw him near any of these patients. This is not a circumstantial web of proof, it is a maze of presumption."

Sybil Moses argued against the defense motion by emphasizing that the accused admitted having the curare in his locker, that no one had seen him do the dog experiments he had cited as justification for having the curare, and that he had been seen in the vicinity at the time of each death. She repeated her earlier contention about Jascalevich's motive: "He wanted to have the power of life and death in this hospital as chief of surgery. He wanted to play God."

On Tuesday, August 1, Judge William J. Arnold acquitted Dr. Mario E. Jascalevich on two of the five counts of murder. Basing his decision on the lack of confirmed evidence of the presence of curare in Margaret Henderson and Emma Arzt, the judge determined that a jury could not properly find beyond a reasonable doubt that the defendant had murdered those two people.

Because the court had heard witnesses testify with reasonable medical certainty that Carl Rohrbeck, Frank Biggs, and Nancy Savino had died from curare, the judge declared that if the jury chose to interpert all of the evidence most favorably to the prosecution, it could properly convict the surgeon in those three cases.

After a little more than five months, two-fifths of Raymond Brown's job was done successfully. He would now have to defend Jascalevich on only three counts of murder.

By the time the prosecution had finished presenting its case, defense counsel Brown had also presented the defendant's position through his own extensive testimony in the guise of lengthy objections and arguments supporting the various motions he made during the previous five months. Brown had stated the defense's case: There was no sure evidence of curare in the bodies, except in one, where curare was found to such a great extent that it had somehow been put there only recently, after the bodies had been exhumed. A conspiratorial group of greedy doctors, ambitious politicians, and an overzealous reporter were victimizing the defendant.

The reason for all this, Brown decreed, was that his client was a better doctor than those who owned the hospital and they were embarrassed by his superior performance and his efforts to elevate the quality of care at Riverdell Hospital to a standard more in keeping with his own than with theirs. Although Mr. Brown had made all these claims clear while the prosecution witnesses testified, it was anticipated that he would now establish appropriate supporting evidence as his turn came to present the defense case. He had said that the only thing that might stand in his way now was that critical evidence had been "lost" by the prosecutor's office and that the newspaper reporter who had played a key role in devising the conspiracy to frame Dr. Jascalevich was now hiding behind constitutional privileges and continuing to resist the extensive efforts to require him to produce evidence in his possession which Brown claimed he needed to defend his client. That is the atmosphere that Mr. Brown had created for the presentation of his case. He had accomplished this by interrupting the prosecution's witnesses and calling most of them liars, by substituting his own testimony for others to whatever extent he was allowed to get away with it—which was most of the time—and by brilliant arguments before the judge advocating a variety of creative motions he had made throughout the trial.

Depending upon the skill of the defense attorney, and the carefulness of the presiding judge, the self-serving statements by defense counsel should not be considered by the jury unless and until they are supported with evidence introduced at the trial. But no judge could conceivably have given a defense counsel such wide latitude as that which Judge Arnold had afforded to Mr. Brown.

The defense began its effort to contradict the testimony of the prosecution witnesses on Tuesday, August 2. The sixteen remaining jurors (two had already been excused) heard the first few defense witnesses, who appeared only briefly. Claire Hartman, once a nurses' aide, and Genevieve Darcey, a former nurse, both of whom were present at Carl Rohrbeck's death, testified that he was pale in color, not blue, as the prosecution witnesses had said.

Betsy Fairly, a former nurses' aide, testified that Frank Biggs was white in color on the night he died, and Barbara Kenderes, the laboratory technician who discovered Nancy Savino's death, said that the child did not look blue either. The recollections of the first and last of these witnesses also raised some doubts about the precise time at which the respective patients had died.

The first expert witness to be called by the defense was Alfred P. Stoholski, an expert forensic chemist and microscopist who was working as an independent consultant. Stoholski had once been on the staff of the New York City medical examiner's office and he, along with Dr. Charles J. Umberger, had been moonlighting when they worked with Dr. Robert Strickman, who ran the laboratory that former Prosecutor Calissi's office had used for scientific tests in 1966. These three scientists were the experts Calissi had consulted just after finding the locker full of curare at Riverdell, which Calissi had turned over to this laboratory team for analysis, along with the additional needles and vials, dripping with blood, that Jascalevich had given to the prosecutor the day after he had gone to Seton Hall to do his last experiment on November 2, 1966.

Mr. Stoholski was allowed to testify and introduce the February 1967 report he had written. Stoholski's report said that samples of nonhuman blood had been found on the syringes and on one of the vials of curare he had tested. The report said that he had also found synthetic fibers and dog hair on one of the syringes. According to

Dr. Stoholski's testimony, he had given all of the notes from his work to Dr. Umberger, who did do more tests, identifying curare and mineral oil among the seized items.

Stoholski explained how he differentiated dog hair from human hair by measuring the thickness of the hair under a microscope and by examining its cell structure. (A difference appears in the size of the core or medulla, and there is a different shape of the scales on the surface of the hairs.)

Dr. Stoholski became the first of the defense witnesses that Sybil Moses was to cross-examine extensively.

She suggested to the scientist that it might be necessary to examine the roots of a hair to determine whether it came from an animal, but Stoholski denied it: "That is not necessary." Mrs. Moses asked the witness whether he could recognize Paul L. Kirk as an authority, to which the witness agreed. At that point, the prosecutor lifted from her table a large reference book entitled *Crime Investigation,* by Paul L. Kirk, a former professor at the University of California at Berkeley.

She brought the book to the seated witness and opened it to some pictures of photomicrographs of dog hair and of human pubic and chest hair, and asked the defense expert whether or not the medullas of these different hairs illustrated in the reference book were of similar size.

Stoholski took his reading glasses from his pocket and put them on before bending down to look at the photographs. After a moment, he looked up and said to Mrs. Moses that he did not accept the photographs, arguing that they may have been selected by one of the professor's students and not by the professor himself.

The prosecutor tried another approach, by leading Stoholski through a similar exercise with photographs that showed very little difference under the microscope in the scales on different types of hair, another of the criteria used to differentiate between dog and human hair; but once again, the witness refused to accept the photographs as being valid or accurate.

When the prosecutor heard Stoholski describe the procedures he had used to determine the presence of blood from the sample bottles and syringes, she charged that his tests were "so old and out of date that modern textbooks don't even mention them." As she continued to press the chemist, he conceded that he was the only one in the New York City medical examiner's laboratory using those tests at the time, and that they was no longer in general use now by other chemists. However, Stoholski testified that he had confirmed his findings of animal blood by having a more detailed test done by the serologist laboratory at the medical examiner's office.

Stoholski was followed to the witness stand by Eve Aarons, the serologist working in the New York City medical examiner's office in 1967 who had identified the dog blood from samples provided to her by Dr. Umberger. However, Mrs. Moses was able to establish that the items which she had tested—a tube of clotted blood, gauze pads, tweezers, syringes, and gloves—had come from the surgical bag that Dr. Jascalevich had given to the prosecutor and not from the contents of his locker.

Dr. Henry Siegel, a bald and severe-looking man, was the seventh and most significant of the defense witnesses to testify. Dr. Siegel, who had worked with defense counsel Ray Brown in other cases, had been consulted by Brown even before the lawyer had agreed to assume responsibility for Dr. Jascalevich's defense. Siegel, a sixty-seven-year-old forensic pathologist, was a graduate of the New York County medical examiner's office, where he had been trained by Dr. Helpern before becoming the chief medical examiner for Westchester County, New York. Only five months had passed since Dr. Siegel retired from that position.

The first case that defense counsel Brown asked him to review was that of Frank Biggs, and Dr. Siegel opined that the fifty-one-year-old patient had died of pulmonary conjestion caused by his liver disease. Anticipating cross-examination, Brown reapproached his witness from another direction, demanding to know if the liver condition had contributed to the death, to which Dr. Siegel responded, "It more than contributed to his death, it caused his death." According to Dr. Siegel, Biggs's liver problem should have been diagnosed before the operation, and he based his view on the patient's hospital chart, which revealed fluid in Mr. Biggs's lungs which to Dr. Siegel signified liver disease. Dr. Siegel's opinion was diametrically opposed to that of Dr. Michael Baden, the prosecution expert who had noted the same symptoms that Siegel talked about, but said they were not serious enough to have caused the patient's death. Siegel charged that there was no basis for Dr.

Baden's recommendation that Mr. Biggs's body should be exhumed, because there was an adequate explanation already available for the patient's death.

Ray Brown also used Dr. Siegel to attack the prosecution's methods of testing for curare. Dr. Siegel argued that you could not have a valid test of ten-year-old curare tissue unless it had been compared with other tissues buried for ten years to determine the effects of decomposition. He characterized the prosecution's tests as "a unique experiment . . . not accepted in the scientific community." However, under the rules established by Judge Arnold, the forensic expert was forced to accept the test results as valid for purposes of answering the prosecutor's questions; so Dr. Siegel responded that even if the tests did find curare, they did not provide sufficient information to conclude that curare was the cause of Mr. Biggs's death, because no one had been able to measure the amount of curare in the body. Dr. Siegel said, "The mere presence of curare is no factor in this man's death, without my knowing the amounts . . . curare may be present in trace amounts and have no effect on Mr. Biggs at all."

On Thursday, August 24, the defense called a witness whose presence would add to the long list of unique features in the case. A judge came to testify—not an ordinary judge, but one who had once been the prosecutor that initiated the investigation eventually leading to the accusation against the defendant now on trial.

Judge Guy W. Calissi raised his right hand and took the oath of a witness. The appearance of the tall, dark, former prosecutor had not changed very much in the decade that passed since the Riverdell directors had first come to visit him in the hall of the same building in which he was now appearing to testify as a witness; there were just a few more lines on his face and somewhat darker circles under his eyes.

Speaking from recollection, Judge Calissi's memory of the additional curare that the detectives had found at the hospital was quite different from that of the two detectives who had testified earlier. They had said that they had found only six vials of curare other than those in Dr. Jascalevich's locker; Calissi's recollection was that they had found some fifty or sixty vials.

Calissi told how his investigation ran into a stone wall when his medical advisors, whom he did not name, said that it was not possible to detect curare in dead bodies.

In recalling his first encounter with the Riverdell directors, Calissi was fair to point out that "they were careful to say that they had no proof."

He explained that after his investigation got started his "suspicion diminished with respect to most of the patients who supposedly died unusual deaths. . . . You don't go before the grand jury with suspicions, you go with proof."

Calissi indicated that when he found his detectives had discovered fifty or sixty additional vials of curare in the hospital, he considered that fact to be a serious contradition, because the Riverdell doctors had assured him that curare wasn't used in the hospital. This discrepancy had seriously challenged the credibility of the other Riverdell doctors in Calissi's mind. (In retrospect, it seems to be a reasonable misunderstanding. None of the physicians who had come to complain to Calissi had been anesthesiologists, and as Dr. DeMarco had testified for the prosecutor, it was only his predecessor in anesthesiology who had used curare. Whether the detectives had found fifty or sixty vials as Calissi remembered, or six, as they remembered (and, from the information I had previously learned, I believe six to be the accurate figure), the fact that the Riverdell directors were genuinely unaware of the presence of curare in the hospital's pharmacy should not be surprising to anyone who knows that thick walls separate the information that medical specialists have about each other's work.

As further explanation for his dropping the investigation, Calissi told the court that "the list of unusual unexplained deaths dwindled" after he had discussed them in detail with Dr. Lawrence Denson, then assistant Bergen County medical examiner, because the two of them had found adequate medical explanations for many of the other patients' deaths. As the former prosecutor put it, "that left 3 or 4 that we didn't have an explanation for."

Judge Calissi also revealed on the witness stand that while he was waiting for the results of the laboratory tests that he had ordered, he was approached by me. He told of my having obtained Dr. Helpern's offer of help and of his giving me the tissue samples and the transcript of the 200-page statement by Dr. Jascalevich. (Calissi did not say that he had already told the Riverdell doctors that he was dropping the investigation.)

The judge testified that he subsequently received the reports of dog hair and blood being found on some of the material he had submitted to the laboratory, which apparently supported Dr. Jascalevich's claim of doing dog experiments, but Calissi also told of Dr. Helpern's continuing interest in the case and the search for additional tissues for Helpern to test, which he was unable to come up with.

When asked the critical question about why he did not consider exhuming bodies to provide more tissue, Calissi said he was told one could not find curare in an embalmed body.

Calissi also said that three years after the original investigation the matter was still on his mind, and he asked one of his assistants to determine if scientists had developed a way to find curare. But the assistant had reported back in early 1970 that nothing could be done.

Judge Calissi was followed to the stand by Superior Court Judge Fred C. Galda. A short, stocky man, Galda enlivened his normally unimpressive appearance that day with a plaid suit, which made him look more like a small-town politician than a judge. As Calissi's first assistant, Galda had the prime responsibility for the Riverdell investigation in 1966 and was most assertative in defending the decision not to prosecute: "Nothing that we had should have been presented to a grand jury. We even considered at one point investigating the hospital." Galda described the investigation they had conducted and said his office had thirty detectives working around the clock for the first three days.

Most of Judge Galda's testimony involved the meeting he had with Myron Farber of the *New York Times,* who had come to the judge's home. Galda admitted that he gave Farber a copy of the detectives' sixty-four-page handwritten summary of the 1966 investigation, after making Farber sign a statement promising to be objective in any stories that he might write.

Raymond Brown also asked Galda for his recollection of the conversation that took place between him, Jascalevich, and the other Riverdell doctors after the Riverdell locker was broken into. According to Galda, "these tapes would tend to exculpate Dr. Jascalevich. . . . He berated the other doctors. He suggested that these doctors were tantamount to being incompetent."

After a brief recess for the long Labor Day weekend, the trial, now in its seventh month, resumed with more testimony from the defendant's expert witness, Dr. Frederic Reiders. He described the mass spectrometry analysis he had done on the tissues of Frank Biggs, Carl Rohrbeck, and Nancy Savino, which had been provided to him by the prosecutor's office. Dr. Reiders offered with "reasonable scientific certainty" that neither Mr. Biggs's liver nor Mr. Rohrbeck's tissues contained curare. His testimony directly contradicted the prosecution's experts who had found curare in these tissues by using two other tests. Dr. Reiders had found curare in the liver tissue of Nancy Savino, but he said that the curare he found was so pure that it could not have survived in that state for ten years. After finding the curare in the Savino case, he had performed other tests which showed that curare was rapidly destroyed by the type of embalming fluid used in Nancy's body.

Dr. Bo R. Holmstedt is a well-known toxicologist in Sweden. His appearance at the trial had been previously heralded in a pretrial newspaper story, and when he came from Sweden to testify on September 12, Dr. Holmstedt denigrated the work of the prosecution scientists, alleging that they had failed to take proper safeguards to prevent errors. It was Dr. Holmstedt's opinion that the presumptive tests the prosecution scientists had used, saying that the drug was probably present through one test and then establishing its presence by another test that was also presumptive, could never justify positive proof. Dr. Holmstedt said positive proof could not come from any number of presumptive tests. The Swedish expert further impeached the work of the prosecution specialists because they had been unable to measure the amount of curare they found: "The presence of a substance should be described in quantities . . . otherwise it would have to be disregarded," because one doesn't know what presence means if it can't be quantified.

Dr. Holmstedt told Brown that he did not believe curare could survive for ten years in embalmed and buried bodies, and he agreed with Dr. Reiders, who had testified that embalming fluid broke down the curare and made it undetectable.

The last of Dr. Jascalevich's expert witnesses was Dr. Valentino D. B. Mazzia, who had served as a consultant to Dr. Helpern's office back in 1966, when he was then chairman of the anesthesiology department at the New York University Medical Center, the medical school with which Dr. Helpern's New York City medical examiner's office has always been affiliated. However, Mazzia did not testify about any involvement in the case in 1966. He had left

N.Y.U. shortly thereafter to practice on the West Coast and was now professor of anesthesiology at the University of Colorado. In the interim, Mazzia had also added a law degree to his credentials, and his testimony turned out to be extensive.

Under the guidance of Raymond Brown's questions, Dr. Mazzia began by accusing the late Dr. Robert J. Baba of mismanaging the anesthesia he had administered to Nancy Savino at the time of her operation at Riverdell Hospital.

Based on his review of the hospital charts, Dr. Mazzia said Dr. Baba had "missed how seriously ill she was" and accused him of grossly inadequate and unsafe practices in monitoring and recording the child's condition during her operation. To support the defense contention that the Riverdell Hospital procedures were inadequate, Mazzia described as incomplete the admission notes on the child's records and criticized the hospital's failure to take an adequate medical history or to conduct an adequate physical examination. He was critical of the administration of phenobarbital, saying the child had needed more attention when this drug was given. Mazzia tried to say that Dr. Baba was a drug addict at one time, explaining that he had known a number of anesthesiologists who falsified patient records by claiming to have administered drugs to patients which they actually used on themselves, and Dr. Mazzia speculated that this had happened in the Savino case, because he could find no justification for the use of Demerol, which was reported on the hospital chart. Sybil Moses objected to this aspect of Mazzia's testimony and persuaded Judge Arnold to instruct the jury to disregard it.

Dr. Mazzia testified that it was a "reasonable medical certainty" that Nancy Savino and Frank Biggs had died of natural causes and said it was his opinion that both deaths were "absolutely incompatible and inconsistent" with curare poisoning. To buttress his position, Dr. Mazzia said a dose of curare that is strong enough to kill would invariably turn parts of the victim blue, and Nancy Savino was reported to have been pale, while the reports on Biggs's coloration varied. He also said, just as Dr. DeMarco had testified earlier, that a patient suffering from an overdose of curare could be revived within twenty minutes, and so if the attempts to resuscitate the patient were unsuccessful, as they were in the Biggs and Savino cases, and if the heart thereafter failed to restart, "it cannot possibly be curare."

To this effect, Dr. Mazzia's testimony was directly in conflict with the prosecution's curare expert, Dr. Francis Foldes, who had said that curare kills within ten minutes and doesn't necessarily turn a victim blue. Dr. Foldes had also admitted that he had been wrong when he testified years ago in the Coppolino case that a person's heart can continue beating for twenty minutes without oxygen.

Like Dr. Foldes, Dr. Mazzia had tested curare on himself and described his experience.

As to the death of Carl Rohrbeck, it was Dr. Mazzia's opinion that Rohrbeck had died of heart failure and that his symptoms were also inconsistent with curare poisoning. Mazzia said that the time lapse of five minutes between Dr. Jascalevich's starting the intravenous feeding on Mr. Rohrbeck and the nurse's finding him dead was not long enough for curare to have completely paralyzed the patient or to have stopped his heart. "Even when they're diseased," Mazzia said, "these hearts take eight to ten minutes to stop."

The cross-examination of Dr. Mazzia may have been Sybil Moses's finest hour. First she elicited from the witness the fact that when he had studied the records on the deaths of the patients he had not taken into account the reported findings of curare in their bodies. He did not at all answer the prosecutor's question, "Isn't it important to take these findings into account?" Since Mr. Brown objected and Judge Arnold ruled that the doctor did not have to answer because he had been called to evaluate the patient's hospital charts and nothing else.

Mrs. Moses was also able to force Dr. Mazzia to acknowledge that he had once made a report to defense counsel Brown indicating that the Savino and Brown deaths were attributable to causes other than the heart failure and abdominal infection ascribed to them by the defense pathologist, Dr. Henry Siegel; but she was prevented from obtaining evidence as to what his earlier conclusion had been. She did get Dr. Mazzia to admit that he did not know how a liver failure could cause a breathing failure, as the defense alleged had happened in the Biggs case, and that the Savino child's symptoms were not usually associated with the type of abdominal infection that Dr. Siegel said had led to her death. Dr. Mazzia was patronizing to Mrs. Moses and on several occasions attempted to instruct her on how best to ask him questions. The epitome of Dr.

Mazzia's hostility was reached when the prosecutor attempted to get him to recognize several different books on medicine as authorities, a necessary procedure before he could be questioned about what the authors said. Dr. Mazzia said he would not accept any authority in the field of medicine. Finally, Mrs. Moses asked him if he would accept his own book as an authority, to which he replied that he would not. Mrs. Moses thus made her point.

The defense side of the case might reasonably be divided into two general aspects: first, the issue of how the patients died and whether or not curare was involved; Second, the role of the *New York Times* reporter, Myron Farber, and the conspiracy alleged by Mr. Brown to have existed between Farber, the prosecutor, the Riverdell doctors, and Dr. Baden to frame Jascalevich. Despite the bizarre allegations against Jascalevich that were being reported on daily, Myron Farber's private war on behalf of a free press gained more attention from the press than did the trial. He became the focal point of the legal and constitutional issues surrounding the defendant's effort to force him to turn his notes over to Judge Arnold to determine if they were relevant to the case. When Farber was jailed for contempt of court during the trial, the issue touched off a national debate, with the press more interested in Mr. Farber's fate than in Dr. Jascalevich's. Farber and the *Times* were held in contempt because he would not surrender his notes or reveal his sources. When the trial testimony ended, Dr. Jascalevich, free on $150,000 bail, went home with his wife to await the outcome of the matter and Myron Farber was in jail for contempt of court.

Insofar as public interests were concerned, whatever testimony Myron Farber gave when the defense called him on September 18 seemed anticlimactic in light of the momentous issues of the legal battle that had pursued the diminutive reporter throughout the previous seven months and had thrust him into the national limelight.

At the inception of his testimony, Farber was forced by Brown's questions to admit that he had misrepresented himself at the office of the Bergen County Narcotics Task Force, where he was sent to review the prosecutor's 1966 file on the case. To gain admission to that file, Farber had identified himself to the officers in charge of the record room as an "official" by so describing himself when he signed the visitor's book. Ray Brown pummelled Farber with questions to get him to disclose how he had obtained information about the case. In response to Brown's questioning, Farber admitted to having spoken with the late Dr. Baba. When Brown asked the reporter for the notes of that interview, Farber said that he had none. Brown consequently asked Farber to describe his conversation with Baba, and the reporter said that the late anesthesiologist had told him that he believed some patients had been murdered with curare. Brown asked, "Did he know who used curare?"

"He thought perhaps Dr. Jascalevich had," the reporter replied somewhat arrogantly.

"In the operating room or to murder people?"

"To murder people, Mr. Brown."

Then Brown began his effort to tie Farber into the Bergen County investigation. He demanded to know about Farber's discussions with former Prosecutor Joseph Woodcock. The reporter remembered meeting him only four or five times, and their conversations were mostly about state and county politics. Brown asked Farber whether Woodcock had discussed his gubernatorial ambitions with him; Farber replied that he hadn't. The *Times* man also said that they had talked about the growth of shopping centers in Paramus, but Farber denied having any specific recollection of sharing information with Woodcock that he had gleaned from the files. Farber did admit giving the missing transcript to Woodcock, although after consulting with his *New York Times* lawyers outside the courtroom, he again refused to answer the defense attorney's question as to whom he had obtained it from, claiming that his duties and privileges as a newspaperman required him not to answer.

The key to defense counsel Brown's conspiracy theory was the relationship that he claimed Farber had with Dr. Michael Baden. Dr. Baden had testified that it was former Prosecutor Woodcock who called him for advice on handling the case, but Brown wanted to show that Farber and Baden had had a long-time relationship which preceded Woodcock's call. Under Brown's rigorous examination, Farber acknowledged that he had known Dr. Baden for about five years, and he recalled having probably spoken to Baden about the Jascalevich case before Woodcock first met with the medical examiner on November 7, 1975. Referring to his discussion with Dr. Baden, Farber commented to Brown, "I suspect that it was before November 7," but he added that he could not remember the details of the particular conversation.

"Because of your poor recollection," Brown asked, "because of your disability, do you have notes on meeting with Dr. Baden?" Farber, who had been refusing to turn over any notes in order to protect his sources, was allowed once again to step down to consult with his two *New York Times* attorneys before answering the question. This time, Farber came back and said that he would check his notes to see whether he could testify with accuracy about the dates of the meetings, but he would not provide the notes for the defense attorney to examine. Judge Arnold directed Farber to check the notes to see what was said at the meeting and threatened to add an additional contempt citation if he did not do so; but Farber respectfully declined to comply. Judge Arnold's order and Myron Farber's refusal would be repeated several times throughout Farber's testimony, a routine bound to have an impact on the jury.

At each point during the examination when Brown requested the reporter's notes, Farber left the stand for a private conversation in the hallway with the *Times* lawyers while everybody waited. Each time he came back and refused, asserting his privilege under the United States Constitution and the New Jersey Shield Law. The procedure was already consuming a great deal of time.

At the very least, Brown had succeeded in creating a picture for the jurors of the bearded *Times* reporter refusing to cooperate and thus appearing to be concealing something.

At this point, Brown raised a surprise issue. After reminding Farber about a *New York Times* story he had written in 1973 concerning the involvement of the New York City medical examiner's office in another murder trial, Brown turned toward the courtroom audience and asked Stephen Delaney, a private investigator working for Brown in the Jascalevich case, to stand up. Pointing dramatically at Delaney, Brown said to Farber, "Did you in November, 1973, speak to this man and tell him that Dr. Baden was your private source of information in the medical examiner's office and that you and Dr. Baden were working together to disgrace Dr. Helpern?"

The first to respond was Sybil Moses, who jumped to her feet and shouted in the judge's direction, "This is an outrage!" But before Judge Arnold could respond, Farber leaned forward in the witness chair and, with more than a touch of indignation, snapped at Brown, "Absolutely not." But Brown did not stop: "Did you receive information on the Carpi case from Dr. Baden?" Farber, his voice rising excitedly, replied, "I did not."

Turning to Judge Arnold, the flamboyant defense counsel said, "I shall put Mr. Delaney on the stand and we will show the continuing relationship of that man on the stand and Dr. Baden."

Mrs. Moses rose to her feet, and in an effort that proved to be as futile as many of the others she had made, objected to what she termed the "irrelevant mud-slinging" on behalf of the defense.

Farber had written an article for the *Times* revealing the preliminary results of the curare testing, but he invoked his privileges again when Brown asked him to reveal his source and provide the notes of his conversation with one of the experts who had tested the tissue in the case. He did the same when he was asked which medical experts he had consulted concerning hospital records.

During his testimony Farber was cited nineteen more times for contempt of court.

The eight-month-old trial was drawing to a close on October 12, when Mr. Brown finished his examination of the beleaguered *New York Times* reporter and allowed him to return to his cell at the Bergen County jail, where he was serving his initial sentence for contempt since the U.S. Supreme Court had rejected his request to stay the sentence.

As promised, Brown's next witness was Stephen Delaney, the former Boston police officer who was now Brown's private investigator. Delaney testified about a long telephone conversation he had had with Farber in 1973, when Delaney was working as a defense investigator in the other New Jersey murder case which Farber had also reported on for the *Times.* Delaney revealed that Farber told him at the time that his source for a series of sensational articles he was then writing about the mishandling of evidence in the New York City medical examiner's office was Dr. Michael Baden. According to Delaney, Farber understood that the articles would prove embarrassing to the chief medical examiner, Dr. Milton Helpern.

Beatrice Helpern, the late chief medical examiner's wife and secretary, was Ray Brown's next witness. The elderly, frail woman was helped to the witness chair by two court attendants; but once she was seated, her usual perkiness seemed to return in force. I had known her ten years ago as the aggressive protector of Dr. Helpern's door and his most ardent admirer. Now she was obviously relishing the opportunity to perform one more act of loyalty to her late husband. She told the court that the locks in her late husband's office had to be changed because Dr. Baden had tried to enter without authority. According to Mrs. Helpern, Baden had been obsessed with the Jascalevich file, which Dr. Helpern had always kept on the windowsill of his office.

(When Baden testified earlier, he denied even knowing the file existed until the 1975 reopening of the investigation. Under Ray Brown's cross-examination, Dr. Baden also denied being a source of information for Myron Farber. When I first spoke to Michael Baden about the affair early in 1977, his recollections of that file and the 1966 investigation were only vague ones, and they certainly were not the recollections of a man who had been obsessed with the file since 1967, as Mrs. Helpern testified. Insofar as I know, Baden had no involvement in the 1966 investigation.)

Mrs. Helpern's testimony that Dr. Baden was the source of Myron Farber's information about the various mistakes in the medical examiner's office during Helpern's reign was identical to the view that Helpern had expressed publicly in 1973, when he charged that Baden was leaking stories to Farber in order to embarrass his boss into retirement. Dr. Baden had denied those stories at the time. In my last discussion with Dr. Helpern in 1976, he had repeated these charges to me.

Mrs. Helpern also testified that she had searched for the missing file that had been in her husband's office after Farber's Dr. X stories had appeared, but she had been unable to find it. This, of course, confirmed my own experience and telephone call with Dr. Helpern in 1976, when I could hear him talking to her about trying again to find the file.

The last witness for the defense was another *New York Times* reporter, Joseph F. Sullivan. Sullivan's story, which appeared in the *New York Times* on January 8, 1976, the day after Farber's first Dr. X story, quoted Joseph Woodcock as saying, with respect to his reopening of the investigation, that information uncovered by the *New York Times* "is actually the thing that tripped it."

Woodcock had told Sullivan, according to the story, that Farber had showed him a deposition "not in our file" and had provided additional information to convince the prosecutor to begin his own investigation. Attempting to use the second *Times* reporter as his foil to crack the resistance of the press, Brown asked for Sullivan's notes on the conversation he had with Woodcock; but Sullivan was able to avoid a confrontation on the issue of reporter's privilege by testifying that he had none, nor did he know the nature of the additional information that Woodcock was referring to.

Brown indicated that he believed the additional information consisted of Farber's putting Woodcock and Dr. Baden in touch with one another, a theory supported by Dr. Baden's earlier testimony that he had been contacted by Farber about the possibility of finding curare in bodies shortly before he heard from Woodcock for the first time. Thus, on a relatively undramatic note, the thirty-third and final week of testimony ended.

CHAPTER XXVIII

The Verdict

It was Friday, October 13, when Raymond Brown announced that he had called his last witness. Mr. Brown informed the court that the defendant would exercise his privilege: Dr. Jascalevich would not take the stand in his own defense. Twenty-two other witnesses had appeared in his behalf, and the state had called fifty-six, making this one of the longest criminal trials on record.

Sybil Moses lost the last round when Judge Arnold denied her the opportunity to call one rebuttal witness. She had wanted to introduce Dr. Werner Spitz, the medical examiner of Detroit, Michigan, to refute some of Jascalevich's scientific witnesses, but Judge Arnold justified his unusual ruling because there were only thirteen jurors left, Ray Brown was threatening a long cross-examination of Dr. Spitz, and the judge's primary concern was to wrap up the trial before any further attrition of the jurors could reduce his jury to less than twelve.

Summation began on the following Wednesday, and Raymond Brown had a lectern placed in front of the jury box for his appeal, which he expected to take up the better part of two days.

In his sometimes emotional plea to the jury, he summarized the case he had presented, both directly and indirectly, and reminded the attentive jurors of how unusual it was.

"This case represents the most extreme form of stretching to make a point that has ever been presented in an American court. There is no proof that this man ever put anything into anybody."

Brown told the jurors that the future of the American system of justice was in their hands, as he reiterated his position that Dr. Jascalevich was the victim of a frame-up initiated by the other Riverdell doctors who, wishing to cover their own inadequacies and embarrassment, had selected Mario Jascalevich because he was not one of the boys and indeed stood above them.

Despite the length of Brown's sometimes emotional speech, the jurors' attention never deviated from his words. He raised and lowered his voice at the appropriate moments and attacked the state's evidence: "There is not one scintilla of proof . . . only speculation."

As Brown weaved the conspiracy together before the enthralled jurors, each of the key witnesses of the past eight months was called to mind again. He outlined his conspiracy theory, referring to it as "political profit, Pulitzer-book profit, prosecutor-judge profit." He told them how Woodcock had cooperated with Farber, because Woodcock wanted to increase his personal fame to justify obtaining the Republican nomination for governor, or even for Congress. Farber, said Brown, was after a Pulitzer prize to distinguish himself as a newsman, and it was his long and close relationship with Dr. Baden, according to Brown, that enabled him to offer New York City's resources to Mr. Woodcock. Brown waived before the jury a letter that Dr. Baden had written to Woodcock on December 30, 1975, encouraging the prosecutor to use Dr. Baden's facilities for the new autopsies and the search for curare. Brown said this offer of help was Baden's "ticket" to become the chief medical examiner for New York City (which he had indeed become during the trial). Describing Dr. Baden's offer, Brown said, "Bring the case to me, I will put the team together, and I will give you a guaranty of finding curare."

Concluding that portion of his summation, which rapped Dr. Baden, Brown called Myron Farber's articles Dr. Baden's "Ad in the *New York Times.*"

The defense counsel also impeached the usefulness of the prosecution's curare tests, persuading the jurors that the prosecution had failed to prove anything about curare.

Brown spent a good deal of his summation time trying to convince the jurors that there were no curare murders and that the patients seemed really to have died of natural causes. Even if this was not clear to the jurors, he told them the state had certainly failed to prove its contentions beyond a reasonable doubt.

"Tell me this, ladies and gentlemen: If there is a difference of opinion between experts, is there proof beyond a reasonable doubt . . . or is there a question?"

He attacked the motives, competence, and integrity of the state's curare experts, demeaning their professionalism by pointing to the hostility or anger that his cross-examination had elicited from them. He compared them with his own scientific experts, who Brown said were working to prevent an injustice.

Speaking of his own approach to the trial, Raymond Brown told the jurors, "The defense has brought you more than a defense, we have brought you an offense."

His eloquent plea took seven and one-half hours, and as he ended it, Brown reached for the hearts of the jurors. Turning to his client, he said, "Please, this man is already destroyed. The man hurt nobody. Tried to hurt nobody. Never had. Never could. Never did. . . . Let him live out his life. . . . This man is at your mercy. This man is but a pawn."

As Brown concluded, the spectators packed in the courtroom broke into applause, until Judge Arnold banged his gavel to quiet them.

The next day, Friday, October 20, Sybil Moses came to the same lectern. Her summation took only half the time that Brown's did; and while she could not match her more experienced opponent in eloquence, it was apparent to anyone who had been there at the beginning of the trial that she had made an impressive comeback, that the lessons she had learned in the past eight months had not been insignificant.

She began by trying to evoke the jurors' sympathy for the alleged victims, showing each of their hospital charts and personalizing them: "This is Carl Rohrbeck, this is a human being." She described the deaths in detail and reminded the jurors that if Nancy Savino had lived she would be starting college next fall.

Sybil Moses found it hard to believe that the jurors could be convinced by some of the arguments that they had heard from Mr. Brown during the trial and the summation. From the prosecutor's perspective, they were incredible; but she knew the lawyer's adage that anything is possible with a jury. So she tried to convince them of her view, and she too turned to the defendant, but only to mock him unsympathetically and with hardness in her voice: "Poor Mario. A cry of frame-up is not an unusual defense. It is the type of defense made by a scared animal." She reminded the jurors how Brown had attacked her own character and integrity as well as that of each of the prosecution witnesses. "That is their way of defending murder, attack, attack, attack. Put everyone else on trial . . . it is ludicrous."

Using almost the identical language that she had for her opening remarks at the inception of the trial, Sybil Moses referred to the fact that Mario Jascalevich was there every time a patient died.

As she reviewed each death, she summarized the testimony indicating that curare was the cause of each death. To support her scientific evidence, she eventually turned to the jurors and asked, "Is it coincidence that prosecution scientists working independently at two laboratories and using three tests found curare in all three bodies when they were exhumed for specialized testing in 1976? The chance that all of these tests could be false is so remote that you have to put it out of your mind."

Mindful of Brown's attack on the motives of the Riverdell doctors, she countered by pointing out that the doctors were well aware of the risk to their hospital from the publicity that would attend them when they pressed charges against Jascalevich. Hitting hard on this point, Mrs. Moses said, "These were not a group of men who said, 'we are going to get a profit out of this.' These men were scared. If they were motivated by profit, don't you think the first thing they would have done is to try to keep the hospital's name out of the newspapers?"

The prosecutor reminded the jurors of the significance of Dr. Jascalevich's 1966 testimony in Mr. Calissi's office. According to Sybil Moses, Dr. Jascalevich's cooperation with the prosecutor and the statement he made was an effort to "cover his tracks . . . the first thing anyone does who's found out." She demonstrated her point to the jurors by reminding them of the unrefuted testimony that dying dogs were not left on the tables of the hospital, as Jascalevich had said they were; that the only employee named Lee who had ever worked as a sweeper at the laboratory had left his employment in January 1966, eight months before Jascalevich had said he stopped his curare experiments on dogs; that the man who was responsible for ordering the hospital dogs testified that the school never ran out of dogs, a refutation of Jascalevich's claim to Calissi that his experiments had ceased in August because the school did not have any more dogs; and finally, she reminded the jurors of the doctor who testified about the day Jascalevich arrived in an anxious state looking for a dog to work on, the day he had been told about the discovery of curare in his locker.

Refuting Brown's claim that his client had been framed, Sybil Moses read the jurors a list of forty people whom Brown had personally vilified during his summation. She said, "Don't you find it incredible that all these people got together to attack this man?"

When Mrs. Moses finished, there was no applause.

The decisive moment had now been reached. However long it would take, Dr. Jascalevich's fate was now in the hands of the jurors.

On Monday morning the judge spent an hour and fifteen minutes instructing the jurors in detail of their responsibilities and outlining for them the applicable law. He told them it was up to them to determine first whether any murder actually took place, or if the patients had died of natural causes. Should they decide, the judge said, that the patients were murdered, then they would have to determine whether Dr. Jascalevich was the murderer. Pointing out that there was no direct evidence that the defendant had administered curare to any of the deceased, the judge said that Jascalevich was "entitled to every inference in his favor which can reasonably be drawn from the facts." He told the jurors that under the laws of New Jersey, "merely suspicious circumstances, no matter how strong they may be, are not sufficient to render a verdict of guilt against anyone." The judge explained that a possibility of guilt is not strong enough; guilt must be proven beyond a reasonable doubt. He described a "reasonable doubt" as an "honest and reasonable certainty as to the guilt of the defendant which exists in your mind after you have given full and impartial consideration to the evidence."

At the request of the defense, Judge Arnold reminded the jurors that the defendant had a constitutional right to remain silent and that they may not draw any inferences of guilt from that fact.

He also told them that they were not bound by any expert's opinion and that they had to determine for themselves which of the experts and which of the scientific tests were reliable.

It was late afternoon when the jurors commenced their deliberations, and after a short time they sent a note to the judge asking for a copy of the testimony of Dr. Frederic Reiders, the defense expert who had testified that curare could not have survived in embalmed bodies for ten years.

The jurors deliberated only forty-five minutes that day before adjourning overnight to the nearby motel. The next morning, after just one more hour of deliberation, the jurors returned the verdict. It was October 24, 1978.

They found Dr. Jascalevich innocent on all charges. Again, the spectators burst into applause. Upon hearing the news, the silver-haired surgeon said, "Thank God justice was done." His wife echoed him: "An innocent man was saved." A stunned Sybil Moses left the courtroom without a word as the familiar crowd of Jascalevich well-wishers began to surround the former defendant.

As the jurors left the room, Dr. Jascalevich rose to honor them by waiving his white pocket handkerchief in their direction.

The six men and six women who served on the jury were interviewed extensively that night, and they spoke freely to the press. They were heard on radio and television, and the many newspaper accounts were full of quotations from different jurors. In summary, they had bought everything that Ray Brown had to sell. They didn't seem to think there had been any murders, they didn't believe the prosecution experts, and, yes, they did believe that there had indeed been a conspiracy to frame Dr. Jascalevich.

One juror commented, "I started out thinking he was innocent and I never wavered." Actually, the jurors said it had taken them only five minutes to find Jascalevich innocent, and they had taken the first ballot when they sat down on Monday afternoon. They had decided to sleep on it to make sure they were doing the right thing, which is why they waited until the next morning to deliver their verdict.

In the morning they discussed only two issues, whether the doctor could have concealed a syringe in his lab coat (something that had never come up during the trial), and whether curare could survive for ten years in the body of a dead patient. The jurors agreed that the answer to both questions was no, and at 11:30 in the morning they delivered their verdict.

One juror told the press that Mrs. Moses had not proved a thing; another expressed the view that the patients were very sick people and had died of natural causes. A third said she could not believe the state's scientific evidence because it had not been used to detect curare before. One of the jurors admitted that she was suspicious of Dr. Baden's motives and had been convinced by Mr. Brown's conspiracy theory: "It is very easy to see how he was framed by ambitious colleagues; it is just like in grade school when a group of big bullies gang up on a small shy boy."

PART VI

CHAPTER XXIX

Epilogue

When the excitement over the trial and the jury's verdict died down, Dr. Mario Jascalevich was still facing a number of problems that were not cleared up by acquittal. Several malpractice claims were pending, some from the families of the alleged victims. The state's proceeding to revoke his license, which had been adjourned to allow him to prepare for trial, was to be resumed shortly.

Ultimately, the verdict of Dr. Jascalevich is of importance only to him, his colleagues, and the families of the dead patients; and this fact touches on the question of why I have written this book. The most significant aspect of the story is its dramatic illustration of the failure of certain elements of the legal and medical institutions which our society should be able to rely upon and which we can improve if we want to. Unfortunately, sometimes it takes a dramatic event to obtain the attention that serious problems deserve. Perhaps the grief caused by the deaths at Riverdell Hospital and the millions of dollars spent in the defense and prosecution of Dr. Jascalevich might still serve some purpose if the experience leads us a bit closer to solving some of the legal and medical problems that came to light during this affair. Now, after telling the story, I feel some responsibility to share my insights about the problems that continue to trouble me, and make some useful recommendations as well.

Suburban law enforcement is frightfully ineffective. With so many Americans living on the edges of our big cities, it's about time that we consider the quality of security protection provided in that setting. Police services are fragmented, outmoded, and unscientific when compared with what is provided in the adjacent urban centers. The reason is simple enough: Because people treasure old values, it becomes good politics to organize police services on the basis of the smallest municipality, thus preserving the myth that such law enforcement is "closer to the people"—which should be translated to mean that the local politicians can have more to say about it. Bergen County in 1966, just like so many other places in America today, tolerated a county prosecutor who could still be involved in private law practice and local politics, which by nature must generate burdensome conflicts.

The capacity for the highest quality professional investigation does not exist, nor do the suburbs have facilities for the professional training of detectives. It is no wonder that most serious felonies remain unsolved. The 1966 Bergen County investigation was hampered by the same lack of a trained forensic pathologist and proper medical examiner's facilities which today plague more than half the counties in America where unqualified people are still performing these functions. The assistant county medical examiner who advised Calissi and who, through the system of seniority but without testing, eventually became the county's chief medical examiner, is not a certified forensic pathologist. Prosecutor Calissi was told in 1966 that it was impossible to detect curare in exhumed bodies, so he did not consider exhumation, despite the fact that at the same time, in a case that would be page-one news around the country, Dr. Milton Helpern and Dr. Charles Umberger were preparing to tell the Coppolino murder trial how they had found succinylcholine, a drug similar to curare, in the exhumed body of Carmela Coppolino. (As this book goes to press, Cappolino's lawyers are seeking to challenge these scientific findings.)

While some improvements in the Bergen County prosecutor's office and the state law enforcement system were made between 1966 and 1978 (additional prosecutors, no more part-timers, more law enforcement responsibility for the attorney general, and the creation of a state medical examiner facility available to all county prosecutors), the inexcusable fact remains that in 1975 the county prosecutor delegated the biggest murder case that had ever been prosecuted in the jurisdiction to his most inexperienced assistant and then gave her almost no help, although it became known that the defendant would be represented by the most outstanding criminal defense lawyer in the state. Mrs. Moses is a capable woman; but in all fairness, she simply did not have the experience to handle such responsibility. What Mr. Woodcock and his successor Roger Breslin did here is tantamount to a general sending a raw recruit into battle without proper training or the weapons necessary to sustain the fight. Such generals usually get court-martialed when the battle is over, and in this case, it is the duty of the governor of New Jersey to conduct an inquiry.

Nor can the black robe of a justice cover Judge Arnold's failure to control his courtroom. He too has some explaining to do, and so does the system that created him. How could a judge allow himself to fall asleep, or even appear to, while presiding over a five-count murder trial? Maintaining order and decorum is a judge's responsibility.

As an attorney, I am justifiably proud of what my profession can be, but I am embarrassed to know that just across the river in New Jersey a trial judge permitted another lawyer to call witnesses such names as "liar" and "quack," to interrupt witnesses' testimony beyond propriety, to make derogatory personal references to opposing counsel, and to give his own testimony during the state's case. Allowing such conduct is a disgrace, not only to the judicial process, but to our civilization. Justice cannot be dispensed in such an atmosphere. Why should we expect future witnesses to come forth in the service of justice if their differences of opinion can lead to personal vilification and character assassination? Counsel has an obligation to be zealous in defense of his clients, but only within the bounds of the laws of evidence and legal propriety. It is up to the judge to assure that he keeps within those bounds. Fairness to both sides and to the sensitivity of witnesses requires that the judge do so. Justice does not require that people should be abused. No judge should permit it—but Judge Arnold did and Judge Arnold should be held accountable.

Means do exist to prevent these problems if the public becomes concerned enough.

As to law enforcement and the judiciary, I have some specific recommendations.

First, modern scientific facilities and all of the services of a forensic pathologist must be readily accessible (without long delay) to every responsible law enforcement official in the country. A crime requiring the services of a scientific detection team is just as likely to be committed in a wealthy suburb or in a poor rural county as in an urban one, and the people there are entitled to quality protection—but they do not always have appropriate facilities available. This can be changed by providing shared services or central facilities at the state level.

The same concept should be applied to professional detective work, which is also unavailable in many jurisdictions. The states should support the creation of highly trained investigators to provide such services where needed and, where the population density warrants it, the training and availability of such experts at the county level. The day of bungled investigations can be ended.

Dealing with defects in the judiciary requires an even greater determination, because judges are so inherently powerful and use their need for independence to justify their resistance to supervision. To obviate the sort of problems illuminated by this case, I recommend: First, that the occupant of any judicial office must meet certain minimal physical and mental standards to assure that each judge has the physical stamina and alertness of mind needed to perform with fairness; secondly, a mechanism whereby judicial conduct is subject to constant scrutiny by an administrative authority. The appellate system alone is insufficient for these purposes.

The case also provides another illustration of the failure of the medical profession's systems for monitoring itself. During my extensive legislative investigations for the New York State Assembly in 1977 and 1978 we found countless examples of this. Doctors claim that the system of accrediting hospitals by state agencies and professional organizations provides patients with a tremendous safeguard. The fact is that these systems don't work. The professional committees are comprised of physicians watching other physicians. It is like trying to run the state prisons on the honor system, but in medicine we are dealing with life and death. Physicians are inducted into the conspiracy of silence during their earliest medical school training, and there is no place in the medical profession for a physician who will report on a colleague.

Patients who impute godlike qualities to their physicians should be aware of the financial conflicts of interest between their medical necessities and their doctors' income. Unnecessary surgery is probably the most horrendous violation regularly perpetrated on Americans by the medical profession. Hundreds of respectable studies have demonstrated its existence. The only argument is whether it constitutes 10% of surgery or 40%, depending upon the type of operation involved, who did the study, and where.

The best surgeons in America do not work in eighty-bed hospitals—they work in large teaching institutions, where they can constantly improve their information and benefit from the insights of their students. Certainly major surgery should not be allowed in hospitals that lack intensive care units, nor those which tolerate employment of referring physicians as surgical assistants. A hospital that started out by awarding an exclusive franchise for surgery to its founder leaves much to be desired, although Riverdell's efforts to correct that situation were honest and commendable. Nor can I countenance surgery by surgeons with a proprietary interest in the hospital, although it is common practice at small proprietary hospitals throughout the country. There is no question that Riverdell Hospital had an inordinately high surgical mortality rate during 1965, 1966, and 1967. Under the existing system the fluctuation in the mortality rates at Riverdell remained unexplained—it shouldn't have.

But there is an answer to the present dilemma. Techniques already exist through the application of simple computer technology to a medical records data collection system, which turns out comparative statistical analysis of morbidity and mortality rates among similar hospitals doing similar procedures. By comparing such performance records, patients and their physicians can know which hospitals and which doctors are having difficulty with which operations. Substandard care and excessive surgery is exposed, and consumers have a reliable basis for identifying the hospitals and doctors to stay away from while governmental licensors take appropriate corrective action. Such a total system is embodied in the Quality of Health Care legislation which has been introduced for study in the New York State Assembly as a result of a two-year-long study by our Medical Practice Task Force. If enacted, it can and should become a model for the nation.

CHAPTER XXX

A Note on Myron Farber

Myron Farber's name has become a household word as a result of Dr. Jascalevich's trial. The press, which creates most of our household words, gave more attention to the plight of a colleague who was jailed than to an accused murderer who was not.

To support his theory that Myron Farber had conspired with Prosecutor Woodcock and Dr. Baden to have Jascalevich indicted, Ray Brown used his subpoena to attempt to get the notes that the reporter made during his 1975 investigation, asserting that the reporter's notes would prove the conspiracy and might also be useful to verify the testimony of other witnesses at the trial. Farber resisted Judge Arnold's decision to review his notes in Chambers to determine if they were relevant to Jascalevich's defense. He claimed that the New Jersey Shield Law (a statute specifically designed to protect reporters' sources) and the constitutional guaranty of freedom of the press gave him the privilege to refuse to surrender his notes to protect his confidential sources. With the full support of the *Times,* Farber contended that if a reporter could be compelled to reveal his sources, the future of investigative news reporting would be jeopardized to the detriment of American democracy.

The New Jersey judges decided that Dr. Jascalevich's right to have whatever he needed to defend himself was superior to the reporter's right to protect his confidential sources, and they found Farber and the *Times* in contempt, for which he was sentenced to stay in jail until he turned his notes over to the court in addition to a six-month punitive sentence. The court fined the *Times* $100, 000, plus $5,000 a day for each day the notes were not produced.

Because Farber had been jailed for twenty-seven days during the trial, the story of a reporter behind bars became a page-one and a

TV news lead every time there was another development in the journalistic legal battle. Columnists and editorial writers across the nation joined the fray. There were clearly conflicting rights at stake: the right of the press to protect its sources versus the right of an accused person to have everything needed to defend himself, both of which were guaranteed by the American and New Jersey Constitutions. The major issue was which of these rights was subservient to the other. Farber's sentence was interrupted by a temporary stay to enable him to appeal, but eventually both the New Jersey and the United States Supreme Courts refused to stay the sentence, and on September 18, Farber went back to jail. The overwhelming majority of the press was sympathetic; U.S. senators and state legislators promised to introduce remedial legislation, and most columnists, editorial writers, and television commentators were supportive of Farber. In the course of a Federal District Court hearing on Farber's application to be released from jail pending an appeal, it was revealed that Farber had a contract to write a book, a fact not previously disclosed to the New Jersey trial court. U.S. District Court Judge Frederick Lacy blasted the reporter and ruled against his application. Judge Lacy said of Farber, "This is a sorry spectacle of a reporter standing on [First Amendment] principles, standing in sackcloth and ashes, when in fact he is standing at the altar of greed." Farber and the *Times* said that the manuscript did not include the names of his confidential sources, and that the federal judge had been unfair; and Farber soon relented to the extent of allowing Judge Arnold to review his manuscript.

Some of the columnists and editorial writers began to equivocate. Sympathetic as they were to the reporter's plight, the American Civil Liberties Union and some columnists, including lawyer-columnist Anthony Lewis of the *Times* itself, agreed that the trial judge should be allowed to review the reporter's notes *in camera* to determine if the defense needed it. They argued that the defendant's rights might be superior to the need to protect confidential sources in particular cases.

With a final decision on the legal issues awaiting a decision of the United States Supreme Court on the day the verdict was rendered, the New Jersey court let Farber go free pending the Supreme Court decision that the *New York Times* said it would pursue the matter in order to test the validity of the heavy fines leveled against the paper. The legal battle had already cost the *Times* $1 million in fines and legal fees. (The State's case against Jascalevich reportedly cost the county about $1 million and experts estimated that Jascalevich's defense had probably cost him more than $250,000 in fees and expenses.)

There was considerable discussion too as to whether Raymond Brown really wanted the reporter's notes or if his entire effort was merely aimed at creating another ground for appeal or to demand a mistrial should that become necessary to protect his client's interest. Even if that were not so, Farber's repeated refusal to answer Brown's questions when he testified at the trial no doubt served Brown's interest by leaving the jurors with the impression that the bearded reporter, accused by Brown of being a conspirator against his client, did have something to hide because he was refusing to respond to legitimate inquiries.

My own experience with Brown's tactics is relevant to this point. Pursuant to the appropriate interstate compact, Brown had filed motion papers in the New York Supreme Court to compel my testimony for the defense and to obtain my notes and the manuscript for this book. (Had he but telephoned, I would have given him all but the manuscript; but he seemed, for whatever reason, to prefer the more circuitous route of the interstate compact, which required the filing of extensive motion papers in both New Jersey and New York courts.) I took the position that Jascalevich was entitled to my testimony and that I would go to New Jersey voluntarily to give it, just as I had already agreed to do for the prosecution. As to the notes of my 1966 investigation, I agreed that some of them might be relevant and, even though he had already obtained most of them from the prosecutor during pretrial discovery proceedings (I had given them to Sybil Moses as soon as she contacted me), he was welcome to whatever I had that he needed. I did not believe the manuscript, all of which was written after the indictment, was of any relevancy to the defense, nor could it meet the constitutional test of materiality. Accordingly, I told the New York Supreme Court that while I would voluntarily comply with the first two demands, I was entitled to a hearing on the relevancy of the manuscript, to which the court agreed. I offered to submit my manuscript to the court for review so that a judge could determine its relevancy. Brown was allowed to withdraw his motion, but was left free to renew it if he chose to do so. Brown never asked me to testify, nor did he ever seek the manuscript again; although he did send Delaney, his investigator, to my office for a few hours to look over my file and take copies of some of the items in it. Other than that, he never pursued the matter, and, in my view, his failure to do so raises serious questions regarding the real purpose of his effort, both in my case and in Farber's.

In 1972 the United States Supreme Court had decided the cases of three newspaper reporters who claimed that they had a constitutional privilege which prevented them from having to testify before grand juries involved in investigating criminal matters which the reporters had previously covered. In a close 5–4 decision, the Court decided in *Branzburg* v. *Hayes,* 925 S.Ct. 2646 (1972), that reporters could be compelled to testify before a grand jury when their testimony was material, relevant, and needed, and when there were no less intrusive means for the evidence to be obtained. In the Farber case, the Supreme Court of New Jersey found that the 1972 *Branzburg* decision governed the situation at hand and that Judge Arnold's offer to review Farber's material *in camera* provided an appropriate means to give the reporter a hearing on the issue of relevancy, materiality, and need. The *Times* and Farber argued unsuccessfully that their case should be distinguished from the 1972 ruling and, by appealing the New Jersey Supreme Court ruling, they asked the U.S. Supreme Court to consider their case separately. On November 27, 1978, the Supreme Court declined to hear the appeal; thus the New Jersey Supreme Court decision stood as the law, at least in New Jersey. Farber commented that the Supreme Court's decision was unfortunate because it left the law unclear. He was wrong. Unfortunately for the interests of the press, the Court left the law very clear.

While the United States Supreme Court is not necessarily predictable and does have the ability to change its mind or to distinguish cases of different circumstances, any objective observer would have to agree that the circumstances at bar did not bode well for Farber's position before the Supreme Court. First, the discussion in the *Branzburg* decision was so complex, extensive, and anticipatory of the case that Myron Farber's situation presented, there was little reason to expect a different result. This argument was buttressed by the comments of two different U.S. Supreme Court Justices, Mr. Justice Marshall and Mr. Justice White, when each of them turned down requests that Farber's jail sentence be stayed pending an eventual Supreme Court determination of the larger issue. Secondly, since the *Branzburg* case, the Supreme Court extended its doctrine to ordering even the president of the United States to turn over his usually privileged executive papers to the Watergate prosecutor.

Finally, and most significant to me, there was an inherent weakness in the Farber case, since it presented the worst possible set of facts to attempt to convince the Supreme Court to afford more protection of any kind to a reporter's notes and/or sources, because this case involved an unusual situation where the reporter's effort was instrumental in prompting the prosecutor to seek an indictment. The case was replete with the reporter's own stories taking credit for that, with other *New York Times* stories taking credit for that, and with the prosecutor admitting under oath that he reopened his investigation as a result of the *Times* investigation, of the *Times* stories, and of the *Times* providing him with material not heretofore in his files (my copy of the 1966 Jascalevich testimony).

Thus Myron Farber did not come to the Supreme Court merely as a reporter who did an investigation and reported on it. Although I believe that Myron Farber's investigative work was admirable, he came to court tainted with testimony that he was in communication with the prosecutor and provided information that constituted a basis for the defense demanding access to his notes.

In effect, Farber's activities became an adjunct to the prosecutor's, thus removing him from whatever protection the press would normally be entitled to.

I know that there is no more important influence on good government than the press. There is no greater protection against tyranny or corruption than the ability of a free press to investigate and publish details of what our government officials are doing, provided that they do so objectively and without destruction to the lives of persons accused before they are found guilty. To the extent that the rights of individuals on trial are not jeopardized, I favor every protection that legislators and judges can devise to stimulate and protect good investigatorial reporting. The law on this subject is still in a critical state of development, and if the Farber case had been heard by the Supreme Court, it could only have resulted in a disservice to those of us who want to preserve for our democracy the most independent press that it is possible to have. To ignore the weakness of the Farber case in the pursuit of this effort is irresponsible and must be recognized for what it is. We must base our hopes on a better set of facts in a future case.

As an institution determined to protect or expand its freedom, the press will be better served to save its next Supreme Court appeal for another day, a day destined to be made brighter by the interests of the press being presented in more favorable circumstances.